THE MAKING OF A COUNTER-CULTURE ICON:
HENRY MILLER'S DOSTOEVSKY

Fedor Mikhailovich Dostoevsky (1872) Artist: Vasily Perov, Tretiakov Gallery, Moscow

MARIA BLOSHTEYN

The Making of
a Counter-Culture Icon

Henry Miller's Dostoevsky

UNIVERSITY OF TORONTO PRESS
Toronto Buffalo London

ISBN 978-0-8020-9228-1

Printed on acid-free paper

Library and Archives Canada Cataloguing in Publication

Bloshteyn, Maria R., 1971–
The making of a counter-culture icon: Henry Miller's Dostoevsky/Maria
Bloshteyn.

Includes bibliographical references and index.
ISBN 978-0-8020-9228-1

1. Miller, Henry, 1891–1980 – Criticism and interpretation. 2. Dostoyevsky,
Fyodor, 1821–1881 – Influence. 3. Nin, Anaïs, 1903–1977 – Criticism and
interpretation. 4. Durrell, Lawrence – Criticism and interpretation.
5. Underground literature – History and criticism. 6. Counterculture
– History – 20th century. 7. Expatriate authors – France – Paris. I. Title.

PS3525.I5454Z6545 2007   818'.5209   C2007-905679-2

University of Toronto Press acknowledges the financial assistance to its publishing program of the Canada Council for the Arts and the Ontario Arts Council.

University of Toronto Press acknowledges the financial support for its publishing activities of the Government of Canada through the Book Publishing Indus-
try Development Program (BPIDP).

Contents

Preface

What does canonic Russian novelist Fedor Mikhailovich Dostoevsky (1821–81) have in common with the controversial American writer Henry Miller (1891–1980)? On the one hand, we have an iconic nineteenth-century Russian novelist whose influence on both Russian and world literature was as extensive as it was complex. On the other, we have an iconoclastic twentieth-century writer who has never been fully accepted into the official canon of modern literature, and is instead viewed as a prominent figure of the American and global literary underground. Unlikely as it may seem, however, the impact of Dostoevsky on Miller was in fact enormous. It shaped his view of the world, of literature, and of his own writing during the most important and creative period of his life, when he was at the centre of a group of equally unorthodox writers, poets, and artists in Paris of the 1930s, later referred to as the Villa Seurat circle. Dostoevsky became the foundation upon which Miller built his vision of a new kind of writing that he believed would break through the conventions of literature and create a revolution in mankind's perception of self and the world. Miller expounded and shared his views about the need for a revolutionary new prose narrative with two of his closest associates at Villa Seurat, Anaïs Nin (1903–77) and Lawrence Durrell (1912–90). Although Miller, Nin, and Durrell would each develop uniquely individual approaches to narrative, their dialogue and their struggles with Dostoevsky during the Villa Seurat period were seminal to their later achievements and to the stunning prose innovation that made them famous.

This book is, first and foremost, a thoroughly documented case study of intercultural appropriation. It analyses Miller's and, subsequently, Nin's and Durrell's, radical understanding of Dostoevsky as the prophet for the new literary underground, focusing on the ways in which Dostoevsky was read, (mis)interpreted, and generally transformed by these three writers. It is the first study to investigate the universally acknowledged importance of Dostoevsky to Miller, analysing his reading of Dostoevsky initially within the context of the historical American reception of the Russian novelist and then within the context of Miller's Parisian milieu in the 1930s. It is also the first book to examine the momentous literary relationship of Miller, Nin, and Durrell at Villa Seurat, as they strove to bring about a revolution in prose narrative inspired by Dostoevsky and, as such, serves as a useful introduction to the work of these key writers. Finally, it documents Dostoevsky's powerful impact on American literature and (counter)culture through Henry Miller's subversive writings and offers insights into the importance that Dostoevsky gained for the literary and artistic underground (especially in America) through Miller's continued publicizing of his version of Dostoevsky in his books.

This study is organized into eight chapters. Chapter 1, 'Intercultural Readings, Dostoevsky's Twentieth Century, and Henry Miller's Literary Ambitions,' introduces the problems surrounding Dostoevsky's twentieth-century reception, as well as Miller's own problematic reputation. Chapter 2, 'Dostoevsky as American Icon,' reconstructs the key features of Dostoevsky's American reception, from first contact in 1881 to the enthusiastic discovery of his rich literary heritage through Constance Garnett's translations of his novels. The third chapter, 'Henry Miller's Road to Dostoevsky,' documents Miller's own encounters with Dostoevsky's texts in America and the evolution of Miller's perspective on Dostoevsky. Chapter 4, 'Henry Miller's Villa Seurat Circle and Dostoevsky,' examines the dynamics and obsessions within a fascinating group of bohemian intellectuals (a group that has largely evaded scholarly scrutiny), Miller's prominence within the Villa Seurat circle, and the place that Dostoevsky occupied in their literary lives. Chapters 5 and 6, 'Post-Dostoevskian Prose at Villa Seurat' and 'Understanding Dostoevsky's "Philosophy" at Villa Seurat,' examine the Villa Seurat writers' interpretation of Dostoevsky's legacy in the areas of literary form and ideas, in the context of both their historical reception and the Villa Seurat writers' ambition to go beyond Dostoevsky's achievements. Chapter 7, 'Writing the Underground,' analyses the importance to Miller, Nin, and Durrell of Dostoevsky's *Notes from Underground* [*Zapiski iz podpol'ia*] (1864) – a complex text that provoked many literary and philosophical reactions during the twentieth century. Finally, chapter 8,

'Pragmatics of Influence, the Dostoevsky Brand, and Dostoevsky Codes,' provides a summary of what has been uncovered by the study and suggests some implications for the understanding of Dostoevsky's reputation in the twentieth century and beyond.

A short bibliographical essay on the work done to date on Dostoevsky's reception in America and another on the state of scholarship on the work of Miller, Nin, and Durrell are provided in appendices. The bibliography includes the location of the main archival repositories of Dostoevsky, Miller, Nin, and Durrell's papers; a list of their major works, correspondence, and interviews; and a representative but by no means exhaustive sampling of biographies and recent criticism. The bibliographic subsection on Dostoevsky also includes a list of English-language translations available up to and including the 1930s, the period when Miller, Nin, and Durrell began their collaboration at Villa Seurat.

I have consistently attempted to use the more familiar English spelling for Russian names in the main body text (I otherwise employ the Library of Congress transliteration system, which I also use in the endnotes and in the bibliography). All references to Dostoevsky's works, unless otherwise noted, are to the standard thirty-volume edition of collected works (*Polnoe sobranie sochinenii v tridtsati tomakh*) published by the Soviet Academy of Science over two decades (1972–90). All translations from Russian are my own, except where otherwise noted. Quotations from most French texts (including Miller's interviews given in French) are left in the original language, except in cases where it is fairly certain that Miller was first exposed to the English-language translation of these particular texts.

This study originated as a doctoral dissertation defended at Toronto's York University. I owe a great deal to Professor Nikita Lary, my thesis superviser, who encouraged me by his enthusiasm for my project and provided me with the needed guidance, while allowing me the freedom to explore the issues of interest to me. I am also greatly indebted to Professor Richard Pope, my secondary superviser, who has been a mentor to me throughout my university years and whose teaching, academic writings, fiction, and poetry continue to be an inspiration in my own work.

Professors Robert Fothergill, Michael Cummings, and Orest Subtelny contributed to the development of my ideas on the subject by asking me probing and stimulating questions at my doctoral defence. Professor Vyacheslav Ivanov, the external reader, enriched my project by offering a number of insights into the subject and by inspiring me to dig deeper and to expand on my work. I am very grateful to him for nominating my thesis for York University President's Award.

I am also grateful to the Department of Graduate English at York University for fostering an environment in which innovative approaches to literary scholarship are encouraged. I am personally indebted to the professors with whom I taught while writing my doctoral thesis, especially Anne Pilgrim and Christopher Innes. I am grateful to the department for supporting the nomination of my thesis for the President's Award and for nominating it for the Governor General's Gold Medal. I thank York University for awarding me the President's Award for my dissertation.

Dr Maya Johnson-Stepenberg contributed a great deal to this book while writing her own. Her knowledge, her generosity, her scholarly finesse, and her sense of humour have been of invaluable assistance to me. Dr Olga Bakich offered wisdom, encouragement, and her own example of integrity, commitment, and creativity as a scholar and a writer. Marina Avisar and Adrianna Oleksienko-Stech have been a source of inspiration, good sense, and good cheer as well as unfailing support over the years. The many talents, many kindnesses, and the friendship of these women have been an undeserved gift that I deeply and sincerely cherish.

I must express my sincere gratitude to Evgeny Dmitrievich Erkovich in Moscow, a truly extraordinary man, who was an enthusiastic supporter of my work from the time I began researching this topic and who selflessly searched out, purchased, and sent me the new Dostoevsky-related materials published in Russia to make sure that I was kept abreast of developments in post-Soviet Dostoevsky studies and all Dostoevsky-related news.

I am also greatly indebted to Professor Robert Belknap, my postdoctoral superviser at Columbia University, where I worked on the subject of Dostoevsky's impact on American literature and culture. His generous feedback allowed me to rethink many of my original assumptions and to further develop my ideas.

I gratefully acknowledge the support I received in the early stages of planning my thesis from Henry Miller biographers Jay Martin and Mary Dearborn. I was assisted in my research by several generous grants from York University, for which I am thankful. In my research at the various archives I was helped by a number of librarians and archival specialists who made my work much easier. I would especially like to thank David

Koch, Shelley Cox, and the staff of the Morris Rare Book Library at the Southern Illinois University for their erudition and genuine helpfulness. During the later stages of preparing this book for publication I benefited, like many others, from the expertise of Karl Orend, whose erudition and expertise on all things Miller related is legendary. Additionally, I would like to extend my gratitude to Jill McConkey, Allyson N. May, and Barb Porter at University of Toronto Press, especially to Jill for her help and support throughout the whole publication process, for her input into the project, and for all her brilliant ideas.

Finally, I would not have been able to complete any of my work if not for my amazing family, who selflessly stood by me, supported me, and cheered me on throughout the whole process. My mother Yevgenia and my sister Irina went above and beyond what could remotely be expected of even the most loving and compassionate family members. My brother-in-law Michael was consistently supportive and generous. My late father Roman Isaakovich Bloshteyn believed in me and encouraged me during his long and difficult illness, which he battled courageously over many years. My husband Stephen was invariably compassionate and supportive, not to mention superhumanly patient, during the lengthy process of manuscript revision as I prepared this book for publication. I have no words in Russian, English, or any other language to sufficiently thank them.

THE MAKING OF A COUNTER-CULTURE ICON:
HENRY MILLER'S DOSTOEVSKY

1 Intercultural Readings, Dostoevsky's Twentieth Century, and Henry Miller's Literary Ambitions

'I should say to any young writer of merit who appealed to me "Read what you like, only don't waste your time reading Dostoevsky. He is the cocaine and morphia of modern literature."'
    Excerpt of a letter written by Edmund Gosse to André Gide in 1926[1]

Fedor Dostoevsky's twentieth-century reception is a topic of keen interest not only to the scholar of Russian or comparative literature and intercultural studies but to virtually anyone interested in the history of ideas. Some of the most important social and cultural movements in the twentieth century defined themselves by reacting to Dostoevsky, placing themselves in opposition to him, or appropriating him as a fellow-traveller or ancestor. Commentaries on his work, epigrammatically brief or expanded into lengthy essays, were composed by such key twentieth-century figures as Albert Einstein, Sigmund Freud, and Jean-Paul Sartre. Dostoevsky's novels have been celebrated, banned, plagiarized, scrutinized publically, and read furtively in underground editions. Countless writers, poets, and artists all over the world, from Turkey's Orhan Pamuk to Japan's Haruki Murakami, from South Africa's J.M. Coetzee to Columbia's Gabriel Garcia Marquez, from such 'elitist' artists as Max Ernst and Jean-Luc Godard to such 'populist' authors as Mario Puzo of the Godfather saga, Anne Rice of the Vampire chronicles, and Patricia Highsmith of the Mr Ripley series, have testified to Dostoevsky's impact on their work.

While the novels of Ivan Turgenev (1818–83) and Leo Tolstoy (1828–1910), two of Dostoevsky's contemporaries and great literary rivals whose stature and esteem during their lifetimes exceeded his, have been relegated to the halls of academia and largely faded out of contemporary consciousness, Dostoevsky managed to remain meaningful to an international readership and his novels continue to be read around the world as eerily contemporary texts. The prominent British Dostoevsky scholar W.J. Leatherbarrow observes in the introduction to his *Fedor Dostoevsky: A Reference Guide* that 'Dostoevsky has always seemed to belong to the present in a way other Russian authors of the nineteenth century have not. It would be difficult, if not impossible, to take the world depicted by, say, Pushkin or Tolstoy for our own. Yet Dostoevsky's novels ... seem unnervingly contemporary if not prophetic ... Dostoevsky himself refuses to settle into the role of venerable "classic."'[2]

It is certainly true that although Dostoevsky's novels have long been established as classics of world literature, his novels, characters, and ideas retain their cutting edge, figuring prominently in today's mass media and popular culture. In America, for example, Dostoevsky was evoked continuously by analysts, editors, and media pundits during the Unabomber case, the Columbine Highschool shootings, and in the aftermath of 9/11. References to Dostoevsky's novels spring up in presidential speeches (for example, President George W. Bush's famous misuse of a line from *The Devils* [*Besy*] in his second inaugural address in 2005). Dostoevsky's characters figure in contemporary graffiti (New York subway's 'Raskolnikov lives!'), in punk rock lyrics (Iggy Pop's version of 'Louie, Louie,' where he professes to be 'as bent as Dostoevsky'), and in contemporary vaudeville (the Broadway juggling troupe known as 'The Flying Karamazov Brothers'). Dostoevsky's novels continue to attract filmmakers (see, most recently, Woody Allen's take on *Crime and Punishment* [*Prestuplenie i nakazanie*] in the film *Matchpoint* [2006] as well as his 1989 film *Crimes and Misdemeanours*) and experimental playwrights (Dan Dietz, Deborah Hay, Andrea Moon, and Jason Neulander, *American Demons* [2000], a dance/theatre piece that interprets the shootings at Columbine High in light of Dostoevsky's *The Devils*).

Dostoevsky's Credo

Despite remaining relevant in the early twenty-first century and continuing to influence a plethora of international thinkers, writers, and artists so many years after his death, it is clear that few other writers have been subjected to such radical misreadings and had their ideological credo distorted to such a dramatic extent. This is all the more puzzling given that the ideas that made up Dostoevsky's world-view in 1859, when he was allowed to return to St Petersburg after his imprisonment and exile, are well known. In the crucible of Siberia Dostoevsky's early atheistic leanings, Westernizing sympathies, and radical impulses underwent a complete about-face (documented and analysed in, among other places, the second volume of Joseph Frank's monumental biography of the novelist) and he resumed his writing career as a believer in the primacy of the Russian Orthodox Church, the paternal rule of the Czar, and the mission of the Russian people as a Messiah unto the nations. Few scholars of Dostoevsky could deny these biographical facts with any conviction. Dostoevsky's commitment to promoting these ideas in his books is also known to anyone familiar with his correspondence and extensive notebooks. He makes it very clear that he sees his writings (fictional and nonfictional) as carefully orchestrated arguments advancing his philosophical position and not as open-ended, free-spirited explorations of religious and philosophical issues.

In a letter written in 1879, for example, Dostoevsky tells Konstantin Pobedonostsev (1827–1907), the ultraconservative Chief Procurator of the Holy Synod, a symbol of reactionary tendencies in Russia of his time and Dostoevsky's personal friend, that he was concerned about whether he could make his arguments against atheism in *Brothers Karamazov* [*Brat'ia Karamazovy*] appear persuasive enough: 'And it is this that worries me. That is, will I be understood and will I attain even an iota of my goal [*khot' kapliu tseli*]' (30/I:236). In other letters written around this time Dostoevsky specifies that his 'goal' in *Brothers Karamazov* is nothing less than 'a destruction of anarchism' and that he is 'preaching God and Nationhood' (30/I:64, 236). In other words, Dostoevsky was attempting to advance his own political, religious, and philosophical agenda in his novels and trying to convince his readers to adopt these same views.

Any student of Dostoevsky's work cannot help then but be profoundly mystified by how this right-wing Russian Orthodox monarchist could have become a mascot for so many left-wing, irreverent, anarchically minded groups (such as, for instance, the surrealists, the existentialists, and the Beats) and a prophet to so many self-confessed members of various fringe groups and cultural undergrounds. The response to Dostoevsky outside of his Russian homeland represents one of the more curious paradoxes in the history of intercultural literary interaction. Dostoevsky remains one of Russia's most successful literary exports; yet

it appears that in traversing linguistic, cultural, and temporal boundaries the cluster of concepts that together form the total construct of
'Dostoevsky' (a corpus of information about Dostoevsky's life, belief
system, and canon of writings) has been radically transformed.

Reading Dostoevsky in Russia

To be fair, Dostoevsky's reception within Russia itself also underwent
some curious twists and turns. Throughout the 1870s and up to
Dostoevsky's death in 1881 – a period marked by increasing social
and political turmoil in Russia – Dostoevsky's novels were avidly
read and hotly debated by Russians from all social milieus. Although
he was widely recognized as one of Russia's greatest living authors,
Dostoevsky faced continued criticism from the Russian liberal intelligentsia and the left-leaning Russian student body, who considered
him a reactionary. Dostoevsky himself had, according to Joseph
Frank, 'always tried to maintain a balance between his opposition to
revolutionary agitation and his recognition of the moral idealism that
often inspired those who stirred up its flames ... [and] saw his [own]
role in relation to the radical youth as that of a sympathetic critic
rather than as immitigably hostile opponent.'[3] Nonetheless, after the
publication of Dostoevsky's so-called pamphleteering novel about
a Russian revolutionary cell, The Devils[4] (1871–2); his assumption
in 1873 of the editorship of an ultra-conservative weekly journal,
The Citizen [Grazhdanin]; and the ongoing publication of his Diary
of a Writer [Dnevnik pisatelia] (1873–81), in which he expressed his
opinions regarding current events (first as part of The Citizen and
then as an independent series), Dostoevsky's personal political,
social, and religious views were a matter of public record. However
Dostoevsky's Russian contemporaries may have felt about him as a
novelist and thinker, they generally had a sense of what he believed
in and championed.

After the Revolution of 1917 and the establishment of the Soviet
regime, Dostoevsky became the subject of heated debate between the
'orthodox Marxists,' who attacked him as a reactionary enemy of the
revolution, and the 'moderates,' who believed that Dostoevsky's depiction of the horrors of life in a large capitalist city made him a precursor to
and a mirror of the revolution (this idea was originally developed by
V. Pereverzev in his quasi-sociological literary study Dostoevsky's Art
[Tvorchestvo Dostoevskogo][5] and espoused by no less than the People's

Commissar of Enlightenment, A. Lunacharsky). After the triumph of Party orthodoxy Dostoevsky was branded 'our evil genius' (Maxim Gorky's infamous phrase) and regarded as an ideological enemy of the state. *The Devils* was deemed to be a particularly vicious example of counter-revolutionary slander. There are many stories about Soviet citizens seen reading *The Devils* and other Dostoevsky novels in the repressive 1930s who narrowly escaped jail or were imprisoned for this suspicious activity,[6] although several important Soviet studies on Dostoevsky, precariously balancing genuine scholarship with Party requirements, did come out during that decade. During the Second World War, there was a reconciliation of sorts, as Soviet powers-that-be encouraged Dostoevsky scholars to thwart the efforts of Nazi propagandists, who tried to use Dostoevsky to further their own agenda, and to show that Dostoevsky was a great Russian writer and patriot. The end of the war saw the publication of many articles and books about Dostoevsky as well as stage adaptations of his novels; in 1946, the 125th anniversary of Dostoevsky's birth, there were widespread celebrations of Dostoevsky and his work throughout the Soviet Union. Already in 1947, however, 'the wave of ideological purges' initiated by the notorious Party boss A.A. Zhdanov 'reached the field of Dostoevsky scholarship,'[7] with new campaigns against 'Dostoevskiism' ('*dostoevshchina*') and its supposed representatives; as a result, Soviet scholarship on Dostoevsky was effectively paralysed for close to a decade. During the so-called Thaw that followed Nikita Khrushchev's revelation of Stalin's crimes at the closed session of the Twentieth Congress of the CPSU in 1956, however, state controls were somewhat relaxed, which had a positive effect on the publication and dissemination of Dostoevsky's novels in the Soviet Union.

A Russian (Soviet) scholar looking back from the perspective of 1993 at the history of Dostoevsky's reception in Soviet Russia sums up the trends in Soviet Dostoevsky scholarship as follows: '[First] Dostoevsky was [seen as] a writer bound to the destinies of the Revolution ... [then he was seen as] the creator of the counter-revolutionary *Devils* and an almost pro-fascist thinker ... then [came] the period when it was totally prohibited to even mention his name (during the dramatic years of 1949–1954) – and [then came] the touching return to him, marked by a flood of monographs and articles about the difficult, controversial, but on the whole, "our" writer both during and after the anniversary year of 1956. Finally, sometime in the middle of the 1960s, Dostoevsky was almost completely rehabilitated and once again allowed into secondary schools as the author of *Crime and Punishment* and *The Insulted and the Injured.*[8] In the 1970s and 1980s, Soviet Dostoevsky scholars were still obligated to set their work within the state-approved framework. In the words of one prominent Soviet (Russian) scholar considering the constraints of that era only a year before the Soviet Union ceased to exist, Dostoevsky continued to be misrepresented as 'a passionate critic of bourgeois society and bourgeois morals, as well as a member of the Petrashevsky Circle, who (despite everything, etc., etc.,) remained loyal to the socialist ideals of his youth until the end of his life.'[9] Generally speaking, however, Soviet readers, skilled as few others at reading between the lines, saw the real situation for what it was, as made evident by a well-known joke about the Soviet government erecting a monument to Dostoevsky with the inscription, 'To Fedor Mikhailovich Dostoevsky From the Grateful Devils.'

Meanwhile, outside of Russia, other radical misinterpretations of Dostoevsky proliferated. He was cast as a proponent of high individualism, as the champion of atheism, as the godfather of surrealism, as the originator of existentialism, and as the representative and champion of anyone alienated and in a state of rebellion against the prevalent world order. The editor of a Soviet critical anthology, *Dostoevsky in Foreign Literatures* [*Dostoevskii v zarubezhnykh literaturakh*], published in 1978 by the Soviet Academy of Sciences, accused Western thinkers, with some justice, of 'attributing their own views to Dostoevsky [and] manipulating his writings into serving as a pedestal for their own future monument.' He also concluded that 'foreign critics who held a bourgeois world view had profoundly distorted [Dostoevsky's] writings.'[10] It hardly needs to be pointed out, of course, that the editor had to remain silent about the ideological slant that he and his Soviet colleagues were bringing to bear upon Dostoevsky in their efforts to make him appear more state-friendly.

Lost in Translation

It is only to be expected that virtually any text undergoing translation into another language will be subject to a certain amount of loss and distortion. Vladimir Nabokov (who, as is well known, had issues both with Dostoevsky and his reputation in the West) called translation a 'profanation of the dead' in his poem 'On Translating *Eugene Onegin*' (1955). Over and above the problems inherent in understanding the many subtle nuances of a complex multidimensional text and then correctly translating them into a target language, cultural differences can also profoundly affect how a certain character, situation, or concept within a text is perceived by readers from a cultural background different from that of the original readership. Geert Hofstede, a scholar of cross-cultural differences and intercultural relations, reminds the reader of his well-known study *Culture's Consequences* (2001) that 'a "message" in one language does not necessarily survive the translation process. Information is more than words: It is words within a cultural framework.'[11]

Cultural differences between Americans and Russians, for instance, cause countless misunderstandings between representatives of the two cultures during contact. O.A. Leontovich, author of *Russia and the USA: Introduction to Intercultural Communication* [*Rossiia i SShA; vvedenie v mezhkul'turnuiu kommunikatsiiu*] (2003), includes the following in her list of barriers to effective communication between the two cultures: 'differences in mentality and national character; divergences in linguistic perception of the world, including the perception of time and space; communicational asymmetry; effect of cultural stereotypes; differences in value structure; divergence in cultural-linguistic norms; differences in presuppositions and background knowledge; culturally specific differences in associations attached to linguistic units; differences in perception of humor, etc.'[12] Although the question of literary contacts between the two cultures falls outside the scope of Leontovich's study, her descriptions of the various barriers to effective communication also apply in the case of Russian texts in translation (including Dostoevsky's writings) read by Americans and other non-Russians.

And yet Dostoevsky's ideas and texts seem to invite distortions so excessive as to suggest the existence of issues beyond those ordinarily expected in the cases of interliterary or intercultural contact. It is useful to keep in mind that it was frequently Russian émigrés – readers theoretically encountering few linguistic or cultural barriers when approaching Dostoevsky's texts – who fostered radical distortions of Dostoevsky's works and ideas outside of Russia. It was, for example, none other than Elena Blavatsky, the Russian founder of Theosophy, who inaugurated the disturbingly popular practice of excising the chapter on the Grand Inquisitor from the *Brothers Karamazov* and publishing it as a separate text (it first appeared in 1881 in her own translation in her English-language journal *The Theosophist*), ensuring that it would be read out of context.[13] What is more, she prefaced her translation by explaining to her ill-informed readers that it supposedly represented Dostoevsky's 'cutting satire on modern theology.'[14] Three decades later, the Russian-born anarchist Emma Goldman featured an English translation of a Dostoevsky story, 'The Priest and the Devil,' in her left-wing American publication, *The Mother Earth Bulletin*. Goldman informed her readers that the story, condemning the workers' exploitation by the ruling classes and their deception by the clergy, was written by Dostoevsky on the wall of his cell during his imprisonment by the Czarist regime.[15] In reality, the story was a crude fabrication, probably written either by Goldman herself or by one of her associates. It is doubtful whether Goldman would have gotten away with any of this in Russia, but in America of 1910 no one called her bluff and her readers trustingly accepted the story as one of Dostoevsky's own.

Misreading Dostoevsky According to Harold Bloom

The problem of extreme misrepresentations and misreadings of Dostoevsky's texts is acknowledged if still largely unexplored in Dostoevsky studies, but the two main theories that are usually advanced as explanations for the proliferation of these misreadings pose more problems than they solve. The first and more general explanation points to Harold Bloom's well-known theory of literary influence. Bloom, probably one of the most famous contemporary American literary critics, proposed the theory more than thirty years ago in his *Anxiety of Influence* (1973). According to Bloom's theory, itself influenced – as pointed out many times – by the Freudian family romance, the 'father' (every 'strong' poet or writer) will necessarily be misread and his message distorted by his 'sons' ('ephebes' or young aspiring poets or writers who come after him and are simultaneously inspired and intimidated by their predecessor's greatness) in an act of creative misreading that Bloom calls 'misprision.' From this perspective, Dostoevsky's case is seen as being representative of any towering writer who attracts many literary followers and, as such, is not perceived to be unusual in any way.

Attractive though it may be, the application of Bloom's theory to the problem of Dostoevsky's extreme misreadings fails to explain why Dostoevsky's famous contemporaries Turgenev and Tolstoy, surely strong writers by any standard, were never subject to such radical misinterpretation and dramatic transformations. The belief systems reflected in the writings of Turgenev and Tolstoy generally remained intact even while their works were translated into other languages and read by people from vastly different cultures. Turgenev, for example, held liberal

Western views and strongly opposed the institution of serfdom; non-Russian readers have thus far not mistaken him for a reactionary right-wing thinker who defended slave ownership. Tolstoy's views on the immorality of war and his ideas on nonviolent resistance were accurately understood by readers from such vastly different backgrounds and cultures as Mahatma Gandhi and Martin Luther King, Jr. Dostoevsky, by contrast, who spoke and wrote repeatedly about how important it was for him to reach readers with his ideological message, has had his credo routinely distorted to the point where it is no longer recognizable. Equally disturbingly, some readers deny the very presence of any ideological credo in his writings.

This is not to suggest that all of Dostoevsky's readers (or all his American readers) misread his writings and misinterpreted his views and beliefs. There were many informed and finely nuanced readings of Dostoevsky by such prominent and dissimilar American writers as Ralph Ellison, Saul Bellow, and Walker Percy (all three, incidentally, included Dostoevsky's novels in the university literature courses they taught), and many others. But many more readings grossly distorted Dostoevsky's novels and subverted his philosophical position or, conversely, flatly denied that Dostoevsky subscribed to any philosophical outlook whatsoever.

An amusing if by no means unusual example of an extreme distortion of Dostoevsky's belief system, life, and writings is found in the Beat writers' and poets' interpretation of the novelist and his works. The group of American writers and poets who later became the nucleus of the Beat movement (including Allen Ginsberg [1926–97], Jack Kerouac [1922–69], and William Burroughs [1914–97]) originally connected because of their mutual appreciation of Dostoevsky and knowledge of his works.[16] They saw themselves as ideological and literary followers of Dostoevsky; established a personal and literary union, and, as it were, the entire Beat movement, on the foundation of their shared belief in the primacy of Dostoevsky and his novels; and planned to remake America according to their understanding of Dostoevsky's concept of Russia as it should be (a 'warmhearted, open, Dostoevskian Alyosha-Myshkin-Dmitri compassion' – an 'open American scene';[17] 'the *endless plane* or plain dotted with endless brothers').[18] They believed that Dostoevsky would have accepted their largely unorthodox lifestyles because, like them, he was supposedly 'mellow in the sense of infinitely tolerant ... infinitely understanding.'[19] Furthermore, they saw Dostoevsky as a symbol of personal freedom and, more eccentrically, as a model for such Beat icons as the blond, muscular vagabond, con man, and womanizer Neil Cassady, who was, according to Kerouac, 'more like Dostoevsky than anybody else ... He looks like Dostoevsky, he gambles like Dostoevsky, he regards sex like Dostoevsky.'[20] Finally, as far as the question of faith was concerned, the Beats, who generally espoused a somewhat watered-down version of Buddhism, believed that their religious vision was also embodied in Dostoevsky's novels: Allen Ginsberg once referred to Dostoevsky's works as 'Dostoevsky's Buddha bibles.'[21]

Alternatively, for an example of a reading that unilaterally denies the existence of any ideological credo in Dostoevsky's writings, one has only to turn to Theodore Dreiser, by no means a naive or inexperienced reader. In a letter Dreiser wrote in 1932 to the head of Amkino, a Soviet film distributor in New York, he states that Dostoevsky's 'observation of life led [him] to no fixed political, social or religious deductions of any kind ... [and that he] reported the idiosyncrasies of man ... without bias and without a personal social plan.'[22] Even if Dreiser's words were intended to make Dostoevsky seem more palatable to a Soviet functionary, his position is both outrageously inaccurate and not at all unique: a surprising number and variety of Dostoevsky's readers echo it.

Misreading Dostoevsky According to Mikhail Bakhtin

When faced with misreadings and misinterpretations this obvious and dramatic, some Dostoevsky scholars point to the explanation provided by the Formalist theoretician Mikhail Bakhtin (1895–1975). Bakhtin's monograph *Problems of Dostoevsky's Poetics* [*Problemy poetiki Dostoevskogo*], first published in the Soviet Union in 1929 and then revised and enlarged for its 1963 edition, is an influential study that proved to be especially popular outside of Russia.[23] In it Bakhtin introduces and expounds the idea that Dostoevsky had created and developed a new kind of novel, which he calls 'polyphonic,' literally meaning 'many-voiced' (defined as a novel consisting of characters that form independent and equal voices, none of which can be fully identified with that of the author himself)[24] – a term that became a fashionable catchword in a number of postmodernist discourses. Bakhtin's theory is complex, multilateral, and controversial (it came in for its share of criticism from Dostoevsky scholars);[25] what is important here is that in the introduction to the 1963 edition of *Dostoevsky's Poetics* Bakhtin addresses the question why Western followers of Dostoevsky include people with wildly divergent ideologies 'frequently deeply inimical to the ideology of Dostoevsky himself.' Readers, he explains, tend to 'monologize [Dostoevsky's] novels ... ignoring or denying [their] intentional incompleteness and dialogical openness.'[26]

Bakhtin was most interested – as he wrote many times in his *Poetics* – in Dostoevsky's innovations in artistic form, rather than his belief system. His explanation for the proliferation of Western misreadings of Dostoevsky's ideology must be seen within the context of both Bakhtin's own precarious position within a repressive totalitarian state as a semi-rehabilitated scholar who had to exercise constant self-censorship (he had already experienced internal exile and was teaching at a small provincial university) and his subject's precarious situation as a semi-rehabilitated novelist with a reputation as a dangerous reactionary ideologue (his novels had already been banned for their unacceptable ideology). Bakhtin's comment about Dostoevsky's misguided Western followers ignoring the 'dialogical openness' of his novels, which supposedly extended to the novel's ideology, may thus have been designed to appease the authorities. At face value, however, the suggestion that Dostoevsky's novels are not only dialogically but ideologically open is deeply problematic.

It is difficult to argue with the observation that Dostoevsky allows many of his characters, including those whose beliefs are the direct opposite of his own, to express their views with a level of conviction and persuasiveness usually reserved for characters who express the cherished beliefs of the author himself.[27] At the same time, one should not ignore Dostoevsky's own explanation as to why he allows his 'negative characters' such power of persuasion in his novels. While it is true that Dostoevsky never offered a direct public *apologia* for his literary/polemical method, it is also true that he came within a hair's breadth of it in the introduction to the first issue of his programmatic *Diary of a Writer*. Towards the very end of the introduction, Dostoevsky recalls the visit he made as a young man to the liberal writer and social critic Alexander Herzen, during which he praised one of Herzen's books, written as a polemical dialogue between Herzen and an opponent. 'What I particularly like,' Dostoevsky supposedly said, 'is that your opponent is also very clever. You must agree that in many instances he succeeds in cornering you.' Herzen replied that this was the whole secret behind writing convincing polemical texts, illustrating his point by recalling his own visit to the famous literary critic Vissarion Belinsky, who read him an article written in the form of a debate between himself and a much weaker opponent. 'So, what do you think?' Belinsky anxiously asked Herzen, who responded, 'It's good alright, and it is obvious that you yourself are very clever, but whatever made you waste your time on such a fool?' In response, Belinsky reportedly threw himself down on the sofa, laughing hysterically and admitting that Hertzen was right in his criticism (21:8). Dostoevsky does not comment any further on this strategically placed anecdote, but the implications are clear: a writer must be allowed to depict the views of his ideological opponents persuasively, and to include their most powerful arguments, if his work is to have any polemical impact at all.

What is more, in letters to those of his correspondents who shared his political and religious views and would have liked to see him craft better propaganda (as, for instance, the aforementioned Pobedonostsev), Dostoevsky points out that he is trying to convince his readers of the correctness of his own position through his art rather than through formal polemics. Thus, Dostoevsky explains that he will be rebutting the arguments in favour of atheism in Brothers Karamazov not by providing a series of counter-arguments, but by creating the charismatic figure of Father Zosima: 'the answer ... is indirect. Here is a representation of something completely contrary to the world view expressed earlier – refuted not point-by-point but, so to speak, by an artistic representation ... [of] a figure modest and sublime' (30/I:122).

Dostoevsky also expounds this concept in a 1862 article 'Mr. –bov and the Question of Art' ['G-n –bov i vopros ob iskusstve'], where he argues that a novelist should never pummel his ideas into the reader's head, as it were, but must convey them indirectly through his art; 'artistry ... is the [novelist's] capacity to express his thoughts so clearly using the characters and the images of the novel, that the reader, having read it, understands the writers' thought exactly in the same way as the writer did when he created his work' (18:79–80). Dostoevsky's own set of beliefs, in other words, was to be extrapolated by his readers from the novels' structure, from the fate that awaited the characters, and from the imagery associated with these characters. This lofty goal (how many people actually make it a practice to read novels in such a close and discriminating fashion?) appears to have been a tall order for some readers, especially those who were approaching Dostoevsky's novels across a linguistic, temporal, and cultural divide and had different perceptions of and associations with the events, characters, and images of the novels than those held by the original Russian readers. No wonder then, that so many readers of Dostoevsky's text veered so far in their interpretations of his novels from his own credo and stated intentions.

If all of the above raises legitimate doubts about the notion of the 'intentional incompleteness and dialogical openness' of the ideology of Dostoevsky's novels, there is a more fundamental difficulty with Bakhtin's explanation. If Dostoevsky's misreadings are predicated on his readers' misunderstanding of the supposed ideological openness of the novels and on their assumption that a single character acts as the mouthpiece of the author (thus, in effect, 'monologizing' his text), then these misinterpretations of Dostoevsky's personal beliefs ought to have been dispelled by the reading of such nonfictional texts as the essays and editorials included in his *Diary of a Writer* [*Dnevnik pisatelia*] and his correspondence, which do not share the artistic mandate with the fictional texts and which present Dostoevsky's own views and beliefs in a much more straightforward and 'monological' manner. James Scanlan, who examines the question of Dostoevsky's beliefs and ideas in his *Dostoevsky the Thinker*, points out that 'in a multitude of texts [Dostoevsky] incontestably speaks in his own voice and expresses views and arguments ... He depicted ... tension in his fiction for dramatic purposes, but his other writings provide unambiguous indications of which side he was on.'[28]

Interestingly, it would seem that some early readers of Dostoevsky had precisely that kind of an eye-opening experience when the translations of his *Diary* and correspondence became available. Scholars trying to account for the sharp drop in Dostoevsky's popularity in England in the 1920s point to these new translations as part of the reason for the decline in his reputation: 'this material that revealed Dostoevsky the man tended to qualify admiration of Dostoevsky the author';[29] 'the translations of novels had come to an end, but the letters ... appeared, followed; by the memoirs of relatives and other biographical material – and Dostoevsky's divinity did not emerge unscathed.'[30]

At the same time, however, other readers of Dostoevsky, while acknowledging that the contents of the *Diary*, for instance, did not harmonize well with their understanding of the novels, refused to let it interfere with their original interpretation. The French novelist André Gide (1869–1951), for example, says as much in his famous book on Dostoevsky published in 1923 (it was considered an important enough contribution to be translated into English only two years later), explaining that the *Diary* is 'profoundly disappointing' and implying that, because Dostoevsky is a novelist, it is the novels that must take precedence.[31] Gide proceeds to reconstruct Dostoevsky's world-view and philosophy from his novels alone, ignoring the diaries, letters, and other material in which Dostoevsky sets out his beliefs. Another French poet, writer, and playwright, Paul Claudel (1868–1955) (Gide's one-time close friend and a prominent figure in the French Catholic Rennaissance) came to very much the same conclusion after reading the *Diary*, deciding that 'when Dostoevsky spoke in his own name, and not as a novelist, he could be discounted.'[32]

Furthermore, we can observe that readers who had the most idiosyncratic interpretations of the novels and subscribed to ideologies most 'inimical to the ideology of Dostoevsky himself' were not only unaffected by their reading of the *Diary*, the correspondence, and related materials, but, in fact, quoted these 'monological' texts in support of their original views. The Beats found nothing in the *Diary* and similar texts to contradict their initial opinions of Dostoevsky's belief system formed after reading his novels. Kerouac, for instance, was particularly fond of the *Diary*, which he referred to as 'Dostoevsky's holy diary.'[33]

Appropriating Dostoevsky

In light of the preceding discussion, my questions remain unanswered and as perplexing as ever. Why have so many iconoclastic writers who consider themselves part of various cultural and literary undergrounds (especially in America) appropriated Dostoevsky as their literary ancestor and mascot even if he had opened himself to radical misreadings? Who, in fact, is their Dostoevsky? How are extreme interpretations of Dostoevsky constructed? What factors are responsible for the perpetuation and proliferation of these extreme (mis)readings of Dostoevsky's texts? The answers to these questions are complex, multilateral, and cannot be derived from the speculations of intertextual study alone (as engaging and illuminating as these may often be). The scholar attempting to address these issues is in danger of either descending into generalities, whereby it is assumed that a writer's encounter with Dostoevsky occurred in a cultural, historical, and linguistic vacuum and little attention is paid to the specifics of the individual reading of a given Dostoevsky text, or conjecture, where, in lieu of specific information about an individual reading of a Dostoevsky text, the scholar's own understanding of a given text is assumed to be the writer's own interpretation as well.

One of the main difficulties, in fact, in approaching these questions in a grounded and credible manner is that often very little information is available about an individual writer's original or subsequent encounters with Dostoevsky, about the shaping of his or her interpretation of Dostoevsky, or even about the specific details of his or her understanding of Dostoevsky. One scholar addressing the question of Dostoevsky's impact on American writers of the 1920s and 1930s notes that this particular area has already been surveyed by other Dostoevsky scholars but points out that their answers cannot be considered conclusive because 'all of the historical-literary material has not been gathered to this day.'[34] It quickly becomes clear to anyone who does the research, however, that much of this 'historical-literary material,' whether relating to Dostoevsky's reception by writers of the 1920s and 1930s or of other decades, *cannot* be gathered because it simply does not exist.

A notorious example of this is William Faulkner (1897–1962). In a number of interviews and question-and-answer sessions given throughout his life, Faulkner seems only too ready to acknowledge his debt to and appreciation of Dostoevsky. In 1957, for instance, Faulkner refers to Dostoevsky as a writer 'who has not only influenced me a lot, but that I have got a great deal of pleasure out of reading.'[35] In several other interviews, Faulkner talks in passing about his respect for Dostoevsky's achievements and mentions his fondness for *Brothers Karamazov*. Many critics and scholars wrote about Faulkner's connection with Dostoevsky (the Belgian Dostoevsky scholar Jean Weisgerber devoted a whole book to the subject.)[36] Despite Faulkner's general willingness to talk about Dostoevsky in interviews, however, the fact remains that he had never *once* written about Dostoevsky, whether in his correspondence (his extant letters do not mention Dostoevsky), essays, prepared speeches, notes, or drafts. Furthermore, in the whole of Faulkner's gigantic literary output there is not a single direct reference to Dostoevsky and only one oblique reference to him in, arguably, a minor text (*Requiem for a Nun* [1951]).[37] Faulkner's extensive and thoroughly catalogued archive in the University of Virginia yields no additional information.

Dostoevsky, Henry Miller, and Friends

In these circumstances it is singularly fortunate that the writer who is universally perceived as being one of the most prominent figures of the twentieth-century literary underground not only admired Dostoevsky throughout his long life and engaged with him regularly during the most creatively important period of it, but also talked and wrote about Dostoevsky at length.

Henry Miller, who was surely one of Dostoevsky's most enthusiastic literary followers, is one of the most intriguing and influential but also one of the most notorious and reviled figures of twentieth-century letters, an icon of the literary underground in America and around the world. Miller first gained both international fame and notoriety for a series of literarily innovative but sexually provocative books published in France during the 1930s books which would eventually capture the attention of millions of readers from all walks of life, electrify the international avant-garde, inspire American writers, rally French intellectuals to defend freedom of expression, and provoke literary debates on both sides of the Atlantic ocean. In the 1930s Miller was at the hub of the Villa Seurat circle, a fascinating set of cosmopolitan writers, poets, and artists who congregated around his apartment studio at 18 Villa Seurat. This circle included two younger members who subsequently became famous in their own right: Anaïs Nin, the writer and diarist who became Miller's patron, lover, and muse, and Lawrence Durrell, a poet and writer who proclaimed himself to be Miller's disciple and who came to Paris from Greece expressly to meet him. Miller, Nin, and Durrell referred to themselves as the Three Musketeers, supported and critiqued each other's work, and comprised the inner circle at Villa Seurat.

While Miller, Nin, and Durrell were the three most famous and important writers to emerge from Villa Seurat, Miller was the undisputed leader during the 1930s. Although he was not the first of the group to be published (both Nin and Durrell had published books to their credit when all he had was a stack of unpublished manuscripts), he was the first to find his own voice and to gain international attention. His first published book, *Tropic of Cancer* (1934), was almost immediately acclaimed by a number of important critics and writers of the day, including the British George Orwell, the American T.S. Eliot, and the French Blaise Cendrars. At the same time, however, it was clear that *Tropic of Cancer* and the Paris books that followed (all of them published by Obelisk Press, a disreputable publishing company based in Paris that specialized in naughty English-language books for the traveller's market) could not be published in the United States or in any other English-speaking country, because they contained passages that were widely considered to be too shocking for the general reading public. Miller's books were smuggled into United States and other English-speaking countries by travellers and returning soldiers until 1961, when *Tropic of Cancer* was brought out by the New York-based Grove Press and became the target of numerous lawsuits under American anti-obscenity laws.[38]

When the dust finally settled, *Tropic of Cancer* was declared to be a work of literary merit by the United States Supreme Court, American obscenity laws changed forever, and Miller became a household name.[39] His reputation in America, however, suffered a blow from which it would never recover. Erica Jong, an American novelist and poet befriended by Miller in his later years, writes that this 'extensive litigation ... fixed Miller in the public's mind as the author of "filthy, disgusting, nauseating trash."'[40] Miller's novels were defended by prominent American intellectuals and he became a hero to many younger writers for his innovative prose, the unusual form of his books, and his fearlessness in dealing with topics that were considered taboo by society at large: Norman Mailer, an admirer of Miller, wrote in 1966 that '[Miller's] influence has been profound on a good half of all living American writers.'[41] At the same time, however, and much to Miller's personal chagrin, since he saw himself as a writer who sought 'to inspire and to awaken,'[42] he acquired the reputation of a writer of dirty books. Mary Dearborn, one of Miller's biographers, writes that 'the public and the press persisted in seeing him as the grand old man of sex,'[43] an image that converged in the American public's consciousness with that of a dangerous, subversive, and corrupting writer (the image painted of Miller by the prosecution in the court cases) and became a part of American popular culture. In Martin Scorcese's 1991 remake of the classic Hollywood thriller *Cape Fear*, Max Cody, a psychopathic criminal, tries to corrupt an underage girl by giving her Miller's *Tropic of Cancer* to read and instructing her to take notes.

Perhaps because of these circumstances, Miller never became a fully-fledged member of the American literary pantheon and remained an underground literary figure, at least as far as the American critical canon-makers are concerned. One Miller scholar points out that 'Miller's reputation in countries other than his native land by far exceeds his posthumous critical reception in America. In Europe (with the exception of the UK), Asia (especially Japan), and South America, Miller enjoys a vigorous critical debate.'[44] Karl Orend, founder of Alyscamps Press in Paris, writer and Miller expert surveying the situation in 2004 for *The Chronicle of Higher Education*, writes that Miller is 'rarely taught on American college campuses ... [despite the fact that] more than 15 major special collections in the United States have built significant repositories of his manuscripts' and concludes that he is 'underestimated and ignored by American universities,' even though his historical importance is much too great and obvious to be denied.[45] Despite all of this, Miller's impact on American culture and letters has been and continues to be enormous. In 1962, a writer in the American journal *Paris Review* explained that Miller had managed to make a deep impression upon his countrymen even before he was legally published in the United States: 'Henry Miller has long been a byword and a legend. Championed by critics and artists, venerated by pilgrims, emulated by beatniks, he is above everything else a culture hero – or villain, to those who see him as a menace to law and order. He might even be described as a folk hero: hobo, prophet and exile.'[46] In subsequent years, countless writers and poets would speak about their admiration for Miller and about his impact on their work and the work of their colleagues. In 2005 Miller scholar James Decker attempted to summarize Miller's influence on American writers and came up with an impressive list that illustrates the extensiveness and pervasiveness of Miller's influence:

> Beyond his indirect impact on such novelists as Nicholson Baker, Kathy Acker, and Bret Easton Ellis, Miller ... inspired members of the Beat movement ... Kerouac, Allen Ginsberg, and Lawrence Ferlinghetti, among others, admired Miller greatly ... Other American writers – such as Roth, Mailer, Terry Southern, and John Updike – saw in Miller a continuation of the realist project, now combined with psychoanalysis and sexual frankness, while authors such as Pynchon, Acker, Robert Duncan, Erica Jong, and Jim Harrison reacted to Miller's violent rejection of modernity. The expansive, teasingly metaphysical style of writers such as T. Coraghessan Boyle, David Foster Wallace, and Jeffrey Eugenides also finds an antecedent in Miller's [work] ... Younger writers continue to read Miller and to debate his project.[47]

One of the main keys to understanding not only Miller's but also Nin's and Durrell's writings and subsequent successes lies in the personal and literary alliance they forged at Villa Seurat. There they developed their outlook on writing, honed their skills, critiqued, inspired, and spurred each other on in their literary journeys. Despite the professional and personal disagreements that the three would experience in later years, they all shared the belief that writing needed to be revolutionized and that they were the ones to bring about this revolution. But if the relationship of these three writers in

Paris was the forge in which they shaped their unique literary voices, the symbolic fire that fuelled it was Dostoevsky.

Miller wrote many times that before encountering Dostoevsky – 'the god, the real one'[48] – he felt disenfranchised and alienated in the America of the 1910s and 1920s (a society he regarded as being concerned solely with economic progress and social conformity) and that in Dostoevsky he finally found a kindred spirit who started him on the road to becoming a writer. Both the place and time when Miller first heard Dostoevsky's name would gain a mystical significance in his eyes, invoked repeatedly in his texts as a life- and consciousness-altering event. In interviews given throughout his life, in his voluminous correspondence, and in his prolific writings Miller provided countless testimonials about his highly emotional and devotional view of Dostoevsky as a brother figure and literary hero. What is more, Miller, whose literary enthusiasms were both numerous and wildly eclectic, remained loyal to Dostoevsky throughout his long life. In one of Miller's last published pieces, 'Mother, China and the World Beyond' (1977), written when he was in his eighties, he explained: 'the writer I most admire is the Russian Dostoevsky ... To me without Dostoevsky's work there would be a deep, black hole in world literature. The loss of Shakespeare ... would not be as great as losing Dostoevsky.'[49]

Miller, however, saw Dostoevsky as more than just a fraternal figure and a source of inspiration. During his years at Villa Seurat, Miller believed that Dostoevsky was the acme he had to reach and surpass in his own work. More originally, at the time when many of Miller's contemporaries celebrated Dostoevsky as the novelist who had inaugurated a new era of the novel, Miller came to believe on the basis of his obsessive reading of Dostoevsky during his early years in New York and, subsequently, in Paris, that Dostoevsky had exhausted the possibilities of the novelistic genre and, in so doing, helped terminate the age of the novel, which was, in any case, no longer able to reflect the apocalyptic realities of the twentieth century. What is more, Miller proclaimed that Dostoevsky had achieved not only all that was possible to achieve within the novel form but, indeed, all that was possible within the confines of literature itself. It was because Dostoevsky achieved the very peak of what could be done in literature that he had to be studied so closely: he was the gateway for the next stage, which was none other than a revolution in prose narrative. Through an in-depth reading of Dostoevsky's work, an intimate knowledge of his characters, and constant meditation on his achievements, one could break through to a new kind of writing. This new prose could be called transliterary in the sense that it would be liberated from the literary constraints and conventions that characterized even such great literary achievements as Dostoevsky's novels (proper plot, three-dimensional characters, clearly defined provenance as fiction, cohesive text) but that no longer sufficed to reflect twentieth-century reality. It is this utopian ideal of a revolutionary form of prose narrative that transcended what had been possible in literature that Miller attempted to attain in his writing.

Miller's position of prominence at Villa Seurat enabled him to effectively promote his views on Dostoevsky and his belief in the need for a prose revolution to fellow writers who looked to him for guidance. Although Dostoevsky never became as all-absorbingly important to the other writers of Villa Seurat as he was for Miller, he still figured largely in the literary and personal exchanges of the Villa Seurat writers, especially in the dialogue of Miller, Nin, and Durrell. This dialogue is well-documented in their letters, diaries, notes, writings, and interviews, which are full of references to Dostoevsky, to their reading and interpretation of his novels, his characters, his style, his philosophy, and his relevance – a treasure trove of practically unmined material for anyone interested in the question of the appropriation of Dostoevsky by the literary underground and counterculture.

An examination of the response to Dostoevsky by Miller and the writers of the Villa Seurat group presents us with several unique opportunities. Helen Muchnic, the American scholar whose pioneering study *Dostoevsky's English Reputation: 1881–1936* (1939) lay the groundwork for anyone considering the question of Dostoevsky's reception by American and British writers, acknowledges in her conclusion that her study provides more insights into the minds of the critics and writers reading Dostoevsky than on Dostoevsky himself.[50] This is a just observation, with one important addition: while a study of this kind rarely provides major new insights into the life and work of Dostoevsky, it certainly provides new and vital insights into 'Dostoevsky' – the constructed total image of the writer and his body of work as it exists in the cultural milieu in which the specific readings of Dostoevsky are enacted.

A study of the Villa Seurat group's reading of Dostoevsky is important on several different levels. First, it allows us a close look into the mind and work of Henry Miller, a fascinating and influential writer, whose *Tropic of Cancer* was included in the Modern Library's list of the most important books of the twentieth century, and, to a lesser extent, into the work of Nin and Durrell, two writers who made their own independent marks on twentieth-century literature. It also provides us with an overview of the structure and dynamics of the Villa Seurat group, an important but still largely unexamined literary and cultural nexus in Paris between the wars. Further, by carefully reconstructing Miller's reading of Dostoevsky *in situ*, as it were, first within the American context of his early encounters with Dostoevsky and then within his Parisian milieu, we can gain an understanding not only of Miller's – and, subsequently, Villa Seurat's – Dostoevsky, but of how this seemingly idiosyncratic understanding was actually a development of a well-established American tradition of interpreting Dostoevsky and his novels. The facts that Miller worked so closely to the pulse of popular consciousness and had such a profound impact on subsequent genera- tions of counterculture writers, poets, and film-makers, and that his opinions on Dostoevsky (so prominently included in his books) were read by multitudes of readers, allow us a better understanding of the importance Dostoevsky acquired for various literary undergrounds (particularly in America) and of the way in which he was interpreted and appropriated by them. Finally, this case study of Dostoevsky's impact on Miller and his friends at Villa Seurat provides insight not only into the importance that Dostoevsky acquired in twentieth-century literary and cultural discourses but also into the transformations that texts undergo when they travel across linguistic, temporal, and cultural matrices and into the whole process of intercultural literary interactions.

2 Dostoevsky as American Icon

> I plunked myself in front of Dostoevsky's portrait, as I had done before many a time, to study his familiar physiognomy anew ... I stood there, as always, trying to penetrate the mystery.
>
> Henry Miller, *Plexus*, 20

In 1872, the famous Muscovite art collector Pavel Tretiakov commissioned a fashionable Russian artist, Vasily Perov, to paint a portrait of Fedor Dostoevsky. Dostoevsky's portrait was pronounced a masterpiece and exhibited in St Petersburg later that year, in Moscow in 1874, and in Paris in 1878 as part of the International Artists Exhibition. It became the most celebrated portrait of Dostoevsky, reproduced around the world as the truest image of the Russian novelist.[1]

Perov sat Dostoevsky in three-quarter profile, his cheekbones sharply defined, his face sickly and gaunt. The novelist is depicted wearing a grey jacket, bulkier and more formless than is typical of the period, more of an overcoat than a tailored frock-coat. His legs are crossed; large hands with prominent veins and square fingers clasp one knee. Only the colours of his cravat, black with blood-red upward rushing streaks, relieve the rigidity of his pose. Darkening the left side of the painting behind and above him is a drab brown backdrop. Dostoevsky's intense gaze turns away from the viewer and travels downward into darkness.

Perov's portrait, which came to represent the writer at the moment of literary creation, brilliantly articulates and combines a number of classic topoi associated with Dostoevsky. The shabby 'overcoat' invokes Dostoevsky's years of penury and exile but also acts as a visual reference to Nikolai Gogol (1809–52), Dostoevsky's literary god-father, whose short story 'The Overcoat' ['Shinel'] (1842) heralded a tri-umphant new epoch in Russian literature. The primal swirling colours of the cravat evoke the intense passions of Dostoevsky's characters and his own life. The background, with its blend of ochre, russet, and umber, recalls the gloom of St Petersburg tenements and the setting of most of his novels. The stern, tense expression of Dostoevsky's face suggests untold suffering. His fixed gaze seems to travel beyond the painting; it seems to look both inward and outward into the heart of a darkness populated by the obscure and downtrodden.

But does the portrait capture the 'essence' of Dostoevsky? After all, the diary of his wife Anna and the reminiscences of some of his close friends depict a man who liked to laugh, enjoyed playing practical jokes, and relished performing comic roles in amateur theatrical pro-ductions. Ultimately, however, it does not matter. As Picasso com-mented after finishing Gertrude Stein's portrait: 'She doesn't look like it now, but she will.' Perov's portrait has become an icon of Dostoevsky that is far more identifiable than any photograph. Dostoevsky's sup-porters and detractors alike insisted that the portrait represented the real Dostoevsky. Hostile Russian critics claimed that it provided unde-niable visual proof of Dostoevsky's mental illness; Russian and inter-national devotees of the novelist said that it revealed his prophetic soul. One Dostoevsky admirer celebrated the portrait as an epiphany on canvas, an icon before which one could lose oneself in adoration: 'The prophet's smouldering, self-consuming ardour burns and stares from these facial features – the stiff, far-seeking gaze of a reclusive seer, a soul whose inspiration and passion were world-embracing, a heart which felt to their depths all human woes, which understood all vice, all ignominy and degradation, as well as all piety, goodness and pure-mindedness.[2] The portrait imprinted its essence upon the viewer's consciousness, becoming not only 'true' but canonical. Even though subsequent artist interpreters of Dostoevsky, from Yuri Annenkov to Ilia Glazunov, had access to many photographs of him, they all responded to Perov's portrait, visually 'citing' and echoing it in their engravings, sculptures, and drawings as the one image of Dostoevsky with which everyone was undeniably familiar.

The cultural icon that is Dostoevsky has a far messier history. Few writers have had such an impact interculturally, or a richer, more fasci-nating historical reception. The 'foreign' veneration of Dostoevsky manifested itself in cultural centres all over the world, from Berlin to

Bombay, Johannesburg to Oslo, Paris to Tokyo. There was even a phenomenon known as the Dostoevsky cult: British literati who revered
Dostoevsky as a literary demiurge who revealed humanity itself.[3] But
if Dostoevsky's impact was felt globally, the United States, just coming
into its own as a centre of cultural production when Dostoevsky's
translations appeared on the scene, was the one country other than
Russia where his work shaped the development of an entire national
literature and influenced popular culture in the twentieth century.

Dostoevsky's American Reception

The translation of Dostoevsky's novels into English occurred relatively
late compared to his translations into French, German, or Italian,
which, in many cases, became available shortly after the original Russian publication. The few English-language translations of Dostoevsky
at the close of the nineteenth century left much to be desired and were
frequently second-or even third-hand translations from German or
French. It was only in the 1910s and 1920s, via the work of Constance
Garnett, the most influential English translator of Russian fiction, that
the way was finally opened to the appreciation of Dostoevsky in countries in which English was spoken and especially in the United States,
where even educated intellectuals tended to be more monolingual than
their counterparts in Britain and could not avail themselves of the various European translations. The excited buzz generated by Garnett's
translations in her circle of London literati attracted many British writers and thinkers to Dostoevsky, but it was the Americans who had a
vested and proprietorial interest in the writer and his works.[4]

Unlike Britain, France, Germany, and Italy, which were widely recognized and respected for having a rich cultural and literary heritage,
the United States, long positioned at the margins of the Western canon
and described in terms of its 'otherness,' had a genuine affinity for
Dostoevsky. Henry James was one of many who saw both American
and Russian society and culture as still being in an embryonic and
emerging state, observing that 'Russian society, like our own, is in process of formation, the Russian character is in solution, in a sea of
change.'[5] A society still in the 'process of formation' could hardly be
expected to produce great literature, and American literature, like its
Russian counterpart, was for a long time denied critical respectability
in Europe. In 1875, an American reviewer of a book about Russian literature observed that Russian literature was ignored and virtually

unknown outside of Russia and concluded that 'in many respects Russia has held to Europe, with regard to its intellectual and literary life, a position analogous to that of the United States.'[6] At the opening of the twentieth century the literature of the United States, like that of Russia, was still being dismissed by many European critics as too jejune to be of any consequence. D.H. Lawrence, writing in the 1920s, pointed out the parallels between the reception of Russian and American literature by Europeans and commented that, for the latter, American literature was still predominantly 'children's tales.'[7] The first Nobel prizes to an American and a Russian writer, finally granting a status of legitimacy, as it were, to their respective literatures, were awarded only in the 1930s and, suggestively, a mere three years apart (to Sinclair Lewis in 1930 and to Ivan Bunin in 1933).

Dostoevsky was one of many Russian writers translated and imported into the United States in the late nineteenth and early twentieth centuries. He was, however, the first to be celebrated by European critics for standing 'apart' from the European literary tradition (ironically so, since subsequent scholarship has amply demonstrated his links to such canonic European writers as Charles Dickens, Honoré de Balzac, and E.T.A. Hoffmann, among many others). His acceptance as a literary 'outsider' was bound to intrigue American writers, who found themselves in a similar predicament, and intrigued they were, leading one scholar of Dostoevsky's American reception to conclude that 'not a single important twentieth century American writer passed by Dostoevsky with indifference.'[8]

In the twentieth century many scholars considered the question of Dostoevsky's impact on American literature, but a full history of Dostoevsky's reception in America has yet to be written, presenting us with certain difficulties when we attempt to reconstruct how any American writer, including Henry Miller, approached Dostoevsky. It is clear that if we aim to learn how an individual reading of Dostoevsky was constructed, we must first understand the cultural iconography of Dostoevsky within the society in which that individual reading was enacted. Unfortunately, even the early history of Dostoevsky's American reception is woefully incomplete. From the groundbreaking but long outdated monograph of the American Slavist Helen Muchnic[9] to more recent work on the subject, most scholars have either opted not to differentiate between British and American responses to Dostoevsky (even though there are important differences between his reception in the two countries), or surveyed the American response to a number of

Russian writers. In so doing they restrict the scope and depth of their investigation of Dostoevsky's impact in America – a subject complex enough to warrant a separate study.[10]

Although Dostoevsky's American reception has only begun to be explored, the key factors that laid the foundation of his iconography in the United States can be identified with relative ease. These include 1) the fact that the first of Dostoevsky's works to reach the imagination of American readers was his Notes from the Dead House [Zapiski iz mertvogo doma](1860–2); 2) the fact that Melchior de Vogüé's insightful but deeply opinionated Le roman russe (1886) served as the most authoritative introduction to Dostoevsky available to American readers; and 3) the fortunate circumstance that the American sociocultural climate between 1912 and 1920 – the time period when Constance Garnett's translations of Dostoevsky were being published – was particularly favourable to the discovery of Dostoevsky by Americans.

Siberian Sensation

In retrospect, it is not surprising that Dostoevsky's Notes from the Dead House caught the attention of American readers. This novel about Russian convict life appealed to the well-established American fascination with Siberia, fuelled by travel writings, the purchase of Alaska in 1867 (making Russia a next-door neighbour), and the ever-popular 'exotic Russia' novels in which delicate heroines were exiled to Siberian wastes. Notes from the Dead House has been described as a 'deceptively objective and noncommital' novel, and today is 'probably the least read' of Dostoevsky's longer works. The neglect into which this novel of Siberian imprisonment and exile has fallen, however, belies its enormous impact and popularity upon publication, both in Russia and in the United States.[11]

Notes from the Dead House narrates the experiences of the wife-murderer Alexander Petrovich Gorianchikov, whose papers were supposedly discovered by chance and introduced to the world by an unnamed editor. Upon its publication in Russia, the novel, intended to constitute a literary comeback, created a 'furore' according to both Dostoevsky's contemporaries and Dostoevsky himself (28/II:115), in part because of its immediate status as 'the most reliable and most interesting information about ... the Russian jail'[12] but primarily because it documented the experience of Siberian imprisonment firsthand. The novel became available in America in 1881, the year of Dostoevsky's death, in the form of a second-rate and second-hand translation by Marie Von Thilo, but demand was so unprecedented that a new 'authorized' translation by H.S. Edwards appeared in 1887. *Notes from the Dead House* thus gained the distinction of becoming the only novel by Dostoevsky available in more than one English translation during the nineteenth century.

American readers were fascinated by what they regarded as an accurate source of information about Siberia and, by extension, about Russia. Its publishers marketed the sensationalist appeal of the novel with a new title, *Buried Alive or Ten Years of Penal Servitude in Siberia*, deliberately playing upon the clichés of Russia engulfed by the snow of its endless winters and the oppressiveness of the Russian regime. *Notes from the Dead House* was packaged to fit an American stereotype of Russia, summed up by one disgruntled Russian as '[the] exotic charm [of] snow and wolves and police agents, with the threatening prospect of Siberia in the background.'[13]

The American publication of *Notes from the Dead House* did much to lay the foundation of Dostoevsky's American reception. American readers, encouraged by the novel's publishers, were never sure which parts were fact and which fiction, and consistently confused the persona of the narrator with that of the author. The novel, announced by its publisher in one circular as 'Fedor Dostoevsky's record of his ten years' exile in Siberia,' was read as a hybrid of journalism and memoir, valuable for the factual information it provided rather than for anything else. American reviewers saw the novel as a straightforward report of Dostoevsky's own experience, a report that lacked both design and stylistic polish. 'There is little attempt at story, and none at all at fine writing,' commented one anonymous reviewer in 1887.[14]

The Outsider

With *Notes from the Dead House* Dostoevsky entered the American consciousness as an autobiographical writer whose literary value resided in the authenticity of his observations and certainly not in his powers of composition. Melchior de Vogüé's *Le roman russe* did little to correct this impression among American readers in 1886.

The French nobleman Viscount Eugène-Melchior de Vogüé was an accepted authority on Russian culture and literature of his time. His appointment in 1877 to the post of secretary to the French Embassy in St Petersburg provided him with the opportunity to become proficient in Russian, personally meet with many Russian writers, and even marry into the Russian nobility. His *Le roman russe* originated as a series of essays on Russian literature that appeared in an influential European journal, *Revue des Deux Mondes*, during the 1880s. When revised and published in book form in 1886 the study was widely acclaimed in Europe, immediately translated into English, and published in America.[15] Given that only a handful of Dostoevsky's books had been translated into English prior to the publication of the translated *Le roman russe*, the latter became simultaneously an introduction to Dostoevsky's work and the most authoritative source of information about Dostoevsky and his novels available to the American readers (in England, a translation of *Le roman russe* was not published until 1913).

Vogüé's critical biases, however, were legion. Fredrick Hemmings, author of *The Russian Novel in France, 1884–1914* (1950) writes that 'the viscount's blend of irritation and enthusiasm, of shortsightedness and penetration, makes it hard to pronounce one way or the other about his Dostoevsky criticism.'[16] While Hemmings may be right, it is still clear that Vogüé's appreciation for Dostoevsky's particular genius was in many ways limited by Russian high society's view of the writer, a perspective that Vogüé himself came to share. Although Dostoevsky was welcomed in the homes of many members of the Russian royal family, he frequently committed various social blunders, leading to anecdotes that amused some and outraged others. There was the story, for example, about Dostoevsky cornering the future Empress, Maria Fedorovna, and, in a dreadful breach of etiquette, absentmindedly twisting a button on her dress while telling her an involved story. In Vogüé's personal reminiscences of Dostoevsky, also included in *Le roman russe*, he writes that in the heat of debate Dostoevsky once shocked Russian ladies by telling them that they were not worthy of holding a candle to the lowliest Russian peasant.[17] Then there was Dostoevsky's famous rivalry with Ivan Turgenev, which led to some embarrassing public scenes. Characteristically, Vogüé took Turgenev's side, explaining that Dostoevsky simply envied Turgenev's groundbreaking portrayal of Nihilism in *Fathers and Sons* [*Otsy i deti*] (1862).[18]

Vogüé himself got into an argument with Dostoevsky, recording in his diary, 'Discussion avec Dostoïevski. Curieux type d'obstiné russe, se croyant plus profond que toute l'Europe parce qu'il est plus trouble.'[19] The argument, which started as a conversation on literary subjects, ended with Dostoevsky declaring that a Frenchman could never understand a Russian, because Russians have 'le génie de tous les peuples et en plus le génie russe ... donc nous pouvons vous comprendre et vous ne pouvez nous comprendre' (Vogüé would later cite these words in *Le roman russe*, wryly commenting, 'Les discussions littéraires finissaient vite avec Dostoïevski').[20] What piqued Vogüé more than Dostoevsky's Russophile arrogance, however, was his lack of good manners and his combination of clumsiness and prickliness, which led Vogüé to memorably describe Dostoevsky in his diary as a cross between a bear and a hedgehog.[21] Unlike Count Leo Tolstoy and the gentrified, wealthy Turgenev (the other two Russian novelists featured in *Le roman russe*), whose status and social graces ensured that they moved easily in the highest circles of St Petersburg society, Dostoevsky was always an outsider, first as '[l]e pauvre petit ingénieur,'[22] then as convict, soldier, and, finally, as a debt-ridden epileptic writer, who simply did not know how to behave in polite company and who, according to Vogüé, could not create a convincing upper-class character.[23]

When in *Le roman russe* Americans read Vogüé's famous essay on Dostoevsky and his novels suggestively entitled 'La religion de la souffrance', they found many confirmations of their original impressions of Dostoevsky gathered through a naive reading of *Notes from the Dead House*. Vogüé claimed that the key to all Dostoevsky's novels is the personal anguish distilled into his writing ('on aurait peine à comprendre ces livres si l'on ne savait la vie de celui qui les a créés, j'allais dire qui les a soufferts; peu importe, le premier mot renferme toujours le second')[24] and that Dostoevsky's writing is largely autobiographical (thus, for example, Vogüé explained that it is Dostoevsky's own intimate history that one finds in *The Insulted and the Injured* [*Unizhennye i oskorblennye*]).[25] Vogüé insisted that the characters in Dostoevsky's novels are incarnations of his own soul,[26] and were to be identified with their creator – especially Prince Myshkin.[27] Significantly, Vogüé reinforced the stereotype of Dostoevsky as an indifferent stylist, whose novels feature 'longueurs … intolérables' and who produced nothing of real greatness after *Crime and Punishment* [*Prestuplenie i nakazanie*] (1866).[28] (This criticism would later be mirrored in Henry James's infamous characterization of Dostoevsky's novels as 'fluid puddings though not tasteless,' because of their 'lack of composition [and] their defiance of economy and structure').[29]

Fortunately, Vogüé's introduction to Dostoevsky consisted of more than criticism of his style and outpourings of respect for authentic if formless suffering. Vogüé provided his readers with a short but fairly accurate biography of the writer, eyewitness accounts of the national exhilaration after Dostoevsky's famous Pushkin speech in 1880 and the national outburst of grief at Dostoevsky's funeral in 1881, which afforded a glimpse of the novelist's stature and importance in contemporary Russia; and a number of close readings of Dostoevsky's texts (most notably of *Poor Folk* [*Bednye liudi*] [1846], for which Vogüé reserved the highest praise). Vogüé also introduced several new features into the rapidly fossilizing stereotype of Dostoevsky in America. The most important of these was his description of Dostoevsky as the ultimate outsider.

While the notion of Dostoevsky's social displacement was already nascent in the reading of *Notes from the Dead House* as autobiography, Vogüé went much further than that. He depicted Dostoevsky not only as a social outsider, an ill-mannered ex-convict, but as a literary and cultural outsider as well, amplifying these concepts to include marvellous and abnormal elements. 'Il faut considérer,' he writes, 'Dostoïevsky comme un phénomène d'un autre monde, un monstre incomplet et puissant.'[30] Vogüé pictured Dostoevsky as a mighty literary barbarian who comes to overthrow the West – 'Voici venir le Scythe, le vrai Scythe, qui va révolutionner toutes nos habitudes intellectuelles,'[31] – but whose ultimate downfall is that he himself is a creature of darkness who can write only of shadows, horrors, and tears: 'C'est un voyageur qui a parcouru tout l'univers et admirablement décrit tout ce qu'il a vu, mais qui n'a jamais voyagé que de nuit. Psychologue incomparable, dès qu'il étudie des âmes noires ou blessées, dramaturge habile, mais borné aux scènes d'effroi et de pitié.'[32]

It is Vogüé's verdict on Dostoevsky that informs the opinions of many nineteenth-and early twentieth-century American literary critics who, like William Dean Howells, felt that Dostoevsky had little to say to citizens of the New World, whose reality was so 'full of shining possibilities and radiant promises,'[33] and whose lives had little in common with their tragic and underprivileged Russian counterparts: 'In a land where journeymen carpenters and plumbers strike for four dollars a day the sum of hunger and cold is comparatively small ... Our novelists, therefore, concern themselves with the more smiling aspects of life, which are the more American.'[34]

This commonplace reading of Dostoevsky through the lens of Vogüé's *Le roman russe* prevented a richer interpretation until well into the twentieth century. Dostoevsky was pigeonholed as a talented maverick whose sufferings were irrelevant to the progressive tenor of Western civilization and, especially, to optimistic and prosperous America. That American reality, however, was about to change.

America Prepares for Dostoevsky

Change in America came so gradually that some, like Howells, can be forgiven for failing to notice it at all. Nevertheless, it would become difficult to ignore. Increased immigration from Europe at the end of the nineteenth century resulted in massive urbanization, overpopulated cities, crowded tenements, and the increased visibility of poverty. A typical tenement block in New York presented a setting as squalid as any found in St Petersburg slums of Dostoevsky's day: '2781 persons on two acres of land, nearly every bit of which was covered with buildings. There were 466 babies in the block, but not a bathtub, except the one that hung in an air-shaft. Of the 1588 rooms, 441 were dark, with no ventilation to the outer air; 635 rooms gave upon 'twilight airshafts.' In five years 32 cases of tuberculosis had been reported from that block, and in that time 660 different families in the block had applied for charity.'[35] Once it had moved to the heart of the big cities, the existence of poverty and disease in the United States was no longer easy to ignore. Americans were slowly awakened to the fact that 'the sum of hunger and cold' in their own country was much larger than they had hoped.

A further blow to American complacency about their role in the free world was delivered by the First World War. As detailed reports of allied casualties and the atrocities in Europe hit the front page, and once the United States entered the war in 1917, Americans began to lose their smiling acceptance of American politics, which now required them to fight and die on the battlefields of Europe. They were also losing their faith in America's economic and social exclusivity, along with their rosy optimism about American progress. Coinciding with these major shifts in the American experience was the rise of psychoanalysis, which rediscovered the psyche as yet another misunderstood and dangerous battlefield. Sigmund Freud sailed to America with Carl Jung and Sandor Ferenczi to lecture on psychoanalysis in 1909; by 1916 about five hundred psychoanalysts were practising in New York City alone.

Shocked by the brutalities of the First World War, uncertain of their future, and apprehensive about what their own psyches hid from them, Americans were ready for their new encounter with Dostoevsky. When Constance Garnett's translations of Dostoevsky appeared between 1912 and 1920, many Americans were inclined to agree with the young T.S. Eliot that they 'have been living in one of Dostoevsky's novels ... not in one of Jane Austen's.'[36]

Garnett Translations and American Readers

There is no doubt that Garnett's translations were superior to those available earlier to Americans, who had been complaining about being forced to read Dostoevsky's novels 'wretchedly translated into English from a wretched French translation.'[37] Relatively few American readers could read the novels in the French translation (after all, not all French translations were 'wretched'). T.S. Eliot, who first read and came to appreciate Dostoevsky in a French translation during his stay in Paris in 1910–11, only did so because his young tutor and friend (the French writer and critic Alain-Fournier [1886–1914]) assigned the texts as part of Eliot's French studies.[38]

Garnett, who had a passion for Dostoevsky's work and a genuine talent for mediating and recreating his novels into a new linguistic and cultural context, translated Dostoevsky from the original Russian. Her translations have had a remarkable staying power; as one scholar recently noted, not only have 'they have remained in print to this day [but] new translators have always had to justify their work against the background of her authoritative body of work.'[39] All the same, it has also been observed that 'of all Russian writers, Dostoevsky is probably one of the most resistant in translation into English'[40] and, as subsequent translators and scholars have pointed out, Garnett took many liberties with Dostoevsky's text, introducing inaccuracies and stylistic distortions for the sake of a more domesticated and fluent reading of his novels.[41]

One has only to compare Garnett's translation of the opening sentence of *Crime and Punishment* with the original Russian text to see how much she was willing to alter to create a smoother read. The Russian original reads:

> V nachale iulia, v chrezvychaino zharkoe vremia, pod vecher, odin molodoi chelovek vyshel iz svoei komorki, kotoruiu nanimal ot zhil'tsov v S-m pereulke, na ulitsu i medlenno, kak by v nereshimosti, otpravilsia k K-nu mostu. (6:5)
>
> [In the beginning of July, during an extremely hot time, close to evening, one young man walked out of his tiny room, which he was renting from the tenants in S-i Lane, onto the street and slowly, as if in hesitation, set off toward K-n Bridge.][42]

Garnett renders it as follows: 'On an exceptionally hot evening early in July a young man came out of the garret in which he lodged in S. Place and walked slowly, as though in hesitation, towards K. Bridge.'[43]

Garnett not only deletes an important piece of information (Raskolnikov rents his room from people who are tenants themselves, which affects the reader's understanding of his social position as well as that of his landlady, who is introduced in the subsequent paragraph), but she also mistranslates certain words (Dostoevsky's narrator does later tell the reader that Raskolnikov lodges in the attic, but here he specifically calls it a *'kamorka,'* which Vladimir Dal's classic nineteenth-century Russian dictionary glosses as 'a tiny room' [*komnatka*] or 'store-room' [*kladovaia*]).[44] Furthermore, Garnett alters the syntax of the original sentence far more than is necessary to render an accurate translation into English; she simplifies it, gets rid of the buildup of modifying phrases, and compresses the sentence, making it appear much more polished and literary but also distorting the conversationally casual, exaggeratedly slow-paced style of the original opening of the novel.

Despite these distortions, most Dostoevsky scholars agree that Garnett succeeded in the challenge of translating such a difficult author: '[she] faced the formidable task of introducing this extremely alien voice into the concert of English literature. She treads a fine line between excessive discordance and excessive fluency, and for all one may say against the resulting text, it achieved its aim triumphantly.'[45] What has not been considered to date, however, is that American readers of the Garnett translations may have had a distinct advantage over their English counterparts.

Paradoxically, one of the main problems inherent in good translations is the very thing that most competent translators seek to achieve: the illusion that a translation is representative in all ways of the original text, with the result being that the readers of the translation feel enabled to confidently pass judgment on the style, form, and language of the original text. At best, however, a translation has a similar correlation to the original text as a reproduction of a painting has to the original painting. Even a very good reproduction of Perov's famous portrait of Dostoevsky, for instance, gives the viewer only an approximate idea of the scale, the colour palette, the paint texture, the brush strokes, and other subtle nuances of the original portrait hanging in the Tretiakov Art Gallery in Moscow, a fact that most viewers of the reproduction readily recognize. Yet the mediation, interpretation, and rewriting involved in producing a translation of a literary text often go practically unnoticed by the readers. Peter France, British translator, literary scholar, and editor of *The Oxford Guide to Literature in English Translation* (2000), observes that 'those reading translations often seem unconscious of the fact, as if in reading

Garnett they were simply reading Dostoevsky – it is easy to overlook the fascinating work of rewriting that translation represents.'[46]

Contemporary translators meditating on their craft frequently talk about the necessity of preserving the 'precious otherness' or 'strangeness' of the original in the translation as a way of both reminding the reader that the text they are reading is a product of a different linguistic and cultural milieu, and also of engaging the reader in the process of imagining what the original text may be like. Lawrence Venuti, award-winning translator, scholar, and specialist in literary translation theory, has talked convincingly about the necessity 'to see the translator in the text, to become aware of a translation as a translation ... to realize that there's another text there.'[47]

Interestingly, the Garnett translations include a number of lexical markers that, while sounding neutral or nearly neutral to Garnett's original readership, come across as peculiarly English to American readers. For an illustration of this, one might turn to her translation of *Crime and Punishment*, which originally appeared in 1914. Even a casual perusal of the Garnett translation yields a number of Anglicisms, while a comparison of these with the original Russian text shows yet again that Garnett was less concerned with accuracy than she was with mediating a more domesticated text for her original English readership.

In the Garnett translation, for instance, Marmeladov's wife finds 'not a farthing' in her husband's pockets when he returns home from his drunken spree.[48] In the original Russian, of course, she finds 'not a kopek' ['*ni kopeiki*'] (6:24). Garnett introduces the expression 'by Jove' (stylistically unremarkable for her original readers but unusual and evoking rich Dickensian associations for her American readers) into the speech of several characters, including Razumikhin and Porfiry.[49] In each case, the original Russian expression is simply '*ei bogu*,' which could be translated 'as God is my witness,' 'God knows,' or, rendered even more neutrally, 'honestly' (6:116, 149, 347). Garnett also shows a fondness for the expression 'capital,' as in 'capital fellow' and so forth, which would have gone largely unnoticed by her original readership but sounds peculiarly English to a North American ear. Again, the original Russian could have been translated in a much simpler, more accurate, and more stylistically neutral way. Thus, Porfiry to Raskolnikov, 'Government quarters ... are a capital thing,'[50] could be rendered more in accordance with the Russian as 'a fine thing' ['*slavnaia veshch*'] (6:256); Razumikhin's emotional praise of Raskolnikov: 'you are a capital fellow, a capital fellow'[51] could be translated more accurately as

'you are a most outstanding person! A most outstanding person!'
['*ty otlichneishii chelovek! Otlichneishii chelovek!*'] (6:339); and finally,
Nastasia's words to Raskolnikov (she is the uneducated village-born
servant in the house where he rents his room), urging him to eat the
'capital soup,'[52] could have been translated more in accordance with
the original as simply 'good cabbage soup' ['*khoroshie shchi*'] (6:26).
Many more examples of this kind can be culled from the Garnett translation, but the important point is that while English readers, faced with
such familiar idioms and expressions, could easily lose the sense that
they were reading a translation, American readers, faced with the same
idioms and expressions, were reminded of it practically at every turn.
It is a matter of conjecture, of course, as to how much this 'Englishing
of Dostoevsky'[53] allowed American readers to speculate about what
the original text may have been like. At the very least, however, they
must have been aware while reading Garnett's translation that there
was, in fact, 'another text there.'

Garnett's translations brought Dostoevsky to the attention of a
wide range of American writers, poets, and critics. In an article that
appeared in New York's *New Review* in 1915, the writer and journalist
Floyd Dell wrote that Dostoevsky's 'importation into the common
stock of literature accessible in English, through the translation of
Constance Garnett ... is likely to be an event of significance in
English and American literature ... it makes us demand as readers,
and should make us desire to achieve as writers, those larger boundaries, those abysmal depths and terrific heights of experience which
Dostoevsky's art includes.'[54]

The Prophet

While the stereotype of Dostoevsky as 'Outsider' remained part of
the American consciousness, his iconic significance was transformed.
The suffering maverick and loner of the earlier decades metamorphosed
into the impartial and wise observer of humanity. Floyd Dell agreed that
Dostoevsky might have a 'peculiar and morbid soul,' but wrote that his
soul embodied 'the soul of mankind.'[55] If Dostoevsky was still an outsider both to society and the literary canon, now this position was seen to
be a privileged one: he was no longer a poor outcast looking in or away,
but a prophet observing the sad reality of human life from a position of
superior understanding and delivering pronouncements of oracular
import that were especially relevant to American society. Dell explained

that Americans were undergoing 'a change' and 'beginning to suspect that we are not really the respectable citizens that we seem ... but a medley of violent extremes of good and evil. A science has already come forward, in the shape of Psychoanalysis, to teach us this. And so perhaps we are ready to learn the same thing from the novels of Dostoevsky.'[56]

The younger generation embraced Dostoevsky with special enthusiasm. One American intellectual reminiscing about his youth recalled that around 1915 the 'enfants terribles of Brooklyn' immersed themselves in Dostoevsky and fancied themselves to be Dostoevskian characters, 'while [their] parents knew nothing or could make nothing of all this.'[57] The response of the American literary intelligentsia to Dostoevsky's novels was also becoming increasingly reverential. Sherwood Anderson called Dostoevsky 'the one writer I could go down on my knees to' and compared Brothers Karamazov to the Bible, adding, 'there is nothing like [it] anywhere else in literature.'[58] Hart Crane extravagantly claimed that a reading of Dostoevsky 'ought to prepare one's mind to handle any human situation ... that ever might arise.'[59]

A sense of awed recognition accompanied American reading of Dostoevsky's novels. Dostoevsky remained a writer of darkness, gloom, and extreme states, but now he also presaged, penetrated, and depicted contemporary American reality for American men and women. Dos Passos was one of many who turned to Dostoevsky after coming to the conclusion that other celebrated writers, in this case Turgenev, had become irrelevant to his generation of Americans.[60] No longer were the readers reading the text, but the text – or rather its creator – was scrutinizing the readers and revealing their true selves to them. A Dostoevsky novel was a ticket to self-discovery. Floyd Dell declared that the 'terribly and wonderfully revelatory' power of Dostoevsky's novels lay in his ability to show Americans for the first time that 'under the petty painted exterior of the ordinary soul may be the lightning-riven gulfs of Dostoevsky.'[61] An American guide to literature published in 1925 concluded the chapters devoted to Dostoevsky by rhetorically asking: 'Even these "abnormal people" in Dostoevsky's world – are they not potentially ourselves?'[62]

Dostoevsky style was still a conundrum. Hemingway recalls considering the question 'How can [Dostoevsky] write so badly, so unbelievably badly, and make you feel so deeply?' during the 1920s.[63] Some, however, began to suggest that Dostoevsky's 'disorganized' and 'inclusive' style might actually constitute his greatness. In a letter to Scott Fitzgerald, for example, Thomas Wolfe elevated Dostoevsky's torrential prose above the architectonic exclusions and silences of the acknowledged masters of prose form like Turgenev and Flaubert, and predicted that he would be among those who 'will be remembered for what they put in' rather than for what they leave out.[64] Sherwood Anderson saw Dostoevsky as an awesome 'river in flood carrying down mud, stones, rails, etc. There is power there' that transcended Turgenev's rather ordinary 'clear stream ... [beside which] you sit down ... [and] wade in.'[65]

Finally, Dostoevsky was still seen to be a largely autobiographical writer who wrote about his own experiences and whose characters were little more than masks that he himself assumed. Theodore Dreiser believed that Dostoevsky's autobiographical characterizations amounted to 'none other than Dostoevsky stalking this earthly mystery.'[66]

Not all American writers hailed the Dostoevsky they found stalking the Garnett translations. Gilbert Phelps correctly observes in *The Russian Novel in English Fiction* (1956) that '[t]here was in fact always a hard core of resistance to Dostoevsky and what he stood for, socially, spiritually, and aesthetically.'[67] Upton Sinclair, for example, admitted that he could not finish even one Dostoevsky novel because he found them all to be 'impassioned, even frenzied propaganda' redolent of Russian nationalism and the preaching of the Russian Orthodox Church.[68] Ezra Pound told Hemingway in the 1920s that he had yet to read anything by Dostoevsky.[69] Pound should have saved himself the trouble, since the result was a conviction that Dostoevsky promoted 'egoistic psychological nuvveling' and set a bad literary example.[70]

What is ultimately significant though, is that the serial publication of Garnett translations which gave Americans the opportunity to love or loathe Dostoevsky also allowed them to view him as a contemporary writer relevant to twentieth-century America. Numerous American writers confirmed the powerful connection between Dostoevsky's writings and the spirit of the age. In 1917, Randolph Bourne commented on Dostoevsky's 'superb modern healthiness' that made it impossible 'not to think of Dostoevsky as a living author when his books come regularly, as they are coming, to the American public every few months. Our grandfathers sixty years ago are said to have lived their imaginative lives in anticipation of the next instalment of Dickens or Thackeray. I can feel somewhat of the same excitement in this Dostoevsky stream.'[71] Seventeen years later, Malcolm Cowley wrote that his generation of American expatriates in the Paris of the 1920s identified closely with Dostoevsky, observing that a novel such as *The Devils* [*Besy*] (1871–2) 'might almost have been written by a young American in Montparnasse as he leaned his elbows on a café table of imitation marble ringed with coffee stains.'[72] This 'up-to-dateness,' however illusory and anachronistic, solidified Dostoevsky's reputation and allowed for his appropriation by members of America's cultural and literary elite, who began to cite Dostoevsky's writings to illustrate and bolster their viewpoints in various sociocultural discourses of the day. References to Dostoevsky's biography and his characters were suddenly appearing everywhere, from studies on psychoanalysis and homeopathic manuals to esoteric tracts and historical monographs.

Dostoevsky was important to American writers not only as a literary model but as the writer who freed Russian writers from the constraints of European tradition and their inferiority complex vis-à-vis the great European canon. Malcolm Cowley, who pondered the reasons for the special American attraction to Dostoevsky, wrote that Dostoevsky helped 'lift ... from the shoulders of Russian literature, a feeling of backwardness and provincialism' shared by the American writers of Cowley's generation, who began their literary journeys 'under a burden of provincialism as heavy and jagged as that which oppressed the compatriots of Dostoevsky.'[73] If Russian writers after Dostoevsky had no need to slavishly imitate the European novel, then neither did the new American authors. They could, in fact, begin to set their own canons and to establish their own traditions independently of the Europeans. It should not be surprising then that Dostoevsky continued to be important to America in the 1920s and well beyond.

The Dostoevsky vogue in the United States never reached the level of 'hysteria and mystical jargon' that characterized the Dostoevsky cult in England.[74] Americans read and discussed the writings of English exponents of the cult, such as Middleton Murry; they attended the lectures given by visiting Dostoevsky enthusiasts from England; and they discussed these viewpoints in literary and scholarly journals. The American response to Dostoevsky, was, however, generally more subdued. The English novelist John Cowper Powys, who lectured on Dostoevsky all across the States, from major urban centres to small towns, wrote about the difficulties of introducing him to American hometown audiences. For Powys, Dostoevsky was 'more than an artist' – he was 'the founder of a new religion'[75] and everything that he produced was holy writ. Looking back on his lecturing experiences, however, Powys suspected that Dostoevsky and his characters, a motley crew of murderers, prostitutes, convicts, and drunkards, were a little too shocking for the denizens of such provincial towns as Young-stown, Ohio, offending their notions of propriety, their religious sensibil-ities, and, more importantly, terrifying them with a glimpse of their own inner darkness: 'I think it was the first time that these busy employers of foreign labour and their hard-working wives had ever had the lid taken off from the terrors of our human soul ... There was a tremendous hullabaloo ... One of the prominent local clergymen there, I think he was a Presbyterian, rose from his seat in the front row and austerely with-drew, not however without banging the door behind him as an aggrieved child might have done.'[76]

The outrage of American small-town audiences aside, the response of American intellectuals to Dostoevsky was more restrained than that of their European counterparts; most likely, this was because it was more divided and conflicted. If New York in the 1910s and 1920s can be taken as a microcosm of Dostoevsky's urban American readership, one immediately notes the deepening rift between the Greenwich Village Bohemian intellectuals, whose literary vehicle was journals such as *The Dial*, and the left-leaning socialist intelligentsia, who con-tributed to magazines like *The Masses*.[77] The former were, generally, warmly receptive of Dostoevsky's novels, while the latter had a very clear line to follow, first from the Russian left and then from Soviet ideologues, whose attitude towards Dostoevsky became particularly hostile. When he wrote for the doctrinaire *Masses*, for example, Floyd Dell had to temper his enthusiasm for Dostoevsky's 'terribly and wonderfully revelatory' novels, expressed only a year earlier in a more moderate and liberal magazine, by acknowledging 'the total wrongness of [Dostoevsky's] attitude toward life.'[78]

The America-Dostoevsky link was strong enough to weather all of these storms and divisions. When the last of the Garnett translations of Dostoevsky came out in 1920s, American interest in Russian literature began to include more contemporary Russian writers like Isaac Babel, Boris Pilniak, and Mikhail Zoshchenko. As the spotlight shifted, how-ever, Dostoevsky consolidated his position at centre stage, remaining the writer who continued to attract and challenge American writers and readers. An extraordinary number of Americans throughout the twenti-eth century testified to the importance of Dostoevsky to their lives and work, raising the eyebrows of such transplanted Russians as Vladimir Nabokov, who found it necessary to point out to interviewers that 'not all Russians love Dostoevsky as much as Americans do.'[79] Dostoevsky's continued high standing in America differed greatly from the fortunes of his reputation in Britain, where the excesses of the Dostoevsky cult years gave way to a jaded indifference if not bitter disillusionment.

Helen Muchnic, who focuses on the English rather than the American response to Dostoevsky in her study, asks how it is that 'Dostoevsky's reputation in England reached a stage of extravagant praise and finally subsided ... to the almost tacit neglect.'[80] She suggests that the rise and fall was occasioned by changes in aesthetic theories and critical focus;[81] that the Russian Revolution of 1917 may have contributed to the decline of Dostoevsky's popularity; and that 'in spite of all the interest in Dostoevsky and the borrowings from him, he has seemed to many to be essentially foreign to the English spirit.'[82] Gilbert Phelps, who also addresses this question in the Dostoevsky chapters of his The Russian Novel in English Fiction (1956), concludes that the English Dostoevsky cult collapsed because it became 'discredited.' The combined damaging effects of the publication of the memoirs of his family members, his own letters, and psychoanalytic analyses of his life and work (including that by Freud himself) 'reduced the saint to very human proportions,' and the Russian Revolution brought about a 'disillusionment with the Russian Soul.'[83] Phelps illustrates the resulting disenchantment by citing the famous excerpt from a 1926 letter to André Gide written by the eminent English critic and writer Edmund Gosse, in which he complains, 'We have all in turn been subjected to the magic of this epileptic monster. But his genius has only led us astray,' and concludes that no aspiring writer should read the addictive but baneful Dostoevsky.[84]

Interestingly, these same events and shifts in aesthetic paradigms failed to tarnish Dostoevsky's reputation in the United States. Dostoevsky continued to be important to Americans as a writer, thinker, and, significantly, as personal inspiration beyond the 1920s. American intellectuals, who discovered Dostoevsky before or during the 'cult' years, usually remained faithful to him. In the 1930s Theodore Dreiser defended Dostoevsky from the attacks of Soviet authorities, writing to a Soviet functionary that 'so great is [Dostoevsky's] gift as an artist, so supreme his analysis of the vagaries of our human dispositions ... [that he] does enormous honor to the race from which [he] springs. Whatever the reason, [he] cannot in my judgement, be safely belittled.'[85] Writing only a year before his death, Dreiser recalled the profound impression made upon him by reading Dostoevsky at the turn of the century, loyally observing that the novels 'thrilled me in my late twenties, and would do so again, I feel.'[86]

Perhaps Dostoevsky appeared less 'foreign' to Americans for all the reasons outlined earlier, perhaps they did not see why Dostoevsky the

writer should be discredited by dysfunctional relatives, personal preju-
dices, inventive psychoanalysts, or tragic events in Russia. But it seems
symbolic that in 1936, the year with which Muchnic closes her account of
Dostoevsky's rise and fall in Britain, a book was published by an American writer who claimed that the moment he heard about Dostoevsky
was the most important moment of his life. The book was *Black Spring*
and the writer, of course, was Henry Miller, who recounted his first
encounter with Dostoevsky in cosmic and apocalyptic terms:

> And then one day, as if suddenly the flesh came undone and the blood
> beneath the flesh had coalesced with the air, suddenly the whole world
> roars again and the very skeleton of the body melts like wax. Such a day it
> may be when first you encounter Dostoevsky. You remember the smell of
> the tablecloth on which the book rests; you look at the clock and it is only
> five minutes from eternity; you count the objects on the mantelpiece
> because the sound of numbers is a totally new sound in your mouth,
> because everything new and old, or touched and forgotten, is a fire and
> mesmerism. Now every door of the cage is open and whichever way you
> walk is a straight line toward infinity, a straight, mad line over which the
> breakers roar and great rocs of marble and indigo swoop to lower their
> fevered eggs.[87]

Black Spring, in which Miller describes this apocalyptic encounter, was,
for the most part, written in Paris in the mid-1930s, the most creative and
important period of Miller's life, the time when he finally found himself
as a writer and exploded on to the literary scene. But if Miller's life in
Paris, the literary partnerships he formed while he was living there, and
the writing goals he set for himself defined what Dostoevsky came to
signify for him, it was his American upbringing and his early exposure
to Dostoevsky in America that served as the background to his understanding of the Russian author.

Miller himself had always emphasized the importance of the
American perspective in his reading of Dostoevsky. In fact, he maintained that he had a special insight into Dostoevsky precisely
because he was an American born and bred, 'just a Brooklyn Boy,' as
Miller self-deprecatingly referred to himself. Miller would also say
that he began his writing career with hopes of becoming an American Dostoevsky. In a later work, Miller's narrator claims that he

> understood Dostoevsky, or rather his characters and the problems which
> tormented them, better, being American-born ... American life, from the

gangster level to the intellectual level, has paradoxically tremendous affinities with Dostoevsky's multilateral everyday Russian life. What better proving grounds can one ask for than metropolitan New York, in whose conglomerate soil every wanton, ignoble, crackbrained idea flourishes like a weed? ... Though millions among us have never read Dostoevsky nor would even recognize the name were it pronounced, they are nevertheless, millions of them, straight out of Dostoevsky, leading the same weird 'lunatical' life here in America which Dostoevsky's creatures lived in the Russia of his imagining.'[88]

Reading Dostoevsky in America and as an American, with the aim of becoming an American Dostoevsky, Miller was fully plugged into the established American stereotype of Dostoevsky, perhaps without fully realizing it himself. It is on this foundation that he would proceed to build his own idiosyncratic vision of Dostoevsky and his works.

3 Henry Miller's Road to Dostoevsky

I became so electrified that I didn't dare move for fear I would charge like a bull or start to climb the wall of a building or else dance or scream. Suddenly I realized that all this was because I was really a brother to Dostoevsky, that perhaps I was the only man in all America who knew what he meant in writing those books. Not only that, but I felt all the books I would write myself, germinating inside me: they were bursting inside like ripe cocoons.

Henry Miller, *Tropic of Capricorn*, 211

Miller's dates (1891–1980) ideally positioned him to participate in the American discovery of Dostoevsky. He first heard of Dostoevsky when he was just coming out of his late teens: a man on the street offered to sell him a Dostoevsky novel. Both the place and time when Miller first heard Dostoevsky's name would gain a mystical significance in his eyes, invoked again and again in his texts as a life- and consciousness-altering event fully appreciated only in retrospect. In *Tropic of Capricorn* Miller's narrator explains that the 'night I sat down to read Dostoevsky for the first time was a most important event in my life,' 'it changed the whole face of the world ... the world stopped dead for a moment, that I know.'[1] Shortly before his death, Miller would write: 'I never tire of rehearsing this introduction to Dostoevsky ... it seems to me that late afternoon in Brooklyn the sun must have stood still in the heavens for a few moments.'[2]

In *Black Spring*, the narrator/Henry Miller persona credits Dostoevsky directly for being his stimulus to becoming a writer. He devoutly recreates the precise moment when he first heard Dostoevsky's name from a Jewish man in New York: 'It was exactly five minutes past seven, at the corner of Broadway and Kosciusko [sic] street, when Dostoevsky first flashed across my horizon. Two men and a woman were dressing a shop window.' He even slows down time and savours a slow-motion close-up of the moment: 'Between [the man's] two front teeth there was more than a usual space; it was exactly in the middle of this cavity that the word Dostoevsky quivered and stretched, a thin, iridescent film of spitum in which all the gold of twilight had collected – for the sun was just going down over Kosciusko street.'[3] Later in the book, Miller describes for the reader his boat journey from London to Paris, the artistic and literary capital of the world, where he was heading in order to finally become a writer, commenting: 'I thought to myself – "the circle is complete now: from the department store window to here."'[4]

In interviews and conversations later in life Miller would readily elaborate on his introduction to Dostoevsky. In the 1970s, for example, when talking to a group of young screenwriting students, Miller revealed that his first taste of Dostoevsky was the result of a misunderstanding. He reflected that back when he was 'just a dumb kid,' he was an avid reader of the so-called dime novels about sensational crimes and that, at first, he thought Dostoevsky's books fitted into that category. 'I was walking along Kosciuszko Street,' Miller reminisced, 'when I met this guy who was holding a book and he asked me if I would like to read a story called Crime and Punishment by a guy named Dostoevsky. I figured it was one of those cheap thrillers. So I took the book home.' Miller discovered his mistake, but by that point he was hooked: 'I couldn't believe what I had read. This was real writing. This was literature. I started to read seriously, for the first time in my life, and that led to my going to Paris to become a professional writer.'[5]

The translation of Crime and Punishment that Miller originally read was most likely the fairly competent rendering of the novel into English by Frederick Whishaw, first published in 1886 and reissued in 1911 (when Miller probably read it) as part of the inexpensive Everyman's Library series distributed in the United States by the New York publishers E.P. Dutton and Company. Miller's interest in Dostoevsky could not have been awoken at a better time. The publication of the first of the historic Garnett translations was just around the corner: Brothers Karamazov came out in 1912 and translation of the rest of the novels soon followed. Miller, an impressionable twenty-something, read many of the Garnett translations as they became available. He also read books about Dostoevsky in his twenties and thirties, as critical works on Dostoevsky were written, translated, and published throughout the following decades.

Miller's literary interests were eclectic from the very beginning. After his introduction to 'real literature' through Dostoevsky, he began to read voraciously and widely. The circle of his personal literary heroes would eventually include Knut Hamsun, John Cowper Powys, Lao Tse, Krishnamurti, Marie Corelli, Georges Gurdjieff, and a host of others, some still well known, others now obscure. All the same, Miller remained loyal to Dostoevsky as the chief deity of his literary pantheon (his 'Holy Philharmonic Synod,' as he refers to it in *Plexus*)[6] throughout his long life, writing as an octogenarian that Dostoevsky was the writer he admired most and that without him there would be 'a deep, black hole in world literature.'[7]

According to Miller, his interest in Dostoevsky and the 'Russians' was reinforced when he met the famous anarchist Emma Goldman (1869–1940) who was lecturing on the subject of great writers throughout the American west in 1913. The twenty-two-year-old Miller also found himself in the west at the time, trying out the life of a cowboy. Whether Miller actually heard Goldman lecture, as he always claimed, or whether he read her works later, which is what some of his biographers and critics believe, the encounter with Goldman's ideas became, in Miller's words, 'a turning point' in his life.[8]

Goldman was promoting Russian drama and literature in America because of its manifest concern with social causes (she said that 'in no other country are the creative artists so interwoven, so much at one with the people').[9] She had, however, a special respect for Dostoevsky, whom she viewed as a political victim of an oppressive regime (she conveniently ignored his subsequent right-wing political and religious beliefs) and whose views she attempted to use to bolster her own. When Goldman featured a supposed Dostoevsky story in her *Mother Earth Bulletin*, in which the ruling classes and the clergy are condemned for their exploitation of the workers,[10] she rhetorically commented: 'who can deny that the same applies with equal force to the present time, even to [America]?'[11] Goldman identified passionately both with Dostoevsky and many of his characters. At one point in her life, when she was in a desperate need of money for revolutionary causes, she found inspiration in an unlikely source: Sonia Marmeladova, the devout young woman in *Crime and Punishment* who turns to prostitution in order to support her alcoholic father, ailing stepmother, and young stepbrothers and sisters.

'Dostoevsky's *Crime and Punishment* ... had made a profound impression on me,' Goldman wrote, 'especially the character of Sonia ... [who became] a prostitute in order to support her little brothers and sisters ... Sensitive Sonia could sell her body; why not I? My cause was greater than hers.'[12] Inspired by Sonia's sacrifice and motivated by her own revolutionary zeal, Goldman resolutely marched out to sell herself, but was stopped by a sympathetic passerby who told her that she was not made to be a streetwalker, gave her some money, and sent her home.

Goldman's passionate love of literature, her enthusiasm for Dostoevsky, and her willingness to follow the lead of his characters made a deep impression on Miller and prepared him for the next turning point in his life. In 1923 Miller met June Edith Smith, who would become his muse and nemesis, appearing in his books under a number of different names as the ultimate femme fatale. Because of Miller's obsession with her (when Anaïs Nin met June Miller later in Paris, she too became enamoured with her and wrote about her at length), June entered the annals of literary legend under her own name. Like Goldman, June was enthralled with Dostoevsky, but for reasons of her own.

Dostoevsky in Greenwich Village

At the time Miller met June, she was desperately trying to reinvent herself as an American success story. Born to a poor Jewish family that emigrated to the United States from Eastern Europe, she was employed variously as a dancing partner (a so-called taxi-girl) in seedy public dance halls and as a hostess at various Greenwich Village nightspots and speakeasies. Her personal ambitions, however, were set upon grander things. June wanted the American dream of fame and fortune. She saw herself as a famous actress or, in the worst case scenario, a successful writer. The first step to achieving her goal, however, was to become part of the Greenwich Village scene, where writers, artists, and actors rubbed shoulders and where intellectualism (or at least the appearance thereof) was considered de rigueur. And so June affected a genteel British accent, informed everyone that she was a graduate of the Wellesley College for Young Ladies, and slavishly followed all the enthusiasms of the Village Bohemians, from psychoanalysis and surrealism to experimentation with sexual identity (as Erica Jong put it, 'in the Greenwich Village of the twenties it was suddenly chic to be gay – and June was nothing if not a modern woman of fashion').[13]

The Greenwich Village Bohemians adored Dostoevsky. In fact, an openly and freely expressed love for Dostoevsky was an identifying badge of true Greenwich Village Bohemians in their ongoing ideological struggle with the city's Marxist intelligentsia. The New York Marxists (many of whom were depraved Village Bohemians themselves before they joined the working masses) railed against the Villagers, condemning their bourgeois cynicism, their lack of political engagement and moral fibre, their decadence and parasitism, and, not least, their Dostoevsky obsession. The *New Masses* (a resurrected version of the original *Masses*, which was shut down by the authorities) was New York's most influential leftist journal and the chief mouthpiece of American Marxists. The journal's contributors and editors thundered against the 'bourgeois cynic[s] ... Greenwich-Village ... parasite[s].'[14] The journal was headed by Michael Gold, who was particularly outspoken against the 'Greenwich village playboy[s]' and their 'gang of literary racketeers who have made of New York such a horrible and dangerous place for the young writer who still respects his mind's integrity.'[15] Gold also made a point of crudely attacking Dostoevsky as a corrupt reactionary writer.

Alfred Kazin, a critic generally sympathetic to the Village Bohemians, wrote that 'one laughed, and indeed many Communists laughed, when ... Michael Gold declared: 'When ... an ex-Czarist officer who has hung and flogged peasants tells us that Dostoevsky shakes him to the very soul, one is perhaps justified in suspecting ... Dostoevsky.''[16] But Gold was not acting of his own accord. Although the *New Masses* was never an official organ of the Communist Party, it faithfully adhered to the line set by Moscow: '[its] editorial line was clearly Communist, policy reflected shifting decisions of the Third International in Moscow.'[17] When Gold claimed that reading Dostoevsky made one politically and morally suspect, he was just following the lead of the Soviet Union, where Dostoevsky was practically banned after 'the victory of the narrowly ideological and hostile view of Dostoevsky as Soviet society and intellectual life settled into the strict Party orthodoxy.'[18]

The Greenwich Village Bohemians, on the other hand, followed no official directives of any kind. They were, however, greatly influenced by the trends set by the newest artistic and literary movements in Western Europe, many of which raised Dostoevsky to the status of a cult hero. Dostoevsky was called one of the patron saints of surrealism, for instance, and the surrealists acquired a devoted following in the Greenwich Village.[19] Oswald Spengler (1880–1936), the German historian

and philosopher, thought that Dostoevsky was one of the greatest prophetic writers of all times and Spengler's works, especially his dark mag-
num opus on the death of civilizations, were extremely popular in the
Village. The local theatres, including the Greenwich Village Theatre, were
successfully staging various adaptations of Dostoevsky's novels, following the success of similar adaptations in London and France.[20] If one
wanted to fit in with the rest of the Greenwich Village Bohemian set,
therefore, knowledge of Dostoevsky's novels was essential.

Originally, Miller had sympathized with the Socialist intellectuals of
the city and envisioned himself as a hard-working proletariat (he
would write to one of the scholars studying his work, 'I must emphasize again that... the Socialist movement ... wielded tremendous
influence over me, not only politically ... but literarily ... Don't
overlook ... *The New Masses*'),[21] but he soon became a part of June's
universe. She convinced Miller to give up his stultifying managerial
position at Western Union and to devote himself to writing full-time in
order to become not simply a writer, but nothing less than the American Dostoevsky, while she took care of their financial needs. Miller
ended up living on June's suspicious earnings, helping her with her
'gold-digging' schemes, revelling in his newly acquired status of a
Greenwich Village Bohemian, and immersing himself in the world of
Dostoevsky's Russian novels, in which, Miller rhapsodized in his own
early attempt at writing a novel, as 'in the Russian soul ... there is God
and snow and ice and talk and murder and epilepsy, where history
leaves off only to make place for nature, where be it only a room there
is space for the biggest drama ever written, space of the invisible host
and for all peoples, climates, tongues.'[22]

At Home with Dostoevsky

Miller wrote about or alluded to his Greenwich Village life with June in
most of his major books, including *Tropic of Capricorn* and *The Rosy Crucifixion* trilogy. According to Miller, most of his writing emanated from
a set of notes he prepared in the late 1920s, when June went to Paris
leaving him alone in New York and he was 'seized with this idea of
planning the book of [his] life ... in about forty or fifty typewritten
pages.'[23] Like many writers Miller was a compulsive myth-maker,
changing the facts of his life as he saw fit, encouraging others to do the
same (he counselled Erica Jong along with his other would-be biographers to 'just make it all up'), and occasionally even setting traps for

future biographers and scholars just for the fun it, as he himself admitted on numerous occasions. The question of the autobiographical veracity of Miller's books is a complicated one, made more difficult by his intentional blurring of distinction between Henry Miller the writer and the 'Henry Miller' persona who narrates his texts, by his contradictory statements about the 'truthfulness' of his texts, and by the dissolving of generic boundaries in his texts, making it frequently impossible to distinguish between a 'non-fiction' essay and a 'fictional' story. The many comments that Miller's autobiographical persona makes about Dostoevsky in the *Tropics* and *The Crucifixion*, however, are so remarkably consistent with statements made in interviews and letters that there can be little doubt that the statements made by 'Henry Miller' the narrator are shared to a large extent by Henry Miller the writer. Furthermore, the Greenwich Village atmosphere that Miller recreates in his novels, especially his account of marathon discussions about Dostoevsky, is an accurate reflection of Dostoevsky's documented prominence in the lives of the Village Bohemians. Thus, for example, in Matthew Johnson's *Life Among the Surrealists: A Memoir* (1962), the author reminisces about his early years in New York when those who fancied themselves young Bohemians, himself included, spent their time not only obsessively reading and discussing Dostoevsky's novels but also impersonating his characters.[24]

June's lesbian lover, who appears as Anastasia in many of Miller's books, is a troubled artist who, naturally, loves Dostoevsky. The narrator and Anastasia are jealous of one another and fabricate incidents from Dostoevsky's novels to test each other's knowledge of his works, hoping to unmask each other as frauds and ignoramuses. Meanwhile, June (who appears as Mona in the book) just sits there 'listening attentively, aware neither of truth nor falsity, but happy as a bird because we are talking about ... Dostoevsky.' Dostoevsky is Mona's 'idol, her god.'[25]

June and the rest of the Villagers see Dostoevsky as a contemporary, a Russian mad genius, writing about people identical to themselves – mad American geniuses, American holy fools. Mona describes Anastasia, who ends up in an asylum, as 'mad maybe, but like Strindberg, like Dostoevsky, like Blake.'[26] When Mona wants to encourage the narrator, she 'will always call me a fool ... Meaning that I am great enough, complex enough, in her estimation at least, to belong to the world of Dostoevsky.'[27] They identify both with Dostoevsky as a fellow Bohemian ('A pity Dostoevsky himself isn't with us!' Mona will sometimes exclaim)[28] and his characters ('all those mad people, all those crazy scenes which flood [Dostoevsky's] novels').[29] When the Millers' marriage finally fell apart in Paris, June's gravest accusation against Miller was that he could not recognize Dostoevskian characters in the world around him and that 'he is nothing, that he failed to be a god and failed to be a Dostoevsky.'[30] Anaïs Nin, who became embroiled in the Millers' complicated relationship and was a confidante of both, recorded in her diary that June told her that she 'had to bring [Miller] his Dostoevsky characters. But he is no Dostoevsky. He could not *see* them.'[31] Miller, for his part, bitterly complained to Nin that June denied his own long-standing Dostoevsky connection, going as far as to tell people 'that it was she who had first made me read Dostoevsky,'[32] a claim he strenuously denied.

Interestingly, there may have been some grounds both to June's claim that she introduced at least some of Dostoevsky's novels to Miller and that it was she who revealed Dostoevsky to him as a literary god. In Henry Miller's letters to friends from the early years of his marriage to June, he wrote that he was almost finished his first reading of *The Devils*, 'supposedly the best of the mad Russian's stuff,' and that it 'reads like a dime novel, for the most part. Would have made good serial stuff … barring an occasional nasty scene.'[33] After he had lived with June for several years, Miller would never again refer to Dostoevsky in such an off-hand manner. Nin, who eventually became Miller's lover, wrote in her diary that 'June wants Henry to be a Dostoevsky, but June prevents him from being one,' adding confidently: 'I can make a Dostoevsky of him.'[34]

The identification with Dostoevsky and his 'mad' Russians had predictable repercussions for the Millers and their friends. Once they saw themselves mirrored in Dostoevsky's characters, tormented men and women living in a variety of undergrounds, they simultaneously positioned his characters as models to follow in everyday life. Miller would later write in an introduction to one of his texts: 'I lived out so many roles portrayed by [Dostoevsky's] characters (good and bad) that I almost lost my own identity.'[35] Nin recorded that June 'was always saying she was like the characters in Dostoevsky'[36] and that Miller was complaining about 'June reading Dostoevsky and changing her personality.'[37] Miller and June (and, subsequently, Nin) emulated many of Dostoevsky's tormented characters. Predictably, June was drawn to Dostoevsky's conflicted and doomed beauties, such as Nastasia Fillipovna of *The Idiot*, while Miller identified with the hopelessly besotted and deluded husband of such a beauty, Pavel Pavlovich Trusotsky of the novella *Eternal Husband* [*Vechnyi muzh*] (1870). Even outside observers noticed the Millers' persistent refashioning of themselves in Dostoevsky's cast. Nin pondered the matter in her diary of 1932: 'The more I read Dostoevsky the more I wonder about June and Henry and whether they are imitations. I recognize the same phrases, the same heightened language, almost the same actions. Are they literary ghosts? Do they have souls of their own?'[38]

Dostoevsky in Paris

Miller was steeped in Dostoevsky both in his broader Greenwich Village environment and in his home life with June. When Miller arrived in Paris in 1930 he may have left America behind, but not Dostoevsky, who, once again, appeared to be everywhere he turned. Dostoevsky was an obsession of the city's large and colourful Russian émigré community, in which Miller had many contacts and which readily accepted him. (Nina Berberova, a Russian émigré writer who, coincidentally, once interviewed Dostoevsky's widow, reminisced about seeing the Millers in a Parisian café and immediately identifying with the two of them.)[39] Many Russian characters appear in Miller's Paris books and he wrote at length about his interactions with their community. Not all Russian émigrés, of course, worshipped Dostoevsky; Nin wrote Miller that her Russian friend, Princess Natasha Trubetskaia, who occupied an artist's studio in Paris, 'swears that Dostoevsky was a great liar and you could hardly find a Nastasia [Filippovna], an "idiot," or a Stavrogin in Russia.'[40] Many influential Russian émigré writers based in France at the time, like Ivan Bunin (1870–1953), Mark Aldanov (1889–1957), and Vladimir Nabokov (1899–1977) sneered at the Dostoevsky worship of in France and considered his novels to be examples of embarrassingly bad writing. Soon after Miller arrived in Paris, however, the entire Russian émigré community came together in commemorating the half-century anniversary of Dostoevsky's death with much pomp, extolling him as the writer who foretold the evils of communism in his novel *The Devils*.

Another Parisian milieu with which Miller became reasonably familiar, the avant-garde of surrealist and Dadaist writers, poets, and artists, was also interested in Dostoevsky and adopted him as a quasi-ancestor. Max Ernst even painted himself sitting on Dostoevsky's knee in his famous 1922 group painting of the surrealists, 'Au rendez-vous des amis.' Miller, of course, had become acquainted with surrealism in

Greenwich Village, where it had many enthusiastic followers, but in Paris he finally had a chance to meet many key members of both movements (although he eventually alienated most of them, many would come to his defence in 1946, during the infamous *L'affaire Miller*, when Miller was charged in France for writing obscenity). While he ultimately rejected the surrealist movement (as evident from his 'Open Letter to Surrealists Everywhere' [1938]), Miller was at first largely ambivalent and at times even enthusiastic about it; certainly, the surrealist influence is evident in many of his central texts, including *Black Spring*. Many years later he would say that he 'was open to everything that was going on when [he] reached Europe ... [He] was infatuated, intoxicated. All this was what [he] was looking for, it seemed so familiar to [him].'[41] Whatever the case (we will have occasion to examine Miller's surrealist connection more closely later on), there is no doubt that at one point Miller definitely wanted to attract the attention of the surrealists and to be hailed by them, writing Nin in 1934 that Marcel Duchamp showed interest in his work and expressing the hope that other surrealists would follow suit.[42]

When Miller's French-language skills improved and he started reading French authors in the original and actually meeting some of them (he was too shy to introduce himself to some of his heroes, like the art historian, essayist, and, notably, devotee of Dostoevsky Élie Faure, who lived in Paris), he once again found Dostoevsky to be a lively topic of discussion.

The French response to Dostoevsky has been examined in such studies as F.W. Hemmings's *The Russian Novel in France, 1884–1914* (1950) and Henri Peyre's *French Literary Imagination and Dostoevsky and Other Essays* (1975). Hemmings, who focuses on the period before the outbreak of the First World War, says that the years following the war withessed high enthusiasm for Russian writers and for Dostoevsky in particular, whose 'significance went on reaching ever greater proportion.'[43] He argues that 'saturation-point was quickly reached ... [t]he influence on the mass of writers is still there, but it has seeped down below surface-level' adds that in the decades that followed, a large number of books and articles were published on the subject of Russian novelists, Dostoevsky included; and predicts that 'it is safe to say that so long as the workings of the subconscious forces in man remain something of a mystery, then readers in France ... will continue to come to [Dostoevsky], as ... to the oracle of Delphi.'[44] Henri Peyre reinforces some of Hemmings's findings and shows that French authors who came into prominence after the First World War, such as François Mauriac (1885–1970) and André Malraux (1901–76), were also readers of Dostoevsky and engaged with him repeatedly in their own writings. Georges Duhamel (1884–1966) was another French writer whose novels bear the imprint of Dostoevsky and his cycle of five novels, *Vie et aventures de Salavin* (1920–32), has a Dostoevskian character at its centre[45] (Miller was a close reader of the Salavin cycle and included his critiques of the novels in his 1930s correspondence).

Not only were the French writers that Miller was meeting and reading interested in Dostoevsky but, in the 1930s, French readers and intellectuals were still trying to evaluate the heritage of writers and critics of previous decades who had wrestled with Dostoevsky. Miller and Nin held passionate debates about the work of Marcel Proust (1871–1922), André Gide (1869–1951), Paul Valèry (1871–1945), Jean Cocteau (1889–1963), Élie Faure (1873–1937), and others, all of whom wrote about Dostoevsky at length. Marcel Proust, for example, includes extended debates about Dostoevsky in *À la recherche du temps perdu*, something to which Miller certainly paid attention; in a letter to Nin, Miller would reminisce that 'immediately' when he and Nin 'started corresponding, it was Proust and Dostoevsky.'[46]

Miller's Dostoevsky

Given the concern with Dostoevsky whenever he turned, Miller's heightened interest in the novelist both during his early years in America and his years in Paris seems almost inevitable. It is far more problematic to establish *who* Miller's Dostoevsky was. As one member of the Villa Seurat circle wryly observed, 'God only knows what [Miller] made of the writers who so *influenced* him ... Whatever he reads becomes automatically distorted, he ingurgitates one thing and excretes another, and it is a safe bet to say that the influence of those writers *on him* is not the least implicit in their works.'[47] While this observation rings true for most readers and readings of complex multifaceted texts, it is perhaps all the more true for Miller, a man who prided himself on his contradictions. Contradictions aside, however, a reader attempting to make sense of Miller's reflections on Dostoevsky will often find them vague, muddled, tendentious, hyperbolic, and, on occasion, simply inaccurate. Miller substitutes Dostoevsky's characters for Dostoevsky himself, confuses Dostoevsky's novels one for another, misattributes words spoken by various Dostoevsky characters, and obfuscates his earlier arguments.

This, of course, is not at all unusual within the larger context of responses to Dostoevsky by other American (and non-American) writers. Miller, however, writes about Dostoevsky at such length, and in so many of his texts, that what may have gone unnoticed about another writer's passing comment on Dostoevsky assumes a heightened significance.

Whatever impression his Dostoevsky pronouncements make upon his readers, Miller himself felt that he was a careful, objective, and informed reader of Dostoevsky. He never pretended to have an exhaustive knowledge of Dostoevsky or his writings; the narrator in *The Rosy Crucifixion* explains that 'there are many things about Dostoevsky, as about life itself, which I am content to leave a mystery' and that he plans 'to leave the last few [unread Dostoevsky] morsels for deathbed reading.'[48] To a young American who complained that there was 'a lot of that Dostoevsky I just don't understand, Mr. Miller,' Miller snapped, 'There are a lot of things in the world you're just not supposed to understand.'[49] All the same, Miller read Dostoevsky voraciously and always claimed the influence of his 'works in general.'[50] From early literary experiments like his novel *Moloch* (written in 1928 and published only posthumously), in which the central character writes a note reminding himself to 'reread *The House of the Dead*,'[51] to the chapbooks written towards the end of his life, an impressively wide range of Dostoevsky's texts is cited and discussed by Miller. His writings of the 1930s include references to *The Devils* (1871–2), *The Idiot* (1868), *Brothers Karamazov* (1878–80), *The Eternal Husband* (1870), and *The Double* (1846); quotations from *Crime and Punishment* (1866); and many allusions to *Notes from Underground* (1864). In his later work, Miller cites Dostoevsky's *Winter Notes on Summer Impressions* [*Zimnii zametki o letnikh vpechatleniiakh*] (1863) and his famous Pushkin speech. Miller always advised his friends and close associates to read as much Dostoevsky as they could get their hands on, pointing out to Lawrence Durrell, for instance, that he must certainly read *The Double* if he never read it before[52] and sharing with Nin the exciting news that, 'Regarding ... those two years of Stavrogin's in Moscow we get so ineffectively ... today there is a book giving you passages and notes on all this which was merely hinted at.'[53]

Both Miller and his autobiographical persona repeatedly claim that Dostoevsky's true legacy extends far beyond his writings. The narrator of *The Rosy Crucifixion* conducts imaginary dialogues with Dostoevsky ('communing' as he calls it) and summons 'the complete Dostoevsky': 'the man who wrote the novels, diaries and letters we know, *plus* the man we also know by what he left unsaid, unwritten ... type and archetype speaking, so to say. Always full, resonant, veridical; always the unimpeachable sort of music which one credits him with, whether audible or inaudible, whether recorded or unrecorded.'[54] Miller explains that the knowledge of 'the complete Dostoevsky' is only possible through a sense of kinship with him and his characters (an idea cultivated earlier by the Bohemians of Greenwich Village). Alfred Perlès, a close friend during Miller's Paris years and beyond, writes in his book of reminiscences about Miller that, almost immediately after meeting him, Miller told him that 'Dostoevsky was his god ... [Miller] identified himself with each of [Dostoevsky's] complicated characters in turn. What he found in Dostoevsky he found in himself.'[55] In order to increase that precious sense of identification Miller was willing to disregard the facts where necessary; he would falsely claim, for instance, to share the same astrological sign with Dostoevsky (Miller was a Capricorn, Dostoevsky was not).[56] Miller's narrator in Nexus maintains that he 'know[s] [Dostoevsky] as one knows a kindred soul,'[57] while the narrator in Tropic of Cancer describes himself as 'really a brother to Dostoevsky' or, only half-jokingly, as 'Herr Dostoevsky Junior'[58] (notably, Miller signed his letters in the mid-1920s as 'Dostoevsky, Jr.').

(Mis)reading the Dostoevsky Critics

Despite the importance that Miller assigned to a sense of identification with Dostoevsky and to an intuitive knowledge of his works, he himself had always drawn heavily from critics of Dostoevsky's works (ironically so, given his general distrust of biographers and especially literary critics, whom Miller labelled 'hideous freaks of nature').[59] Miller's readings in Dostoevsky criticism were extensive and his list of cherished Dostoevsky commentators included a number of English, French, Germans, and Russians. Miller especially appreciated the enthusiastic paeons to Dostoevsky penned by the novelist John Cowper Powys (1872–1963) and the Slovenian-born English scholar Janko Lavrin (1886–1987), two champions of Dostoevsky who continued to celebrate his works well after the demise of the English Dostoevsky cult. Thus, Powys, one of Miller's favourite writers and lecturers (Miller wrote that '[l]eaving the hall after his lectures, I often felt as if he had put a spell upon me'),[60] who originally acclaimed Dostoevsky's 'demonic power of revelation' during the height of the cult years in 1915,[61] continued to extol him as a 'formidable psychic pathologist' more than thirty years later.[62] Lavrin, whom Miller called an 'old favorite and eye-opener,'[63] praised Dostoevsky as a 'great writer and seeker in one, [who] deepened our awareness of man and life to such an extent that his work forms a landmark ... in the European consciousness.'[64] Miller would correspond with both men later in life; he would also echo and expand their praises in his own scattered writings on Dostoevsky.

The Russian religious philosopher and critic Nikolai Berdiaev (1874–1948), who was living in exile in Paris at the same time as Miller, was another favourite Dostoevsky commentator (Berdiaev would be the first Russian intellectual to pay serious attention to Miller's own work).[65] Berdiaev's volume of Dostoevsky criticism, Dostoevsky's Worldview [Mirosozertsanie Dostoevskogo], was translated into English from a French translation and published in 1934, the same year as Miller's Tropic of Cancer. Berdiaev's theories and especially his 'intuitive' philosophical and literary method were, according to Miller, 'right up [his] alley.'[66] Miller declared to Durrell: 'I love Berdiaev. It's like my "alter ego" writing.'[67] Miller's interest in Berdiaev's work is evident from the extensive quotes in The Rosy Crucifixion relating to Berdiaev's comments on Dostoevsky's eschatology and his perception of evil.[68] Certainly, Berdiaev's key assertion that 'to "get inside" Dostoevsky it is necessary to have a certain sort of soul – one in some way akin to his own,'[69] corresponds to Miller's views on the subject.

Miller also paid special attention to Oswald Spengler's pronouncements on Dostoevsky. Spengler's philosophical, apocalyptic, and quasi-historical treatise Decline of the West, published between 1918 and 1922 and first translated into English in the years 1926–8, generated a cult of its own in Greenwich Village during the late 1920s. During the Villa Seurat years Miller regularly recommended Spengler's books to Nin and Durrell and engaged in spirited discussions of various aspects of his work. Spengler considered Dostoevsky one of the most portentous writers ever, a completely autonomous figure,[70] a 'symbol of the future,' and, mystically, a writer through whom 'Bolshevism' would be conquered.[71] Miller refers to Spengler's views on Dostoevsky extensively (as, for example, in the piece 'Balzac and His Double' of the Wisdom of the Heart collection)[72] and approvingly cites him in The Rosy Crucifixion as the originator of the idea that 'Dostoevsky's Russia would eventually triumph.'[73]

The commentators of Dostoevsky who proved to be most important for Miller's own reception and understanding of the writer were neither professional literary critics nor philosophers, however, but writers themselves: D.H. Lawrence (1885–1930) and André Gide, neither of them particularly reliable guides to Dostoevsky's work, but both of them passionate and deeply opinionated readers of Dostoevsky. Miller was well aware of Lawrence's complex love-hate relationship with Dostoevsky. (Lawrence opposed the excesses of the Dostoevsky cult in England, perceiving Dostoevsky somewhat enigmatically as 'a marvelous seer' but 'an evil thinker').[74] Before the publication of *Tropic of Cancer*, Jack Kahane of Obelisk Press asked Miller to write a short brochure on Lawrence to be issued in advance of the novel, in order 'to give [Miller] the sort of prestige as a thinker which would disarm the critics in advance and force them to take the novel seriously.'[75] Miller had little sympathy for Lawrence at the time and saw the brochure as his chance to show all that was wrong with Lawrence as a writer and a man (in a letter to Nin, at the early stages of his work, Miller gleefully wrote, 'I see now what a hellish grip I have got on him. Everything falls into whack. And with a vengeful clip').[76]

In the process of Miller's work on the project, however, his attitude to Lawrence changed from contempt to devotion. Ihab Hassan, whose study *The Literature of Silence: Henry Miller and Samuel Beckett* (1967) situates Miller within the tradition of the avant-garde, even concludes that Miller's admiration for D.H. Lawrence was exceeded only by his admiration for Dostoevsky.[77] Unfortunately, Miller's projected brochure on Lawrence soon grew into a massive heap of fragmented and contradictory notes. Miller finally gave up on his attempts to produce a cohesive study – those friends to whom he turned with it were unable to help – and settled for the publication of several of the more harmonious fragments separately (in a curious twist, the Lawrence book, which was to have been Miller's first published full-sized work, became his last published work in 1980, after the heroic editorial efforts of two dedicated Miller scholars). Nonetheless, in the year that Miller spent working on the project, he became well acquainted with Lawrence's body of work and, significantly, with Lawrence's writings on Dostoevsky.

Miller himself believed that Dostoevsky was the single most significant author for Lawrence, an insight later confirmed by the work of such scholars as Peter Kaye, whose chapter on Dostoevsky and Lawrence in his study *Dostoevsky and English Modernism, 1900–1930* (1999) convincingly shows that 'the spur of Dostoevsky' initiated in Lawrence a rivalry 'crucial to the development of [his] own art.'[78] In Miller's opinion, Lawrence was 'tremendously influenced by Dostoevsky. Of all his forerunners, Jesus included, it was Dostoevsky whom he had most difficulty in shaking off, in surpassing, in "transcending."'[79] Miller also tried to provide some insights into Lawrence's public rejection of Dostoevsky. What Miller produced, however, is an idiosyncratic narrative, that ultimately says more about his Miller's own views on modern life than it does about Lawrence's views on Dostoevsky. In one characteristic sampling Miller writes that 'What Lawrence detected in Dostoevsky ... was man's attempt to forestall the death process ... [Lawrence] regarded the lives of men about him as wasted in a sort of eternal twilight of the womb, their energies frustrated in a vain struggle to break the walls that shut them in,'[80] a passage that has little to do with Lawrence's professed dislike of Dostoevsky for hiding at the feet of Christ,[81] but says a great deal about Miller's own ideas on millennialism and the human condition.

Lawrence's opposition to Dostoevsky proved to be valuable for Miller because it forced him if not to re-examine his own presumptions about Dostoevsky and his novels then, at the very least, to articulate them more clearly. Conversely, Gide's reading of Dostoevsky became important to Miller because it was analogous to his own. Gide's study of Dostoevsky, based on a series of lectures he gave in 1922, was published in a single volume in 1925, the same year it came out in an English translation with an enthusiastic introduction by Arnold Bennett. According to Miller, this was one of the most important books he had ever read (it is the only book by Gide included in Miller's 'The Hundred Books Which Influenced Me Most' list of Books in My Life).

It is not clear when Miller read Gide's book for the first time, but he was discussing it with Nin as early as 1932, suggesting that he probably read it first in the English translation.[82] Miller reread Gide's study throughout his life and quoted it frequently in his own writings. Gide's interpretation of Dostoevsky was highly personal (Gide wrote that he 'gathered from [Dostoevsky's] works what I needed to make my own honey'[83] and that he had 'sought, consciously or unconsciously, what had most intimate connection with my own ideas');[84] it was precisely this intimate, personal quality that had always appealed to Miller in literary criticism. An extra attraction lay in the fact that many of Gide's statements about Dostoevsky could also be applied to Miller himself (Gide, incidentally, was one of the French writers to come to Miller's defence during L'affaire Miller). Gide wrote, for example, that 'Dostoevsky never deliberately states, although he often insinuates, that the antithesis of love is less hate than the steady activity of the mind,'[85] and despite Miller's love for abstruse and esoteric subjects, he was avowedly 'anti-intellectual' both in his approach to writing (he claimed to write spontaneously, taking down a mysterious 'dictation') and painting (he produced thousands of watercolours in a deliberately primitive, childlike style that are now exhibited in a number of museums worldwide). Gide's observations on Dostoevsky provided Miller with a respected authority to support his own position on the matter and to make his *own* honey, so to speak.

Although the critics, philosophers, and writers read by Miller on Dostoevsky often espoused mutually contradictory visions, there was one point on which they all agreed: they all felt that Dostoevsky was a momentous writer for world literature. From Miller's perspective, these commentators shared another important characteristic: they were all important writers or cultural figures themselves who weighed in on the continuing debate about Dostoevsky, and their books were read, reviewed, and widely discussed both in United States and in Europe.

Miller was learning that Dostoevsky and his novels were culturally relevant and close to the centre of public attention wherever he went, that discussions of Dostoevsky by intellectuals and writers continued unabated, and that those who wrote about Dostoevsky would also have the public's ear and interest. The time was coming when Miller would contribute his own views on Dostoevsky.

Writing about Dostoevsky

Miller's output of critical writings on a legion of subjects was enormous. His projected book on Dostoevsky's 'Grand Inquisitor' chapter in *Brothers Karamazov* never materialized, but he repeatedly turned to Dostoevsky and his novels in his own texts, comparing and contrasting him with Balzac, Lawrence, Proust, Whitman, and many others. Despite Miller's vast output of criticism, however, he frequently lamented – especially in the early days – that he had no critical abilities. In a letter written in the early 1930s to Michael Fraenkel, benefactor, friend, and collaborator during his Villa Seurat years, about one of Fraenkel's philosophical tractates, Miller writes, 'Alas, I am only too well aware that I have no critical faculty. I have only the creative instinct ... violent passions, hates, aversions, etc. What I would write about your book would not be criticism. It would be only a register of my emotions.'[86] It is difficult to judge now whether Miller genuinely believed that he had no critical faculty, was indulging in false modesty, or was simply attempting to evade the onerous task of writing a lengthy analysis of Fraenkel's book. At some point, however, Miller decided that he was in fact a good critic, in part because he came to believe that true criticism implied becoming enamoured with one's subject in a 'full surrender to author or Author.' In support of this idea, Miller would often cite John Cowper Powys's comment that criticism can never be anything other 'than an idolatry, a worship, a metamorphosis, a love affair.'[87]

Many of Miller's own critics concurred with his original opinion, citing, among other things, the disaster of Miller's never completed study on D.H. Lawrence. Mary V. Dearborn, one of Miller's biographers, writes pointedly that Miller's criticism is 'uniformly riddled with encomiums, the subject always "a great man," his art ... the best of its kind. Critical writing was never Miller's strong suit.'[88] It is true that Miller's surrender to his subject frequently resulted in gushy passages that expressed little beyond his love for the author and his fervent belief that everyone should read his or her books. Norman Mailer, a champion of Miller and his self-proclaimed student, observes that '[Miller's] literary criticism can be pompous and embarrassingly empty of new perceptions ... In fact it would be tempting to say that he writes well about everything but his enthusiasms, which could explain why the ventures into literary criticism are not as good as one might expect.'[89]

In contrast, however, some Miller scholars, including John Parkin, author of *Henry Miller: The Modern Rabelais* (1990), believe that Miller's critical writings are not held in higher esteem because they are simply too unconventional for many readers, presenting 'a multifaceted, polytextual display of tastes, responses, quotations, intuitions ... [Miller's] authorial voice becoming not a scientific instrument capable of precise and objective observation, but rather the kind of criss-cross of absorbed voices that Bakhtin was ... analysing in his studies of ... Rabelais and Dostoevsky.'[90] Parkin also argues that Miller's work should be taken no less seriously than the more orthodox approaches to literary criticism: 'That these readings are repetitive, circular, enthusiastic to the point of hyperbole is offensive only to those who demand interpretation which is positive, linear and sober (to the point of bathos?), and such criticism could scarcely accommodate even the very use of language which Miller adopts and extends.'[91]

Whichever position on the subject one espouses, it is clear that Miller's criticism shares much in common with the watercolours that he painted throughout his life: it is colourful, sometimes naive, at times insightful, and always exuberant. His writings about Dostoevsky, taken as a whole, clearly do not belong in the category of empty rhapsodizing, even though they fall far short of a systematic, let alone rigorous, analysis of Dostoevsky's life and work. (It is highly unlikely, of course that Miller had ever aspired to produce a formal critical examination of Dostoevsky's major novels employing a sophisticated conceptual apparatus and an orderly, methodical evaluation of his writing.) On the other hand, those readers who, theoretically, want to understand Dostoevsky through Miller's criticism and commentary will find themselves frustrated and with good reason. Many of Miller's comments about Dostoevsky *are* hyperbolic as well as hazy and inconsequential. What does it mean, for instance, that Dostoevsky reveals 'the eternal youth of the spirit'[92] or that 'Dostoevsky was the sum of all those contradictions which either paralyze a man or lead him to the heights?'[93] Miller seems incapable of articulating or perhaps even recognizing some of the complexity of the ideas addressed in Dostoevsky's writings. Here, for instance, is what he writes on the subject of Dostoevsky and faith in one of the essays included in *The Books in My Life*: 'We know that the great problem with Dostoevsky was God ... Dostoevsky had virtually to create God – and what a Herculean task that was! Dostoevsky rose from the depths and, reaching the summit, retained something of the depths about him still.'[94]

For a reader interested in the dynamics of Dostoevsky's reception, however, Miller's comments are a source of invaluable information, because despite the problems inherent in his criticism they allow for insights into the origins, construction, and perpetuation not only of Miller's reading of Dostoevsky but of unorthodox readings of Dostoevsky in general. Miller's comments about Dostoevsky tend to fall into two general interrelated categories: the formal features of Dostoevsky's novels and prose and his philosophical outlook. It is to Miller's credit that he did not see these two categories as binary opposites (probably due to his reading of Berdiaev) – a typical fallacy of Dostoevsky reception in Europe and America. It quickly becomes evident, however, that it is the American vision of Dostoevsky that provides the foundation for Miller's reading of Dostoevsky, and that all the key features of an American interpretation of Dostoevsky are found in Miller's interpretation of his work.

Thus, Miller envisions Dostoevsky the man as an outsider, one 'who obviously preferred the lowly life, a man fresh from prison.'[95] Moreover, as a genius, 'the tragic, unprecedented artist,'[96] Dostoevsky, according to Miller, is already far removed from society and any moral order: 'the man of genius is a monster, a traitor and a criminal, among other things ... the more abnormal he is – the more monstrous, the more criminal – the more fecundating his spirit.'[97] In Miller's interpretation, Dostoevsky's outsider status is a privileged one, allowing him to see what insiders did not. He extols Dostoevsky as the ultimate commentator on the condition of humankind, whose opinions were especially relevant and liberating to contemporary Americans. Further, he sees Dostoevsky as primarily an autobiographical writer, writing through and of his own suffering, identifiable with his characters from Stavrogin ('the ideal image of himself')[98] to Zosima ('alias the real Dostoevsky').[99] Notably, Miller's interpretation of Dostoevsky's style includes both the concept of Dostoevsky resigning control over the stylistic elements in the text (obviously related to the widespread belief that Dostoevsky was a 'bad' stylist) and the idea that something very important was gained by this supposed release of controls (the notion advocated by Sherwood Anderson and some other American writers).

Nonetheless, at the heart of Miller's American reading of Dostoevsky lies a more original concept, if the notion of originality is applicable in the case of a writer who discounted it altogether, explaining: 'We invent nothing, truly. We borrow and recreate. We uncover and discover.'[100] Whereas most Dostoevsky proponents in America and England argued that he had *opened* a new era in literature, Miller professed that Dostoevsky had, through his person and writings, both expressed and *terminated* an epoch in world literature and history. One of Miller's characters articulates this view when he says that 'with Dostoevsky's death, the world entered upon a complete new phase of existence. Dostoevsky summed up the modern age much as Dante did the Middle Ages.'[101]

The closest any contemporary critic came to Miller's vision of Dostoevsky was Middleton Murry, who wrote in his almost embarrassingly effusive *Fyodor Dostoevsky: A Critical Study* (1916) that in Dostoevsky and Tolstoy 'an epoch of the human mind came to an end.'[102] Miller was familiar with Murry's ideas, if only through his reading of D.H. Lawrence, who responded to Murry's book with little enthusiasm (in fact, the book would spell the end of the two men's friendship). In a well-known letter to Murry Lawrence wrote that '[a]n epoch of the human mind may have come to the end in Dostoevsky: but humanity is capable of going on a very long way further yet, in a state of mindlessness – curse it,' and concluded with the infamously grotesque image of Dostoevsky with 'his head between the feet of Christ ...

waggl[ing] his behind in the air.'[103] Miller decided that the most important thing in this epistolary exchange was that Lawrence finally 'realized that ... Dostoevsky had brought to an end a great epoch of the human mind.'[104] Miller himself intended to push this idea further. In 'Balzac and His Double' Miller expressed his long-held views on the subject as follows: 'The study of society and the psychology of the individual, which form the material of the novel in European literature, served to create the illusory world of facts and things which dominate the neurotic life that began with the 19th century and is now reaching its end in the drama of schizophrenia ... Dostoevsky gave expression to the conflict ... Indeed, *it is with him that the novel comes to an end*' (emphasis added).[105]

The argument that the novel is dead or dying and that literature itself is dead or dying was not a new one even when Miller expressed it. Long before the death of the novel became a subject of national and cultural controversy in America and England in the 1960s, T.S. Eliot argued in his 1923 essay 'Ulysses, Order and Myth' that, after James Joyce, 'the novel is a form which will no longer serve.'[106] Miller may have had some personal reasons to deny Joyce's pre-eminence in anything literary (Joyce, only ten years Miller's senior and an acknowledged literary master, was exploring some of the same ground in his own texts and Miller frequently found himself being compared unfavourably to Joyce), but he consistently situated the locus of the novel's destruction not in Joyce's literary experiments but in Dostoevsky and his nineteenth-century novels. Miller's belief that Dostoevsky put an end to the novel and literature itself, however, posed an obvious problem for an aspiring writer: if the novel was depleted and obsolete, so were novelists. Miller's solution to this conundrum was that it was literature – not writing, and novels – not books, that were made obsolete by Dostoevsky. According to Miller, Dostoevsky enabled new writers to discard literature, with all its staid conventions and formalities, and to create a different kind of writing, more intimately entwined with life itself. Miller never fully defined this new writing or even referred to it in a consistent fashion and the concept itself remains hazy to this day. Miller's own writing fits into this new category, and despite the best efforts of critics and literary scholars to come up with an appropriate moniker and description for it for it it still remains frustratingly vague (some of the less successful ones include 'faction,' 'long autobiographical narratives,' and 'novel in first person' – the last one suggested by George Orwell). Reflecting on his own works shortly before his death Miller would say, 'I was definitely not a novelist.

Good or bad, from the very beginning of my literary career I thought of myself as a writer, a very important writer to be. I had no use for fiction, though many of my readers regard my work as being largely fictive. I myself am at a loss to give it a name.'[107] Erica Jong, who believes that Miller revolutionized writing, refers to him as a writer of narratives.[108] Whatever one calls the books that Miller was working on in Paris, it is important to recognize that Miller regarded himself as a post-Dostoevskian writer who had to invent writing anew, and that it was the radical vision of Dostoevsky as the last rather than the first prophet of the novel, the last writer of *literature*, that Miller expounded during his Paris years to his friends and disciples at Villa Seurat.

4 Henry Miller's Villa Seurat Circle and Dostoevsky

In Paris we made something, by God. There was a good, firm free-masonry
laid there between us all.
> Lawrence Durrell to Henry Miller, August 1938,
> *The Durrell-Miller Letters, 1935–1980*, 131

Henry Miller's new studio at Villa Seurat quickly became a hub of creative activity, a kind of an iconoclast salon, attracting intellectual noncon-
formists from Paris and beyond. But where Gertrude Stein's famous
salon at 27 rue de Fleuris has been studied and exhaustively documented
as a locus of tremendous intellectual ferment, a place where international
writers, artists, and poets gathered, argued, and exchanged ideas, 18 Villa
Seurat remains a tantalizingly blank spot on the literary and cultural
map. The street where Miller finally found a home after years of peripa-
tetic sojourns (he complained to Nin that *Tropic of Cancer* was 'written on
the wing, as it were, between my 25 addresses')[1] was located in Paris's
fourteenth arrondissement. It was an artist's haven: a quiet cul-de-sac
lined by brightly coloured houses with spacious sky-lit studios. In the
1920s and 1930s, it housed the studios of Marc Chagall, Salvador Dali,
and Chaim Soutine. The apogee of Villa Seurat, however, came in the
mid-1930s, when 18 Villa Seurat was taken over by an eclectic group of
writers, poets, and philosophers – or in the words of one of its members,
'cranks, nuts, drunks, writers, artists, bums, Montparnasse derelicts, vag-
abonds, psychopaths'[2] – all brought together by Henry Miller.

Villa Seurat played an almost mystically important role in Miller's
life. He first stayed at 18 Villa Seurat in 1931, sleeping on the floor of
a friend's studio apartment. It was here that he began writing *Tropic*

of Cancer (an early manuscript of his book opens with the words 'I am living at the Villa Seurat,' later changed to the now-canonical 'I am living at the Villa Borghese'). Three years later, he moved into a studio of his own on the top floor of 18 Villa Seurat; the date was 1 September 1934, the day when *Tropic of Cancer* was published. The studio served as Miller's home base for several critically important years. It was at Villa Seurat that Miller forged friendships that would last a lifetime; it was also here that Miller completed *Black Spring* (1936), *Max and the White Phagocytes* (1938), and *Tropic of Capricorn* (1939), together with *Tropic of Cancer*, books that shocked, delighted, and challenged their readers, changing the landscape of American literature in the process.

Miller's friends were a motley and cosmopolitan group. Naturally, many of them were American expatriates, like Walter Lowenfels (1897–1976) (an American poet and experimental writer who shared *This Quarter*'s Aldington Poetry Prize in 1931 with e.e. cummings), Michael Fraenkel (1896–1957) (an American businessman turned philosopher and publisher, who wrote about spiritual death), and Richard Thoma (an American poet who had been one of the assistant editors on the *New Review* with Ezra Pound). Other Americans included artists such as the illustrator Abe Rattner as well as the young abstract painter and heiress Betty Ryan, who came to Paris to study art and who lived in the studio on the ground floor. The circle also brought together expatriates from other countries, like Alfred Perlès (1897–1990), an Austrian-born novelist and Miller's sidekick in numerous Parisian escapades; David Gascoyne (1916–2001), a young British poet associated with the surrealist movement; the Hungarian-born Frank Dobo, literary agent par excellence; Gregoire Michonze, a Bessarabian-born artist who painted what he called 'naturalistically surrealist' paintings; and Brassai (1899–1984) (the pseudonym of Gyula Halász), who was born in Hungary and went on to become one of the most acclaimed photographers of Paris and the chronicler of its underworld of brothels and seedy cafés. Many French writers and poets were also attracted to 18 Villa Seurat; these included Raymond Queneau (1903–76), an experimental poet and novelist who would become a pataphysician but who started out as a surrealist; Georges Pelorson, translator and editor-in-chief of the important Parisian literary magazine *Volontés*; and the poet, novelist, and irrepressible adventurer Blaise Cendrars (1887–1961), who hailed Miller upon the publication of *Tropic of Cancer* with a rave review titled 'Un Ecrivain Américain nous est né.'

The nucleus of the Villa Seurat circle, however, consisted of Henry Miller himself and Anaïs Nin, Miller's lover, muse, and fellow writer, whose patronage and support made Miller's Villa Seurat studio and the whole circle possible.[3] Miller and Nin met in the early 1930s, when Miller found himself living the life of a literary derelict in Paris, after being shipped there by June, who was determined to help him become a writer at any cost. At the time of first meeting Miller was desperately trying to live up to his literary potential. He had already completed several book-length manuscripts in New York, including two derivative novels titled *Moloch* and *Crazy Cock*, which he was trying to revise and publish but would eventually abandon (like *Crazy Cock Moloch* would only be published posthumously). He was also beginning to write about his Parisian experiences and it is in these short texts, including his story 'Mlle Claude,' written in the first person and describing a well-known Left Bank prostitute, that a powerful new voice was beginning to emerge. The expatriate community was taking note and Miller became a local celebrity, featured in 'La Vie de Bohème' column of the *Paris Tribune* as the prime example of a happy-go-lucky Bohemian, a vision of himself that he definitely wanted to encourage, since he ghost-wrote that particular instalment of the column. More importantly, he was tenaciously working on the 'Paris book,' which would eventually become his famous breakthrough, *Tropic of Cancer*.

Nin was an aspiring writer as well. By the time she met Miller she had been writing steadily for more than fifteen years but most of her work went into a monumental diary, which numbered over forty volumes by the early 1930s. She thought that her diary writing had literary merit but was uncertain as to whether or not it made her a real writer. Nin believed that she needed to produce a distinct literary work, which she had already tried but failed to do, abandoning several fledgling novels. She had been more successful in her attempts at literary criticism. In *D.H. Lawrence, An Unprofessional Study* (1932) she defended Lawrence at a time when he was still considered a scandalous writer. While her literary criticism was impressionistic and not particularly accurate (she repeatedly misquoted titles of his books), it was passionate and frequently insightful, and her study would eventually earn high praise from some Lawrence scholars. But the book – subsidized by her adoring banker husband – was largely ignored on publication and the few reviews it garnered were disappointing.[4]

Both Miller and Nin were working desperately towards a literary self-discovery and their meeting in December 1931 proved a pivotal event in their writerly lives. For all the complications of their personal relationship, Miller was the first to pay serious attention to Nin the writer, attention that became more important as his own literary fame grew. Shortly after their original meeting Miller started commenting on Nin's writing and correcting her work, explaining that he did not intend to 'cramp [her] style' and that 'only when the meaning is distorted or the beauty marred ... would [he] hazard a friendly counsel.'[5] At the beginning of their association Nin wrote with amazed delight in her diary that Miller, 'this giant,' was reading her work 'with such comprehension, such enthusiasm, talking about the deftness of it, the subtlety, the voluptuousness, shouting at certain passages, criticizing, too.'[6] Nin pored over Miller's notes about her writing; Miller, she said, was 'the one who has most pushed me in my work.'[7] Deirdre Bair, one of Nin's biographers, credits Miller both for supporting Nin and helping to shape her literary vision: 'Henry gave her respect for her talent, faith in her literary endeavors, and enough sustained criticism to nudge her – forcefully at times, gently at others – into the writer she eventually became.'[8] Miller not only nudged her into becoming a writer but provided her with material: Nin's first published 'fictional' work, *House of Incest* (1936), was loosely based on her relationship with the Millers (and especially with June, who arrived in Paris, was duly introduced to Nin, became intimately involved with her, and finally left for America after deciding to file for divorce) and written with Miller's encouragement. Notably, although Nin claimed that all her fictional texts were really a distillation of the material she included in her diary, both Nin and her critics considered *House of Incest* 'the primary source of everything fictional that followed.'[9]

Despite Nin's lesser success and fame (she would become known in wider literary and public circles only in the late 1960s, with the publication of her diaries, while her first best-seller, a book of proto-feminist erotica, did not appear until after her death), she played a crucial role in Miller's work, not only as a muse, patron, and appreciative reader (she wrote that 'modern writing belongs to [Miller]; he does it better than any[one]'),[10] but also as a constructive critic, sending him letters in which she discussed the weak points of his prose and vision, and helping him prune and edit his texts.[11] Early in 1932 Nin tactfully inquired of Miller whether he would allow her to 'weed out' his early novel *Moloch*, which he had given her to read: 'I'll chisel it out a bit,' she suggested.[12] *Moloch* proved beyond salvation (it would be published only in 1992, capitalizing on a spike of interest in all Miller-connected things around the centenary of his birth), but Nin played an important role in editing the books that he wrote throughout the 1930s, including the *Tropics* and *Black Spring*. Nin wrote in her diary that she helped Miller to 'evaluate ... throw out ... [to follow] a discipline in cutting,' adding that 'he has a folder of pages I have extracted because they were just tantrums ... I will not let him make the faults of bad taste which marred Lawrence's work.'[13] If her impact was not as large as she herself believed (she would boast in her diary, 'I promised Henry he would not be a failure, that I would make the world listen to him, and I kept my promise'),[14] it was still substantial. Nin's influence is felt in a number of Miller's texts, especially in *Black Spring*, which he dedicated to her. Miller began a study of D.H. Lawrence inspired by Nin's own work on the British novelist. Moreover, Miller's *Scenario (A Film with Sound)* (1937) is, essentially, a rewrite of Nin's *House of Incest*, a connection that Miller acknowledged in his prefatory note. One of Miller's many subsequent biographers would write, 'Henry regarded [Nin] as "[his] equal in every way," and she was treated thus, staying up drinking and participating in the all-night talk sessions and tactical discussions on the assault on posterity.'[15] Noël Fitch, another one of Nin's biographers, marvels about 'the extent of [Miller's and Nin's] remarkable mutual enrichment of each other's intellectual and artistic capacities,'[16] which became all the more evident when scholars and biographers gained a fuller access to their writing.

The period when Miller and Nin's literary association began to bear fruit coincided with Miller's move to 18 Villa Seurat in 1934. In fact, Nin helped him rent the space on a more-or-less permanent basis. Miller's first real home in Paris provided him, finally, with a room of his own where he could work and create without the fear of being kicked out in the morning. 'One can sleep almost anywhere,' explains Miller's narrator of *Tropic of Cancer*, 'but one must have a place to work. Even if it's not a masterpiece you're doing. Even a bad novel requires a chair to sit on and a bit of privacy.'[17] The studio, along with the recognition that he began to receive for his work, inspired him to begin an avalanche of literary projects, which involved a number of his friends. Nin wrote that the 'activity Henry has created is extraordinary.'[18] Eighteen Villa Seurat hummed and pulsated with creative energy. To Lawrence Durrell, a young poet-novelist who arrived at Villa Seurat on a pilgrimage to meet Miller after reading his *Tropic of Cancer* in Greece, the place seemed 'an immense factory – rather like the Walt Disney studio – with [Miller] at the center.'[19]

Durrell, only twenty-three years old when he sent Miller a brilliant and effusive fan letter about *Tropic of Cancer*, was well on his way to becoming a man of letters. He had already published a book of poems, a satire on the formidable G.B. Shaw (by then a stodgy one-man institution), and written two novels, both of which found a publisher. Nonetheless, Durrell would repeatedly say that it was only after reading Miller that he truly discovered his own destiny as an ambitious literary innovator rather than the 'proud father of cheap romance, wishy-washy stuff'[20] or a middle-brow commercial author with 'vague premonitions of facility, mediocrity, and perhaps later, prosperity.'[21] Durrell wrote to Miller that '*Tropic* opened a pit in my brain. It freed me immediately ... I tell you – two years ago – God couldn't have prophesied more than a Hugh Walpole income for me: now I don't know.'[22] Many years later Durrell would say that Miller 'in a way, invented me ... gave me the courage to exist ... fulfilled my needs as an artist perfectly.'[23]

Miller's philosophy, his outlook on both life and text, proved immensely important for the young Durrell. Scholars of Durrell's work explain that in the 1930s he 'came up with a formula of his own that would prove a motif in all his major novels from *The Black Book* on: "Chaos is the score on which reality is written;"'[24] it is sometimes overlooked, however, that Durrell derived this formula from the opening pages of Miller's *Tropic of Cancer*: 'When into the womb of time everything is again withdrawn chaos will be restored and *chaos is the score upon which reality is written* [emphasis added].'[25] Durrell asked Miller half-jokingly not to 'lose sight of the ardent disciple in [him],'[26] because in the 1930s he was still a chela looking for a guru, and Miller was ready and willing to fulfil the role.

When Durrell finally came to Villa Seurat with his wife Nancy, a painter, after an intense correspondence with Miller and Nin and countless manuscript exchanges, he was immediately accepted as a friend and close associate. Nin wrote in her diary that she felt she had 'known Lawrence Durrell for a thousand years'[27] and that there was 'instant communication. We skipped the ordinary stages of friendship, its gradual development.'[28] Miller was even more warmly welcoming. Not only was theirs an instant three-way friendship, it was a friendship built on respect for each other's literary abilities. If Durrell was Miller's 'first real disciple,'[29] writing to Miller, 'Anything positive I have as a writer I owe to your books,'[30] Miller regarded Durrell's work with a self-confessed mixture of 'terror, admiration, and amazement,' hailing him as '*the* master of the English language'[31] and a genius. 'You are a very old man in a boy's skin,' Miller proclaimed to Durrell, 'You are really Buddha or John of the Cross.'[32] If Durrell rejoiced in Nin's work, writing her admiringly, 'what a splendid writer you are ... A salute of 400 guns ... MARVELOUS. ABSOLUTELY MARVELOUS,'[33] and calling the text that she sent him 'the first book in Europe which belongs to a female artist,' [34] Nin saluted Durrell's work for his ability to 'reach ... a world so subtle, almost evanescent ... the dream life directly through the senses, far beyond the laws of gravity ... Magical phrases. You wr[ite] from the inside of the mystery, not from the outside.'[35] Nin concurred with Miller that Durrell was old beyond his years, a 'seer, child and old man' in one.[36]

Durrell joined the literary and artistic debates at Villa Seurat even before he came to Paris, writing long letters to Miller and Nin from Corfu. Nin's diary records Durrell's arrival and marathon talks between the three about literature in general and each other's work in particular. The three provided each other not only with friendship and support, but also with a literary sounding board. Durrell's biographer, Ian MacNiven, observes that Miller, Nin, and Durrell 'fitted together like a jazz trio,'[37] an apt comparison, if only because the independent voices of the three writers were not overwhelmed by their friendship but enhanced and accentuated.

It was not all idyllic, of course. There were tensions in the relationship of Miller and Nin, precipitated, according to her biographer, by her 'resentment of his success'[38] and by their complicated love lives. Nin did not relish the way in which Miller and Durrell would occasionally join forces to criticize various aspects of her work.[39] Nin's mammoth diary was subtly threatening the others; Durrell's wife Nancy, who was having a hard time fitting into the Villa Seurat scene, would later reminisce that the 'diary was almost like another person ... [Nin] talked about it; everybody talked about it – everybody was afraid of Anaïs's diary ... a terrific *monster* of a thing lurking in the background.'[40] Durrell sheepishly asked Nin not to write his private confidences into her diary, but despite all her assurances to the contrary, it was clear that she would include them. Miller was not pleased with Durrell's decision to take the 'schizophrenic route,' as he called it, dividing his literary output into 'real' work on the level of *The Black Book* and 'literary gardening,' which included essays, travelogues, and more cheap 'romances' under the pseudonym of Charles Norden (a character in Miller's *Tropic of Cancer*). Miller admonished him that 'You can't write good *and* bad books. Not for long ... The toll is "disintegration."'[41] Durrell was finding the constant parties and interruptions at Villa Seurat draining, telling Nin that he hated Bohemianism and recoiling from some of the Villa Seurat habitués[42] (what sympathetic Nin called 'the slippery, greasy, putrid world of Fred [Perlés], [Gregoire] Michonze, Brassai, et al').[43]

Nonetheless, the association of Miller, Nin, and Durrell at Villa Seurat would prove to be a definitive one for their lives and writing careers, just as they became the three most famous writers to come out of the Villa Seurat circle. In subsequent years they would dream about recreating that 'old constellation,'[44] along with the dynamism, collegial atmosphere, and 'freemasonry' of the Villa Seurat period. Durrell would nostalgically write to Miller a decade later, 'Can't we all meet and create a little of the warmth and fury of the Villa Seurat days; a glass of wine and the pleasant soft furry murder of typewriters going.'[45] At Villa Seurat Miller, Nin, and Durrell started calling each other the Three Musketeers, spurring each other to new projects and new literary heights. Eighteen Villa Seurat assumed the aura of a separate world, impenetrable to outsiders. Upon visiting England in 1937, Durrell admiringly wrote to Miller and Nin that 'you have created such a bubble around yourselves there in Villa Seurat, talk such a personal and strange language, that you cannot even conceive the bewilderment of people who sit outside in London for example, and listen.'[46]

Within that protective bubble of Villa Seurat things were possible that were impossible elsewhere. Durrell confided to Miller that he 'always wanted to be in with people, feel myself a part of a band of people. It's chilly work sitting all by yourself in the dark.' The problem was that most artistic and literary movements of the day were political – and Durrell was 'tired of political people [who] have confused the inner struggle with the outer one' – or else exacting in their demands on individual members to conform to the group credo. The surrealists, for example, were constantly pronouncing anathemas on renegade members.[47] Durrell explained to Miller that he did not want 'any movements made up of people who agree with each other even on first principles'[48] and described himself as committed to high individualism: an 'ardent Durrealist.'[49]

At Villa Seurat personal freedom was not only encouraged but celebrated and individual expression was championed over group identity. The residents and visitors of Villa Seurat formed a loose and unstructured alliance. Peripheral members came and went as they pleased. There was no programmatic credo. Miller and Perlès once wrote a parody of group manifestos called 'The New Instinctivism,' which, among the list of things rejected and supported, rejected itself. The same exploit would be repeated with Durrell's participation; this time they were also against 'hygiene,'and 'any form of activity which might lead to success.'[50] Miller always explained that he was congenitally 'against groups and sets and sects and cults and isms and so on.'[51]

At Villa Seurat, however, one could be highly individualistic but still receive the encouragement and support of a group of peers with similar interests and feel oneself a member of a warm band of creative people. Members of Villa Seurat bolstered one another in the face of a largely hostile literary establishment and an indifferent readership. They understood what the individual members were trying to achieve and shared in their excitement of discovery and creation. They enthusiastically collaborated with each other. They also promoted each other's work.

Even a casual look at the activities of all these writers, artists, poets, and photographers throughout the 1930s reveals the extent of their involvement with each other's projects. Miller's early biographer, Jay Martin, provides a representative if abridged overview of the situation:

> [Raymond] Queneau reviewed *Tropic of Cancer* and *Black Spring* in the [*Nouvelle Revue Française*]. Miller became the editor of the 'Siana Series,' books to be distributed through Obelisk Press ... Nin supported the series financially ... [Miller's] *Aller Retour New York*, the first volume published, was followed by ... [Richard] Thoma's *Tragedy in Blue* and Anaïs's *House of Incest* ... [Miller] did write a preface for Fraenkel's *Bastard Death*, wrote about Nin's diary in *The Criterion*, and printed the essay – 'Un Être Etoilique' – in a separate pamphlet in 1937. With Nin's encouragement he planned to edit a series of 'Booster Broadsides,' including ... *En marge des sentiments limotrophes* by Perlès, *Incognito in America* (poems) by [Richard] Osborn, and *The Neurotic at Home and Abroad* by David Edgar.'[52]

Members of Villa Seurat published together in various British, French, American, and, oddly enough, Chinese journals; co-wrote books (Miller, Perlès, and Fraenkel collaborated on a project called *The Hamlet Letters* [1939, 1941], which started off as a three-way meditation on death and creativity); photographed and painted each other; wrote essays about one another; and attempted to boost each other in their own journal, *The Booster*.

The Three Musketeers of Villa Seurat

Miller, Durrell, and Nin were especially involved with each other's work and projects. Miller and Nin's literary dialogue began in 1931, shortly before they began their famous affair, but while their personal relationship was already in decline during the period when Miller finally settled at Villa Seurat, their literary relationship became increasingly important as their projects started to materialize. When Durrell made his appearance he added a new dimension to their literary alliance and provided a connecting bridge between their often conflicting perspectives. Nin wrote that Durrell was 'divided between Henry and me, sharing Henry's hardness, laughter, masculine objective world, and yet better able than Henry to put himself in the place of a woman with a sensitiveness Henry does not have'[53] and that he 'could have been, symbolically speaking, the writer child of Henry and myself.'[54] In her diary Nin reflected about how much the alliance was giving her personally – 'Henry and Larry are the ones who give me impetus and activity'[55] – and how much the Three Musketeers were giving each other at Villa Seurat: 'Beautiful flow ... It is while we talk together that I discover how we mutually nourish each other, stimulate each other. I discover my own strength as an artist ... Henry's respect is also reawakened by Durrell's admiration for me.'[56] Durrell would later say, 'Henry and Anaïs Nin completely transformed my intellectual landscape ... the association with Henry and Anaïs was a great blessing for me.'[57]

The friendship of Miller, Durrell, and Nin would undergo various vicissitudes after the Villa Seurat period, but despite occasional disagreements, both personal and creative, it remained important to them until the very end of their lives. Durrell, who eventually settled in France, would even accept an offer to lecture at the California Institute of Technology because, according to him, that was the only way that he could be 'living within a few kilometres of Miller and more or less the same distance from Anaïs Nin' and in so doing have the opportunity to 'reforge and revive an old and important friendship.'[58]

Miller's importance to both the Villa Seurat circle as a whole and to the Three Musketeers cannot be overemphasized. Ian MacNiven writes that each of the three writers benefited from 'the Villa Seurat nexus [which] was of inestimable importance to them all' but acknowledges that it was Miller who was 'the most secure among the three of them in having found his artistic voice.'[59] Miller was the only one of the three writers to achieve an international literary status of sorts during the Villa Seurat period (in his case, a mixture of celebrity and notoriety), which allowed Nin and the much younger Durrell as well as many other members of the circle to look up to him as an authority on literary matters. If 18 Villa Seurat was, according to Durrell, an immense creative factory, Miller was unquestionably, its foreman. As Miller testily responded to Durrell's enthusiastic comparison: 'Yes, this is a sort of factory, but *without* assistants. I do everything myself, and I'm half dead,' adding more philosophically, 'But I'm in the plenitude of my powers now and one has to make hay while the sun shines.'[60] It was Miller who 'sat in the Villa Seurat like the ruler of a magic kingdom'[61] and it was his presence that attracted and unified the others. As Nin wrote, 'He lives in a whirlpool, drawing everyone to him.'[62] If Durrell was the precocious and impetuous D'Artagnan of the three, and Nin the elegant, mysterious, and intrigue-prone Aramis, then Miller was an amalgam of Porthos and Athos, earthy and possessed of a large appetite for life's good things, but also older, more experienced, and the undisputed leader.

The Three Musketeers of Villa Seurat were much more than a mutual admiration and promotion society. To a greater degree than the other members of the circle they were united by a common language, a common medium, and a common mission, which was grounded in a sense of dissatisfaction with contemporary literature and an almost Messianic belief that they were destined to create a new and radically different writing. The texts each of the three writers produced in the 1930s are remarkable for their differences rather than similarities: Miller's raw scenes, wild associative passages, and lengthy philosophic digressions do not seem to have much in common with the rarefied exoticism of Nin's fictional texts, or with the naturalistic and hyper-observant writing of her *Diary*, while Durrell's poetic playfulness and lexical baroque differ markedly from Miller and Nin's own techniques. This, however, is to be only expected of a group of writers who prized individual expression to the extent they did and who struggled to be true to their own individual voices.

Miller found his voice in *Tropic of Cancer*, but Durrell and Nin were still struggling to discover their own individual voices and negotiating their own identities as writers. Despite calling *Tropic of Cancer* 'the copy-book for [his] generation,'[63] Durrell was particularly concerned about not sounding like a younger Miller with a British accent. When Durrell sent Miller the first version of his *Black Book* he wrote that 'technically it's very influenced by you: but after millions of anxious nights Nancy [Durrell] says that she sees a distinct personality in it which is not Miller.'[64] When Durrell wrote a preface to *The Black Book* in 1959 he again acknowledged Miller's influence but also pointed out that 'in the writing of it I first heard the sound of my own voice, lame and halting perhaps, but nevertheless my very own' and that the book came out of a period when he was struggling to 'discover myself, my private voice and vision.'[65] Nin was also trying to discover her own voice, along with what she called 'a woman's way of writing,' and was concerned about not being absorbed or overly influenced by either Miller or Durrell. During one discussion at Villa Seurat when Nin felt herself 'suddenly attacked' by Miller and Durrell for her ideas on writing, she told them that she would have to find her own way of writing, 'the woman's way.'[66]

The Three Musketeers' emphasis on individuality and their struggles to be true to themselves in their prose should not obscure the fact that the three writers played an important role in shaping each other's literary production in the 1930s, whether by direct editing or by suggestions, many of which are preserved in their epistolary exchanges. Although Miller, Nin, and Durrell admired each other's work intensely, they were as merciless in their critiques as they were lavish in their praise. Miller, for instance, took exception to Nin's passages of 'exotic' purple prose in her fiction, writing her that 'When you go off into what seems like the cerebral atonalities of the Hindu ragas – your Hispano-Suiza style – you do give the impression of one who has suddenly become tone deaf.'[67] Nin told Miller that much in his writing is 'flat, lifeless, vulgarly realistic, photographic ... not *born* yet'[68] and criticized his general ethos in her diaries as 'his world of "shit, cunt, prick, bastard, crotch, bitch."'[69] Miller wrote Durrell to cut the verbiage in *The Black Book* and informed him that he 'overshot [his] wad ... talk[ing] too much about and around.'[70] The imagery that accompanied these critiques was frequently that of professional boxing or warfare, which reflected the belief of the Three Musketeers that serious literary battles lay ahead.

The criticisms that the three writers were levelling at each other, after all, were simply practice sessions in the literary gym to prepare them for the great war ahead. Thus Miller writes to Nin, 'Better that I tap you lightly on the chin ... than that you enter the ring unprepared and get all your teeth knocked down your throat! ... I'm toughening you for the final bout.'[71] Miller's literary advice to Durrell is to '*Move in closer* and deliver good body blows. Aim for the solar plexus, always. If you deliver a foul now and then you will be forgiven – because your intentions were good. But don't pull your punches – that's unforgivable.'[72] When Nin's manuscripts were rejected, Miller rallied her to

'Get out the *House of Incest*, dust it up and send it round to someone else ... Don't be discouraged. *This is war.*'[73]

The pugilistic rhetoric was all part of the Three Musketeers' preparations to make a stand in their prose against contemporary writing, which they all found intensely disappointing. They were waging an attack and prose was both their battlefield and weapon. In Durrell's 1937 letter to Miller, written around the time of the publication of his *Black Book*, he announced, 'We are all opening fire now on different fronts. Boom Boom. Great puffs of prose. The battle is on.'[74]

While the smaller targets of the attack led by the Three Musketeers included individual contemporary writers, such as Gertrude Stein and the members of her salon, their larger battle was waged against what they perceived as the monolith of contemporary prose, which included most British and American writers of the day, as well as the influential literary movements of the time, such as surrealism. Contemporary prose, according to the writers of Villa Seurat, was both boringly predictable and depressingly uniform. In Miller's *Black Spring* he lumps together the works of Aldous Huxley, Gertrude Stein, Sinclair Lewis, Hemingway, Dos Passos, and Dreiser only to dismiss them as substitute toilet paper.[75] Durrell writes Miller that Eliot's *The Waste Land* reminded him of 'those little printed exhortations to muscular development students on how not to masturbate'[76] and that the work of their contemporaries 'from Joyce to Eliot' was merely 'whim-wham and bagatelle.'[77] Later in life, Anaïs Nin would withdraw her sponsorship of an experimental theatre in New York because they produced plays by modern writers, including one by the doyenne of modern literature, Gertrude Stein.

The Three Musketeers believed that the world was ready for a revolution in writing. Durrell's original fan letter to Miller hailed *Tropic of Cancer* as the first of these revolutionary texts: 'I did not imagine that anything like it could be written ... yet ... [it is] something which I knew we were all ready for ... *Tropic* turns the corner into a new life.'[78] Miller agreed wholeheartedly: 'The world *is* ready for something different, something new,'[79] he wrote. This new writing would create a revolution not only in text but in life itself. Miller asserted that there would be '[a] little drop of coloured ink which will stain the whole body of life; a work which will accomplish by silent osmosis what revolutions are powerless to bring about. A chemical metamorphosis because the little drop of ink comes directly from God's fountain pen. Because the chemical here is divine.'[80] Nin also believed that 'the artist must do ... the clockwork to put the soul in tune with the external revolution ... by mysterious routes of language to formulate and arouse that which the soldier and mystic have violently inscribed in the sky with flames and blood.'[81] And if a revolution was imminent, then the writers of Villa Seurat were obviously meant to be the ones to herald it and bring it about.

But if the Three Musketeers all agreed that there needed to be a revolution, the vexing conundrum was how to achieve it. Miller proposed that there needed to be, first of all, a revolutionary freeing of the self. For him, that self-liberation was to be gained by and through text – the first step being a reading of the texts of writers before him who managed, in Promethean fashion, to steal the divine fire for others, both liberating and inspiring them, just as his own *Tropic of Cancer* had for Durrell. If Miller, Nin, and Durrell had little praise for the writing of their time and refused to identify with their contemporaries, they had many heroes in writers and poets past, from Rabelais and Lao Tse to Whitman and Proust. All three wrote about D.H. Lawrence, and Durrell was engrossed in a private study of the Elizabethans. But Miller, whose position in the group made him particularly effective in promoting his views and enthusiasms, had one literary ancestor that he persistently identified and claimed as his liberator: Fedor Mikhailovich Dostoevsky. It was, in fact, Dostoevsky whom Miller proposed as the greatest ally of Three Musketeers in their attempt to create a personal and literary revolution.

Dostoevskian Allusions

During the Villa Seurat period Dostoevsky figured prominently in Miller's discussions with Nin and Durrell. Nin's diaries from the early 1930s mention many instances when she and Miller obsessively discussed Dostoevsky into the early morning hours 'while the cock crows.'[82] By that point Miller no longer wanted to become the American version of Dostoevsky but believed that, since the world, as he put it, 'had evolved to a point far beyond that of Dostoevsky – *beyond* in the sense of degeneration,'[83] a new voice and form needed to be developed that would go beyond Dostoevsky's own achievements, an idea that he expounded to Nin and Durrell. The highest personal praise Miller himself could offer to Nin and Durrell was to tell them that they were reaching that goal. For example, reflecting on Nin's *Diary* in his tribute to her, 'Être Etoilique' (1938), Miller would say that it reminded him of 'the raw pith of some post-Dostoevskian novel.'[84] In a letter to Durrell after the first reading of a manuscript of his *Black Book* (1938), Miller approves of the fact that Durrell 'breaks the boundaries of books, spills over and creates a deluge which is no longer a book but a river of language ... You have written in this book which nobody has dared to write ... You've crossed the Equator ... From now on you're an outlaw,'[85] reserving as his highest praise of Durrell's writings the compliment that 'sometimes this stuff seems to me to outdo Dostoevsky.'[86]

Miller's letters, essays, interviews, and practically all of his books, including such central works as *Tropic of Cancer, Tropic of Capricorn,* and *Black Spring,* as well as *The Rosy Crucifixion* trilogy and later writings, testify to the important place that Dostoevsky occupied in his literary and personal universe. Hundreds of references and allusions Dostoevsky, his novels, and his characters are scattered throughout Miller's 'fictional' books, which function variously as a tip of the hat and loving homage to the Russian author (beginning with *Moloch,* where the protagonist quite literally tips his hat to a portrait of Dostoevsky hanging in a store window),[87] parodic pastiche, or even as sly metatextual commentaries on Miller's own writing. For instance, Dostoevsky's famous detective Porfiry Petrovich, who torments Raskolnikov but also sympathizes with him, is evoked by Miller's portrayal of O'Rourke both in *Tropic of Capricorn* and *The Rosy Crucifixion.* O'Rourke works as a detective for the 'Cosmodemonic Telegraph Company' in New York City. In *Tropic of Capricorn* the narrator tells Curley, one of the company employees who has been involved in stealing money from the till, O'Rourke is 'wise to you.'[88] Curley retorts that if O'Rourke knew anything he would have confronted him long ago. By way of response, the narrator explains that O'Rourke is not a typical company detective but 'a born student of human nature.' His preferred method is a cat-and-mouse game which he plays with his suspect, 'giving [him] plenty of rope' but studying his every move: 'And out of the clear blue he'll suddenly say – you remember ... the time when that little Jewish clerk was fired for tapping the till? ... and abruptly change the conversation to something else ... until you feel as though you were sitting on hot coals ... and finally, when you think you're free ... he'll say in a soft, winsome voice – *now look here, my lad, don't you think you had better come clean?* And if you think he's only trying to browbeat you and that you can pretend innocence and walk away, you're mistaken.'[89] In *Sexus,* where O'Rourke reappears, the narrator adds that 'He was a detective because of his extraordinary interest in and sympathy with his fellow-man ... He sought to understand, to fathom their motives, even when they were of the basest.'[90]

Although a legion of fictional detectives share O'Rourke's methods and characteristics, Miller refers the reader to Dostoevsky's Porfiry Petrovich of *Crime and Punishment*, a student of human nature with an extraordinary interest in his fellow-man who plays cat-and-mouse games with Raskolnikov: '[O'Rourke's] knowledge of literature was almost nil. But if, for example, I should happen to relate the story of Raskolnikov, as Dostoevsky unfolded it for us, I could be certain of reaping the most penetrating observations.'[91] This metaphoric tip of the hat to Dostoevsky both indicates O'Rourke's fictional predecessor and proudly acknowledges Dostoevsky's influence.

Miller makes different use of the iconic scene in *Crime and Punishment*, where Raskolnikov and Sonia Marmeladova read the Bible together. He first alludes to the incident in *Moloch*, which contains both a reference to Sonia and Raskolnikov together and a direct quotation from the novel about their relationship.[92] In *Tropic of Capricorn*, however, the incident is parodied when Curley tells the narrator about being seduced by his aunt, Sophie, a woman known for her questionable morals: 'He said she had seduced him,' comments the narrator, 'True enough, but the curious thing was that he let himself be seduced while they were reading the Bible together.'[93] The reference to *Crime and Punishment* is more oblique here than in other of Miller's texts. Nonetheless, sufficient allusions are provided to make the reference to the Dostoevsky novel recognizable: the reading of the Bible by the young criminal and the quasi-prostitute; the aunt's name (Sophia, of course, is Sonia's official name – in her papers she is Sophia Semenovna Marmeladova); the familiar image of O'Rourke, a Porfiry Petrovich type character, looming threateningly in the background. Instead of Curley being inspired and potentially reformed by the reading of the Holy Book (as Raskolnikov is in *Crime and Punishment*), however, he is seduced and sexually corrupted by the woman who persuaded him to read the Bible in the first place. This kind of subversive textual parody of Dostoevsky's novels occurs frequently in Miller's books; it serves both as a game played with his readers, challenging them to recognize the text alluded to, and as a manifestation of his refusal to view the writings of his favourite author as sacrosanct, inviolable texts.

Another important use that Miller makes of Dostoevsky's texts is that of referring to a Dostoevsky character in order to provide an ironic commentary on his own characters and, ultimately, on his own text. To draw upon *Tropic of Capricorn* once again: a philandering character named Kronski becomes widowed when his wife dies on the operating table. Kronski is utterly despondent, sobbing dramatically, 'I knew it would happen … It was too beautiful to last.'[94] Just the previous day, however, as soon as Kronski's wife was taken to the hospital, Kronski ran off to see a woman whom he was trying to bed. On the evening after his wife's death Kronski tells the narrator an improbable story about having sex on the grave of a woman he once loved. The narrator, concerned for his sanity, tries to distract him, telling him about 'Anatole France at first, and then about other writers,' with no success. Finally, he 'switche[s] to General Ivolgin, and with that [Kronski] beg[ins] to laugh … [until] tears were streaming down his eyes.'[95]

General Ivolgin, of course, is the grotesque character in Dostoevsky's *The Idiot* with a pathological need to relate outrageous things that supposedly happened to him but never actually did. Kronski's laughter serves as an acknowledgment of the humour in Dostoevsky's novels, something that Miller – unlike many of his contemporaries – always appreciated (as Miller writes in *Books in My Life*: 'There are passages in Dostoevsky … which still bring tears of laughter to my eyes').[96] Allusions to Dostoevsky's grotesques are found in many of Miller's texts and highlight his own use of the grotesque or, in Bakhtinian terms, the carnivalesque element, with its overturned order, anarchic freedom, wide-reaching parody, comic violence, and an accession of a rowdy group of social outcasts. To this sphere belongs Miller's evocation of Smerdiakov from *Brothers Karamazov* as 'General Smeridakov' in *Black Spring*[97] (Miller reinforces the connection between Smerdiakov and Ivolgin by also referring to the former as a general). The narrator does not elaborate on who General Ivolgin is, other than calling 'a poor drunken sap' several pages later.[98] Nonetheless, a reader familiar with General Ivolgin's character, who knows about his propensity for creative lying, can derive some insight into Kronski's character from the juxtaposition of the two. Kronski's laughter at the mention of General Ivolgin serves as an ironic footnote to both his teary-eyed insistence that his marital relationship was too beautiful to last (as contrasted with his callous philandering behaviour) and his highly improbable story about wild sex on the grave of his former beloved with her sister.

The reference to General Ivolgin is also important on a metatextual level. General Ivolgin's willingness to tell elaborate anecdotes about himself that turn out to be outrageous lies raises the issue of the truthfulness of any autobiographical account, oral or written. Given that

Miller himself writes texts which are purportedly autobiographical, but in which he consistently blurs the boundaries between fact and invention, truth and falsehood, the reference to General Ivolgin becomes especially suggestive. It carries even deeper metatextual implications concerning the similarity of the need to invent and relate stories about oneself that never happened ('inspired' lying) and the need to invent and write stories as a part of a literary text (inspired 'lying'). The reference to General Ivolgin within a creative text in which the categories of truth and falsehood are constantly problematized acts as Miller's playful and self-reflexive comment both on *Tropic of Capricorn* and the act of literary creation itself.

References to Dostoevsky are not as prominent in Nin and Durrell's writing as they are in Miller's work, but they can be found. Meditations on the meaning of Dostoevsky's novels and characters abound in Nin's letters and, more significantly, in her diaries (as reflected both in their expurgated and unexpurgated publications), which Nin eventually came to recognize as her real legacy as a writer. Locating obvious traces of Dostoevsky in Nin's *House of Incest* and *A Winter of Artifice*, however, is more problematic, as the allusions are more tenuous and veiled and could be as much a reference to other intermediaries as to Dostoevsky. The theme of the double in Nin's 'fictional' works, for example, has many connections with Dostoevsky but also owes much to Otto Rank, her analyst, associate, and lover. Rank, a renegade Freudian who shared Freud's admiration of Dostoevsky, cites Dostoevsky's *The Double* (1846) as the greatest literary treatment of the theme in his own famous study of the Double (*Doppelgänger* [1914]), which was well known to Nin.[99]

Durrell's *Black Book* includes several allusions to Dostoevsky and his novels. None are explicit, some are parodic, others are possibly affected by a number of intermediaries (Otto Rank's study of the Double was also well known to Durrell, who incorporates the doubling device in all his work), but most are still identifiable, such as the instance when Death Gregory, the diarist of *The Black Book*, smirkingly refers to 'the critical point' in his relationship with his wife, 'as when, in any Russian novel, the Christian protagonist, having speculated for pages on the properties of murder, actually *does* poleax his grandmother'[100] – an obvious spoof of *Crime and Punishment*.

Some of Durrell's allusions in *The Black Book* can be positively linked to Dostoevsky's novels only after a fair bit of literary sleuthing. For instance, when Death Gregory describes Lobo, a character obsessed with bedding women, he comments, 'To Lobo sensual lust ... To insects sensual lust.'[101] The quotation is an oblique but undeniable reference to *Brothers Karamazov*, where Dmitry Karamazov is citing the Russian poet F.I. Tiutchev's rendering of Friedrich Schiller's poem 'An die Freude' ['Ode to Joy']: *'Nasekomym sladostrastie/Angel bogu predstoit'* ['To insects sensual lust/{but} An Angel stands before God'][102] (in the German original, the phrase reads 'Wollust ward dem Wurm gegeben,/und der Cherub steht vor Gott' ['{Nature} gave the joy of life to the lowliest,/And to the angels who dwell with God']). Since Tiutchev is virtually unknown in the West and was not even fully translated into English in the 1930s, Durrell could not have come upon this poem in a volume of Tiutchev's poetry. Similarly, Durrell is not quoting directly from Schiller, because the original poem never mentions 'insects' – this is introduced in Tiutchev's rather free rendering of Schiller's original. It is clear that Durrell can only be citing the Garnett translation of Dostoevsky's novel. Needless to say, Durrell does not make it easy for his reader to recognize, let alone identify, this allusion, which is typical of the way in which he incorporates most Dostoevskian references in his texts, offering them as a reward only for the most careful and erudite reader.

Generally speaking, Durrell delights in challenging his readers and keeping them on their toes. In *Tunc* (1968) he slyly advises his readers in an author's note at the very end of the novel that 'attentive readers may discern the odd echo' of his other books and that 'this is intentional,' presumably with the aim of making his readers go back and reread his text more carefully.[103] Durrell continues the trend of challenging and playing with his readers in the epigraphs he chooses from Dostoevsky's writings for his own texts. Occasionally, he cites obscure translations of Dostoevsky's titles instead of the more easily recognizable ones; his contribution to *Art and Outrage* (1959), for instance, includes a reference to *Notes from Underground* cited as *Letters from the Underworld*,[104] an unfamiliar translation of the title and sure to confuse his readers. At times, as in *Tunc*, he cites Dostoevsky in French rather than English, confronting his Anglophone readers with the mystifying and unfamiliar Dostoevsky title *Voix Souterraine*, which once again turns out to be a French translation of *Notes from Underground*. At other times he appears to intentionally mislead the reader by citing a different Dostoevsky source than the one he is actually using; Durrell's *Key to Modern British Poetry* (1952), for instance, includes an epigraph identified as from Dostoevsky's *Notes from Underground* which is actually a quotation from his *Raw Youth [Podrostok]*.[105]

While the deciphering of individual quotations and allusions to Dostoevsky in the works of the Three Musketeers can be an interesting literary exercise, it is more important to recognize that texts produced by Durrell, Nin, and Miller during the critical period of their lives at Villa Seurat represent their attempt to break through to a revolutionary new writing, and that Dostoevsky figured prominently in that project, especially for Miller. Miller's *Tropic of Cancer, Tropic of Capricorn, Black Spring,* and his famous short pieces of those years and, to a lesser but still significant extent, Nin's *House of Incest, Winter of Artifice* (1939), and diaries of the 1930s; as well as Durrell's *Black Book* – in other words, texts pivotal to the *oeuvre* of each writer – may be viewed as an almost utopian attempt to create a new, post-Dostoevskian writing, emanating from but going beyond Dostoevsky.

5 Post-Dostoevskian Prose and the Villa Seurat Circle

There are some volumes [of Nin's *Diary*] ... which are like the raw pith of some post-Dostoevskian novel.

Henry Miller, 'Un Être Etoilique,' 289

During Dostoevsky's lifetime fellow writers, newspaper columnists, and critics frequently attacked his novels for their flawed diction, prolixity, and cumbersome form. His prose style and novelistic form were judged by his Russian contemporaries (even by those who admired his novels) to be inferior to those of Turgenev, Tolstoy, and the other prominent Russian novelists of the time. One nineteenth-century Russian reader, who had actually met Dostoevsky and considered herself a devotee of his work, explained that for her 'he stood incomparably higher than other writers,' adding, as a matter of course, 'naturally not when it came to style or artistry.'[1] Turgenev and Tolstoy commented privately on the shortcomings they perceived in Dostoevsky's stylistic craftsmanship. Turgenev, for instance, referred to Dostoevsky's *Raw Youth* [*Podrostok*] (1875) as 'chaos' filled with incoherent 'mutterings.'[2] Tolstoy, who felt that Dostoevsky's novels contain 'astonishing pages' that 'enthral' the reader, still questioned his 'appalling form.'[3]

Russian literary critics concurred. Beginning with Vissarion Belinsky, the foremost Russian critic of Dostoevsky's era, who called his work 'at times insufficiently polished, at others overly decorative,'[4] most Russian literary critics of the nineteenth century either derided Dostoevsky's literary style or else ignored it in favour of the social and philosophical issues raised in his novels. In the first period of Dostoevsky's literary activity (before his imprisonment for his role in the Petrashevsky affair) critics of prominent Russian journals 'made fun of the "monotony and mawkishness" of [Dostoevsky's literary] language.'[5] After he came back from exile and started publishing again, the reaction to the style of his novels remained unchanged. The radical critic Nikolai Dobroliubov wrote of Dostoevsky's *Insulted and Injured* [*Unizhennye i oskorblennye*] (1860) that 'one would have to be too naive and uninformed in order to analyse ... the aesthetic significance of a novel ... that demonstrates a lack of any claim to artistic significance.'[6] A year after Dostoevsky's death the influential critic Nikolai Mikhailovsky wrote an article in which he provided an overview of Dostoevsky's life work, claiming that 'with the exception of *Notes from the Dead House* and two or three of the minor stories ... everything else written by Dostoevsky fails to overwhelm us by its clumsiness, long-windedness, measurelessness (if one can put it this way) only because we have gotten too accustomed to his manner of writing.'[7]

Dostoevsky himself complained about never having enough time to rewrite and hone his material as much as he would have liked. In a letter to his favourite niece Sonia, after he radically changed his plans for *The Idiot*, destroying everything that he had written in a whole year, Dostoevsky lamented: 'I know for certain that had I two or three years [to work] on this novel, like Turgenev, Goncharov, or Tolstoy, I would write a book [still] talked about 100 years from now! ... But what will happen [instead]? I know it in advance: I will write this novel in 8 or 9 months, mangle it and ruin everything ... There will be many instances of lack of restraint [*nevyderzhek*] and drawn-out passages' (29/I:136).

Some Dostoevsky scholars have argued more recently that he 'became defensive about the artistic quality of his work and excused himself by having had to write hurriedly' because he was 'not blessed with laudatory reviews.'[8] It is certainly true that early in Dostoevsky's literary career he insisted that his style was exactly suited to his subject and his characters. In a letter to his brother Mikhail of February 1846, in which he discussed the criticism he was facing over his debut novel *Poor Folk*, Dostoevsky wrote that 'the public ... cannot understand how anyone can write in such a style ... but they do not even understand that it is Devushkin talking, not myself, and that Devushkin cannot talk any other way. They are finding the novel drawn-out, but it does not contain a [single] unnecessary word' (28/I:117–18). The fact remains, however, that after his return from Siberian exile Dostoevsky worked under increasing financial and temporal constraints, and that he bitterly complained to relatives and friends until the very end of his life about the pressure that prevented him from properly editing his work. On many occasions the first instalment of his novel was already published while he was still deciding how its plot would unfold. His wife wrote in her memoirs that 'very frequently,' having just reread 'an already published chapter of his novel,' Dostoevsky 'would clearly perceive a mistake he had made and become despondent, realizing he botched something he planned.'[9] What is more, Dostoevsky himself agreed with the deeper criticism of his literary form offered by such friendly critics as Nikolai Strakhov,[10] conceding to Strakhov that his 'chief fault ... [was] cram[ming] a multitude of separate novels and novellas into one, so that there is neither measure nor harmony.'[11] While working on *Raw Youth*, Dostoevsky wrote to his wife that upon examining his plan for the novel, he realized that 'its main defect' lay in its 'multiplicity,' so that it was really 'four novels strung together,' something that 'Strakhov had always seen as my weakness' (19/I:338).

In early twentieth-century Russia the issue of Dostoevsky's style and literary form was hardly a primary concern. Debates raged around the content of Dostoevsky's novels – the psychology of his characters, the philosophical and metaphysical dilemmas facing them, his depiction of society and class conflict, and so forth. A pioneering study of Dostoevsky's style and prose form was written in 1911 by the symbolist critic Vyacheslav Ivanov (1866–1949), *Dostoevsky and the Tragedy-Novel* [*Dostoevskii i roman-tragediia*], in which Ivanov theorized that the seeming chaos in Dostoevsky's novels is in fact a complex and subtle organization of the text using the technique of contrapuntal development of the theme in musical composition.[12]

After the Revolution of 1917 the question of Dostoevsky's style moved further into the background, as the new regime made it clear that the issues at stake were not Dostoevsky's style or form but his 'dangerous' ideology, his attitude towards the revolutionary movements of the 1870s, and the corrupting effect his novels might possibly have on the embryonic Soviet man. All the same, important work in the area was done by Leonid P. Grossman (1888–1965), who began publishing on the problems of Dostoevsky's style and prose form before the Revolution and continued to work actively on related issues throughout the 1920s (in 1925 he published a book of collected essays on Dostoevsky's form under the title *Dostoevsky's Poetics* [*Poetika Dostoevskogo*], arguing that Dostoevsky's novel form, far from lacking cohesion, represents a breakthrough in the European novel, weaving multiple heterogenous threads of narrative around a single idea. In 1929 Mikhail Bakhtin polemicized and built upon Grossman's work in his own *Problems of Dostoevsky's Poetics* [*Problemy poetiki Dostoevskogo*],[13] a study that received wide international acclaim when it became better known in the second half of the century, arguing that Dostoevsky came up with a novel form that was not only unprecedented in European literature but which was perfectly suited for his philosophical perspectives. Although Ivanov, Grossman, and Bakhtin espoused radically different visions of Dostoevsky's style and of the form of his novels, they all praised what earlier critics and scholars berated or, at best, excused.

Towards the second half of the twentieth century the tide of opinion about the style and form of Dostoevsky's novel generally began to turn (not least because of the popularity of Bakhtin's work).[14] While strong dissenting Russian voices remained both within the Soviet Union and in the West (one thinks of Vladimir Nabokov's extreme aversion to Dostoevsky's novels), more and more important Russian scholars, writers, poets, and critics expressed their appreciation for Dostoevsky's literary style and the form of his novels. No less a connoisseur of Russian language and style than the poet and Nobel Prize laureate Joseph Brodsky praised Dostoevsky's prose for its 'feverish, hysterical, idiosyncratic pace'[15] and proclaimed Dostoevsky to be 'the very best Russian stylist.'[16] After the Soviet Union fell apart and the constraints of literary and scholarly censorship fell away it became more common to extravagantly celebrate Dostoevsky's literary style than to criticize it. For example, when Liubov Dostoevsky's memoirs were first published in Moscow in 1992, the editor, a Russian scholar, felt obligated to point out that her eccentric remarks about her father's literary style (she claims that his literary style and, in fact, his written Russian were faulty because his ancestors were not ethnically Russian)[17] represent 'a complete misunderstanding of Dostoevsky's style' and that Dostoevsky has 'a special, spiritual style, the style of the fourth dimension, of spirituality,'[18] without any further explanation of what any of this means.

Outside of Russia the issue of Dostoevsky's style was further complicated and obscured by the fact of translation itself (often twice removed from the original)[19] and by the liberties taken by the translators. Mindful readers of translated Russian prose have always realized, of course, that they were at a disadvantage when it came to judging the style of Dostoevsky's novels; Virginia Woolf, for example, wrote in *The Common Reader* (1925) that 'we have judged a whole [Russian] literature stripped of its style' and questioned the validity of any conclusion a reader of translations might come to about Dostoevsky.[20] Constance Garnett, who took up the Herculean task of mediating the style of Dostoevsky's novels for the Anglophone reader, was almost universally praised for her effort and accomplishment. There is no doubt that Garnett succeeded in providing translations of Dostoevsky's novels into English that were not only better by far than anything available earlier but also largely stood the test of time; as we have already seen, however, she was willing to distort Dostoevsky's style in her quest to offer a more accessible and domesticated text to her readers.

Unlike Woolf, many non-Russian readers exhibited a remarkable naiveté when it came to expressing opinions about Dostoevsky's style. Several decades after Woolf had observed that non-Russian speakers were ill-equipped to consider the issue, Truman Capote, who did not speak Russian, declared that Dostoevsky's style in the Russian original was simply terrible.[21] When it came to the form of Dostoevsky's novels, the verdicts of such acknowledged literary experts as Vogüé and Henry James, both of whom criticized Dostoevsky's drawn-out passages and lack of streamlining (as James put it, his novels' 'lack of composition [and] their defiance of economy and structure'),[22] became accepted as authoritative in a number of countries. With the passage of time, these original critical opinions became divorced from their sources and uncritically accepted by the general readership.

Generally speaking, Dostoevsky's novels continued to be viewed by Russian and non-Russian readers alike as binary systems consisting of 'content' and 'form,' with the former outweighing the latter in importance. Because of this emphasis on 'content,' many of the non-Russian critics of Dostoevsky who were interested in his form continued to ignore it in favour of his ideas and the social significance of his works. André Gide, for instance, admits in his book on Dostoevsky that 'carried away in my enthusiasm to discuss his ideas, I am afraid I have neglected all too much his wonderful skill in exposition'[23] but, with the exception of a panegyrical paragraph or two, goes on comfortably neglecting both the 'exposition' and the formal features of the novels.

Writing Like Dostoevsky

When it comes to the subject of writers themselves claiming to be influenced by Dostoevsky's style and literary form, it would seem that there are more examples of this outside of Russia than in Russia itself, although many Russian writers' techniques were retrospectively linked to Dostoevsky by scholars and critics. In Soviet Russia, probably the only group of writers that claimed to be stylistically influenced by Dostoevsky was the young, irreverent, and eventually state-suppressed group of absurdist writers and poets active in the late 1920s under the name OBERIU (the Russian acronym for 'Association for the Art of Reality'). Even their lone claim needs to be qualified, as members of the OBERIU professed to be influenced not by the prose style of Dostoevsky's novels but by the versification of Dostoevsky's Captain Lebiadkin in *The Devils* [*Besy*], such as his comically inept 'Once there was a cockroach/A cockroach from childhood/And he fell into a glass/Full of frenzied fly-hood [*mukhoedstva*]' (X:141).[24] As Soviet authorities clamped down harder on dissenters Dostoevsky became a dangerous writer to emulate within the Soviet Union, whether that emulation was of his ideology or of his literary style.

Outside of the Soviet Union, of course, writers could and, in some cases, did talk about being influenced by the style and form of Dostoevsky's novels. In the revised edition of *Problems of Dostoevsky's Poetics*, Mikhail Bakhtin states that 'Dostoevsky's novels are possibly the most influential of all models in the West. Individuals ... follow Dostoevsky the artist.'[25] Bakhtin does not specify whether he believes that this Western literary emulation of Dostoevsky the artist occurs at a level of any depth or sophistication. Some scholars who have examined the question more specifically argue the opposite, writing, for example, that 'it is hard to find one British or American writer who, as literary artist, has learned from [Dostoevsky's] art,' and concluding that any 'following' has been limited to superficial imitations of the kind of narrative devices found in his novels (feverish inner monologues of Raskolnikov-like antiheroes, claustrophobic man-in-hostile-cityscape scenes, variants of Svidrigailov's nightmares, and so forth).[26] Further, they show that most of these borrowings cannot be ascribed to a careful study of Dostoevsky's form or prose style (even as mediated by the canonical Garnett translations), and that the latter was generally 'put down to a fall from the Turgenevan ideal.'[27]

Whatever the case, it is clear that in the 1930s – the decade that saw the birth and apogee of the Villa Seurat Circle – there was a scarce handful of prominent writers who wrote in English and who were sympathetic to Dostoevsky as a prose stylist (most prominently, the Americans Thomas Wolfe and Sherwood Anderson) but practically none who claimed to identify with, learn from, or be influenced by his prose *style* in their own works. Miller and the Villa Seurat writers' sustained focus on Dostoevsky's prose form and literary style and their attempt to learn from it is unique for the period and must be understood within the context of their rejection of contemporary prose writing. (We will leave aside for now the questions of how accurately Miller and his disciples had actually understood Dostoevsky's prose form and style and how coherent and incisive they were in their analysis.)

Prose Innovation in 1930s

In the 1930s prose innovation was widespread and almost an exigency upon every serious author; models of revolutionary prose were seemingly everywhere. A brief survey of writing produced in English during the decade shows just how momentous a period it was for experimental prose. In England, the ban was finally lifted from Joyce's *Ulysses* and sections of *Finnegan's Wake* were being published (the completed book came out in 1938). In the United States William Faulkner produced his macabre *As I Lay Dying* (1930), written as stream-of-consciousness. John Dos Passos wrote the *U.S.A.* trilogy (1932–8), which incorporated collages of newspaper headlines, popular songs, and advertising slogans as well as impressionistic passages. John Steinbeck experimented with a neo-Aesopic mode in *Of Mice and Men* (1937). In France, American expatriates were continuing their work in prose innovation. Djuna Barnes's lyrical *Nightwood* was published in 1936. In Paris, Gertrude Stein wrote the playful *Autobiography of Alice B. Toklas* (1933). Elsewhere on the continent Stein's erstwhile disciple Ernest Hemingway was aspiring after 'the kind of writing that can be done ... a fourth and fifth dimension that can be gotten' in the *Green Hills of Africa* (1935).[28]

One of the most common critical assumptions made about the work of Miller, Nin, and Durrell is that they shared the literary and aesthetic sensibilities of their contemporaries. This assumption ignores their outspoken disappointment with the work of other writers active in America and England in the 1930s. Miller, for instance, proclaims in the Autobiographical Note of 1939, 'On the whole I dislike the trend of American literature ... As for English literature, it leaves me cold ... it is a sort of fish-world which is completely alien to me.'[29] Durrell scornfully writes in a letter of 1937, 'Been to the Café Royal [a literary gathering spot in London] a lot and confirmed the opinion I always had of English writers.'[30] Elsewhere, he accuses American writers of 'descending from over-exuberance to mannerism and cheapness very easily.'[31] Nin, for her part, had always maintained that she found contemporary English and American literatures uninspiring, referring to the latter privately as the 'miserly, sterile, frigid, plain, homely, prosaic, stuttering world of American writing'[32] and publicly as 'the most literal, the most one-dimensional [literature] in the world.'[33]

The Villa Seurat writers' dissatisfaction with contemporary English and American literatures extended towards other expatriate writers living in France and producing experimental prose in English. As far as they were concerned, the expatriate writers who became famous in the 1920s were all written out and finished by the next decade. In the late 1930s Miller compared 'the brilliant ones of a decade ago' to 'burnt out planets' because they were 'so definitely dead.'[34] Shortly before her death, Anaïs Nin explained to an interviewer that, as a young writer in the 1930s, she felt little affinity for the key expatriate writers because 'they were passé, too 1920's. We were trying to be our own writers, and we didn't have much respect for Hemingway or Fitzgerald.'[35]

One does not need to delve too deeply into the realm of psychoanalytic conjecture to observe the obvious: at least part of the Villa Seurat writers' dissatisfaction with and ultimate rejection of the work of their contemporaries (as Nin, in fact, suggested) had to do with their desire to be major literary figures in their own right, not some arrivistes who came on the literary scene too late to make an independent impression and were doomed to follow in the footsteps of their betters. Their dismissal of Joyce, whose prose was among the most radically innovative available at the time, and with whom they actually had much in common in the realm of prose experimentation (and by whom, perhaps, they felt most threatened), is representative both of their disappointment with other experimental writers and their determination to make their own way in literature. Durrell discarded Joyce's writing as 'whim-wham and bagatelle.'[36] Nin decided that Joyce was too elitist: '[Joyce's prose is] so clever that it was undecipherable for me and I didn't want to study it in terms of scholarship, just as language or mythology'[37] (she graciously conceded that he had a 'lovely voice' as a singer).[38] Miller engaged with Joyce's writings most strenuously of all the circle members, applauding the portrait of Molly Bloom in *Ulysses*[39] (mythologized as much as the June figure in Miller's own books) and holding up the final chapter of the novel as 'a free fantasia such as has never been seen before in all of literature.'[40] Nonetheless, Miller rejected Joyce even more vociferously than the others, writing in his 'Universe of Death' that *Ulysses* was 'vomit spilled by a delicate child,'[41] that Joyce's *Work in Progress* (the future *Finnegans Wake*) was an example of global schizophrenia,[42] and that Joyce himself was 'the high priest of the lifeless literature of today.'[43] As Miller wrote to Durrell in an obviously self-congratulatory mood, 'Joyce must know what I think of him, which is not very flattering – or haven't you yet seen my "Universe of Death" chapter from the Lawrence book? Anyway I've just flattened him out. I've made a shit-heel of him.'[44] For Miller and the rest of the Villa Seurat circle, Joyce, Hemingway, Fitzgerald, other expatriate writers, and contemporary British and American writers all belonged to one hopelessly outdated and essentially homogenous generation of writers, in which one did not search for allies.

Surrealism and the Writers of Villa Seurat

The writers of Villa Seurat had considerably more sympathy for the prose experimentation of French writers, especially those connected with the surrealists and with Dada, which preceded surrealism, but ultimately rejected them as literary models as well. In the 1930s the surrealists, a movement born in Paris in the 1920s, were stepping up their efforts to become an international phenomenon. Their main target for conversion was Anglophone writers. In 1936 *Surrealism*, the famous anthology of French and English essays on the subject, was published in London. The anthology was brought out in England by Durrell's publishers Faber and Faber and included pieces by André Breton, Paul Éluard, and Hugh Sykes Davies, as well as reproductions of the works of Salvador Dali, Man Ray, René Magritte, and Joan Miró, all chosen by the prominent English literary critic, Herbert Read. In it, André Breton, as the unofficial spokesperson for the movement, outlined the surrealist program and welcomed the 'English poets and artists who ... are now with us, agreeing to pool all their intellectual resources with ours.'[45] The surrealist theories, then, provided yet another compelling model of literary prose innovation in the 1930s, not only for French writers, but for those writing in other languages, especially English.

All the writers of the Villa Seurat circle had, at one time or another, produced prose incorporating such surrealist standbys as automatism, free association of random images, and symbols from the realms of Freudian and Jungian psychology. Miller's *Tropic of Cancer* is full of surrealist passages where random and often deliberately shocking images are brought together in lengthy automatist lists, which are used to describe characters, places, events, or moods: 'Tania is a fever, too – *les voies urinaires*, Café de la Liberté, Place des Vosges, bright neckties on the Boulevard Montparnasse, dark bathrooms, Porto Sec, Abdullah cigarettes, the adagio sonata *Pathétique*, aural amplificators, anecdotal seances, burnt sienna breasts, heavy garters, what time is it, golden pheasants stuffed with chestnuts, taffeta fingers, vaporish twilights turning to ilex, acromegaly, cancer and delirium, warm veils, poker chips, carpets of blood and soft thighs.'[46]

Miller's *Black Spring* (1936), comprised of ten self-contained short texts, is probably the most surrealist-flavoured of Miller's books. In fact, it was singled out by George Orwell in his famous essay about Miller, 'Inside the Whale' (1945), as a prime example of Miller sporadically 'slid[ing] away … into the squashy universe of the surrealists.'[47] One of its shorter pieces, 'Into the Nightlife,' had its start as a dream diary kept by Miller at Nin's insistence, and consists of a thirty-page record of incongruous and often nightmarish images of old hags with their hair 'full of rats' and young girls with blood 'bubbling from [their] temple … something stirring inside … It's a cuckoo!'[48] Miller himself was conscious of the surrealist facet of the book; in a letter to Durrell of 1936, just before the publication of *Black Spring*, Miller writes that 'I got somewhat surrealistic myself [in the book] … As you will see.'[49]

The abundance of surrealist imagery in *Black Spring* and Miller's other works led some scholars to conclude that 'there is no disputing that Henry Miller was a surrealist.'[50] Miller did hope at one point to attract the attention of the surrealists; in 1934 he wrote to Nin that 'Marcel Duchamp … expressed unprovoked & unstinted admiration for the [*Tropic of Cancer*], had great pleasure in reading it, etc. I think thru him, and Raymond Queneau & Jacques Baron, I may finally get the attention of the Surrealist gang.'[51] Nonetheless, already in *Black Spring* there are indications that while employing surrealistic techniques Miller is not a full-fledged surrealist; in longer pieces like 'The Fourteenth Ward' and 'The Tailor Shop,' about his childhood and early youth, he demonstrates that autobiography, the everyday, and portraits of real people interest him more than automatism, the marvellous, and randomly chosen subjects. In another letter to Durrell written in 1936 Miller confides, 'I have used the [surrealist] method here and there, when it came naturally and spontaneously … I don't start out by trying to be Surrealistic. Sometimes it comes at the beginning and sometimes at the end.'[52] Miller also expresses his belief that the surrealists have not come up with anything new in their literary theories: 'what constitutes Surréalisme is a permanent thing in art, more especially in literature. Swift was a good one, and so was Lewis Carroll in my opinion – and Shakespeare too now and then.'[53] Durrell, whose work shows the least surrealist tendencies of all the Villa Seurat writers, but whose *Black Book* abounds in such typically surrealist moves as an 'elegy in swan's-down, ferroconcrete, postmen, Lobo, foetus, halfpenny stamps'[54] standing in for a description of a winter morning, agrees with Miller wholeheartedly (in his response, he writes: 'A definition of the word surrealism, please ... Breton etc. Very true, but surely as ancient as Oedipus?').[55]

Nin's fictional prose of the 1930s (as opposed to her diary writings) has more connections with surrealism than the prose produced by either Miller or Durrell during those years, so much so that some hostile critics have called Nin's writings 'Surrealist Soap Opera'[56] (Nin herself always believed that the surrealist label was applied to her 'as an expression of ostracism').[57] Even in Nin's case, however, the surrealist affiliation is ambiguous and her affinity for surrealist images and techniques more complicated than it appears at first glance.

One of Nin's most surrealist works is *House of Incest* (1936), her so-called prose-poem, a highly poetic and allegorical first-person narrative of a woman's journey through various states of consciousness towards self-knowledge. The text itself is strongly marked by a kind of surrealist Orientalism, which juxtaposes exotic Eastern images ('Alhambra,' 'simoun winds,' 'Moorish chants,' 'Chinese bells,' 'Indian bracelets,' etc.,) in an exploration of solipsism, incest, and lesbianism, and where dreams are used as elaborate representations of inner states. At the time of working on the *House of Incest*, Nin was conscious of writing 'in a surrealist way ... [it] gives my imagination the opportunity to leap freely,' as she noted in her diary.[58] Nonetheless, even while writing the book, she knew that she was resorting to surrealist techniques for reasons other than a genuine identification with their movement (in 1935 she wrote in the diary, 'More and more I'm against surrealism ... The surrealists just want to laugh at the unconscious. *Ce sont des farceurs*').[59] Much later, in 1957, Nin would confide to her psychoanalyst that she 'went into surrealism as a method of equivocal truth telling.'[60] Seen from this perspective, the opaqueness of surrealist imagery provided Nin with an acceptable way to write publicly about the 'Unmentionable Events' in her life that she was recording privately in her diary: a lesbian liaison with June Miller, who appears as the character Sabina, and an incestuous affair with her own father, which is transmuted in the *House of Incest* into a description of a painting of Lot and his daughter ('Lot with his hand upon his daughter's breast while the city burned behind them ... all crackling with the joy and terror of their love').[61] All the same, Nin's ideological differences with the surrealists (as well as the upsetting fact that André Breton dismissed her as a mere 'bourgeois banker's wife'),[62] made her emphasize that she did not have much in common with the movement. In 1936, Nin wrote emphatically in her diary, 'I am not a surrealist,'[63] elaborating later, 'Surrealism bothers and irritates me. I am near them but not one of them.'[64]

Surrealism then was quickly reduced by the members of the Villa Seurat circle from the status of a comprehensive philosophical and aesthetic system claimed for it by its adherents (what Miller referred to as 'the societal-politico-economic-mumbo-jumbo theory of the Surrealists')[65] to that of a mere literary technique, one among many available. As Durrell argues, 'everyone uses ... surrealism etc AS HE WANTS IT. But to make such a stink about it is like me starting a league for more conditional clauses in poetry.'[66] What is more, Miller, Durrell, and Nin would eventually claim that their use of the 'technique' was different from the way the surrealists proper employed it. When Miller read the manuscript of Durrell's *Black Book* in 1937 he hastened to note that 'Superficially there are analogies between your technique and [that of the Surrealists]; but only superficially! The real difference is vast, a chasm veritably.'[67]

Two years after the publication of *Black Spring* Miller finally addressed his position on surrealism publicly in his 'Open Letter to Surrealists Everywhere' (1938), begun as a review of the already mentioned anthology, *Surrealism*. Herbert Read, the editor, whose introductory essay was one of the lengthiest and most ponderous pieces in the anthology, was well known to Miller. In fact, Read was the one who sent him the book. Although Miller was sympathetic to some of the statements made by the essayists (the loneliness of the poet mourned by Paul Éluard, for example) and generally approved of the artwork, he found the collection of essays infuriating on the whole. Miller still wanted to get the attention of the surrealists in the interest of self-promotion but his response to the collection cannot be called complimentary; writing to Durrell, Miller explains that 'Herbert Read sent me the new book, *Surrealism*, which I am answering immediately with a broadside, in the hope that his gang of English and French surrealists will have the guts to publish it in one of their forthcoming manifestos or what not.'[68] Although the 'Open Letter' is a typically labyrinthine and often self-contradictory text, it clearly amounts to Miller's declaration of independence from the surrealists; in another letter to Durrell Miller characterizes the 'Open Letter' as his 'attack' on the surrealists.[69]

In the 'Open Letter' Miller raises several objections to the surrealist movement. According to Miller, the surrealists have lost their sense of humour and become oracular – a sad departure from their irreverent Dada roots, as far as Miller is concerned, and a dangerous one, since 'without a healthy scepticism there can be no real significance in a work of art, or in life, for that matter.'[70] Miller also protests against surrealist self-righteousness, exemplified by Read's moral high-horsing about the 'undesirable elements' among the surrealists.[71] Miller takes issue most strongly, however, with the surrealists' efforts to become an international millennial movement to which nations would flock 'to learn, to find enlightenment.'[72] Miller writes, 'What strikes one as pathetic, lamentable, deplorable and ridiculous ... is the "effort to get together"'[73] and points out that the 'seeming discrepancies between the language of Breton and Lenin, or Marx, are only superficial.'[74] In all cases, according to Miller, the danger lies both in the subjection of the individual to the group and in the dictatorial imposition of a single ideal for everyone to uphold (Miller writes that 'the Surrealists are guilty of ... trying to establish an Absolute').[75] Finally, the surrealists are dismissed by Miller as 'merely the reflection of the death process ... one of the manifestations of a life becoming extinct.'[76]

It is against this background of the Villa Seurat writers' dissatisfaction with the writing of their famous contemporaries, of their rejection of the key models of experimental prose that were available to them in the 1930s, and of their desire to be 'their own writers' that Miller and, subsequently, the other writers of Villa Seurat turned to Dostoevsky's prose style for inspiration and guidance. The distance – temporal, cultural, and linguistic – separating the writers of Villa Seurat from Dostoevsky, and the fact that his novels were not regarded as obvious models of experimental prose in the 1930s, made Dostoevsky appear more rather than less attractive to Miller and his fellow iconoclasts, who were intent on emphasizing their independence from contemporary movements and their distinctness from other, more established contemporary writers. More surprisingly, Miller made his interpretation of Dostoevsky's prose style and form into the foundation not only of his philosophy of how to write but of how to create a revolution in prose narrative.

Dostoevsky and Stylistic Breakdowns

Miller had always paid special attention to a writer's style, holding that a writer is 'revealed in his style, the language which he has created for himself.'[77] Characteristically, however, he never acknowledged that relying on a translation was somehow a hindrance to his understanding of a text, or that a translation might seriously distort the original. In a later essay included in his *Books in My Life* (1952) Miller argues in a rather obscure fashion that 'the understanding of a language is not the same as the understanding of language. It is always communion versus communication,' going on to claim that '[e]ven in translation some of us understand Dostoevsky ... better than his Russian contemporaries – or, shall I say, better than our present Russian contemporaries.'[78] Needless to say, Miller himself felt that he was in direct communion with Dostoevsky. From more a critical perspective, however, it is clear that even though Miller's ultimate interpretation of the key features of Dostoevsky's style was highly idiosyncratic, in his 'communion' with Dostoevsky in matters of style, he was affected both by the American understanding of Dostoevsky's style and by the comments of his favourite critic of Dostoevsky's work, André Gide.

By the time Miller was ensconced at Villa Seurat his understanding of Dostoevsky's style had undergone a major evolution. When Miller first read Dostoevsky's novels in New York, he did so from the conventional American perspective of viewing Dostoevsky as a careless or indifferent stylist who fell far behind Turgenev and other Russian novelists in matters of novelistic artistry. In a February 1932 letter to Nin from a lycée in Dijon, where Miller was temporarily teaching English, he writes about the transformation of his understanding of Dostoevsky's style. He tells Nin that he used to irritate June back in New York by 'pick[ing] flaws in [Dostoevsky] [and] point[ing] out his bad artistry.'[79] At a certain point, Miller began to excuse Dostoevsky's style, deciding that he was too hassled by creditors and generally much too rushed to properly revise his novels (information that he culled, no doubt, from the biographies and articles on Dostoevsky that came out in the 1920s): 'Dostoevsky had neither time nor money. He was writing for money which he always used up in advance. His life was terrible, terrible. No chance to fashion things out artistically.'[80] Then Miller began to find things to appreciate in the supposed disorder of Dostoevsky's style; he concludes his 1932 letter to Nin by remarking, 'Finally, I feel about Dostoevsky now that anything he did was all right. I not only forgive, I applaud, I admire.'[81]

More interestingly, Miller eventually came to believe that Dostoevsky deliberately avoided revisions of his work and relinquished tight control over his prose to achieve a sense of spontaneity and immediacy in his novels. Dostoevsky's prose style (which Miller still saw as marked by chaos) now represented a different kind of artistic perfection than one achieved by acknowledged masters of prose. This hermeneutic shift is reflected in the opening pages of *Tropic of Cancer*, where the narrator celebrates Dostoevsky's style: 'I have made a silent compact with myself not to change a line of what I write. I am not interested in perfecting my thoughts, nor my actions. Beside the perfection of Turgenev I put the perfection of Dostoevsky.'[82] Instances of chaotic textual breakdowns within Dostoevsky's literary prose were now especially prized by Miller. In a published section of his Lawrence study Miller wrote that 'wherever in [Dostoevsky's] works there is chaos and confusion, it is a *rich* chaos, a meaningful confusion; it is positive, vital, soul-infected.'[83] Miller went as far as to eroticize instances of Dostoevsky's textual chaos in his own *Tropic of Cancer*. In what surely must be the most unorthodox commentary ever written about Dostoevsky's literary style, Miller's narrator, who is in the midst of a sexual encounter with several women, compares Dostoevsky's prose breakdowns to an orgasmic release: 'When the eyes waggle then will I hear again Dostoevsky's words, hear them rolling on page after page, with minutest observation, with maddest introspection, with all the undertones of misery now lightly, humorously touched, now swelling like an organ note until the heart bursts and there is nothing left but a blinding, scorching light, the radiant light that carries off the fecundating seeds of the stars.'[84] Besides shocking the reader (a practice that Miller would later also come to associate with Dostoevsky), the *Tropic of Cancer* passage celebrates Dostoevsky's stylistic chaos as both erotic and life-affirming – the moment of breakdown and dissolution prior to the inception of new life. In a later essay, Miller again combines these two notions when he calls Dostoevsky 'chaos and fecundity.'[85]

Nin was initially antagonistic to Miller's celebration of disorder and chaos in Dostoevsky's prose, even as she criticized her own reaction as 'terribly, terribly French ... [and] the effort of clarity fighting obscurity.'[86] Nin also began reading Dostoevsky from the conventional perspective of viewing his prose style as inferior. In an early letter to Miller, Nin writes that when she first read Dostoevsky at Miller's recommendation she 'laughed and cried together and couldn't sleep, and didn't know where [she] was' but recoiled afterwards because she had 'a feeling against complete chaos,' something that Miller was relishing, 'thank[ing] god for the living chaos.'[87] By October 1933, nonetheless, Nin was writing in her diary that 'the elements I do not like, which leave me cold [are] logic, order, construction, classicism, equilibrium, control. I wanted to shout: I admire imperfections, Dostoevsky.'[88] Dostoevsky's style, she also came to eventually believe, reflected 'the chaos of nature'[89] and life itself. Like Miller, who praised Durrell's work by noting its similarities to Dostoevsky, Nin wrote Durrell admiringly that his prose 'breaks ... [into] a *fever*. Sensation overflows from its vase ... read Dostoevsky and it will give you the same feeling.'[90]

Miller took the idea of Dostoevsky's stylistic spontaneity further still, however. According to a concept Miller developed at Villa Seurat, Dostoevsky had not only given up rigorous stylistic control over his text, deliberately breaking down his prose until he achieved the spontaneity and fertile potential of textual chaos, but he also did so as a natural result of his reaction to the 'disintegration of the world.'[91]

Deteriorating World, Disintegrating Text

The idea of the world and civilization deteriorating was hardly a new one in the 1930s, and would have been familiar to Miller if only from his early years with June in New York, when Nietzsche's writings and Oswald Spengler's *Decline of the West* were all the rage among New York Bohemians. At Villa Seurat, however, this idea had a fanatic adherent in the face of Michael Fraenkel, a close associate of Miller. Fraenkel, who became wealthy after he emigrated to America and who subsequently came to Paris to live the life of a literary gentleman of leisure, developed a theory about living in the midst of a dying civilization that made an indelible impression on Miller and other members of the circle. Fraenkel's central belief was that everything within the Western civilization was actually dead – sapped of vitality and creative forces, existing by inertia rather than being vibrantly and meaningfully alive – and he expounded it rigorously in his writings, such as his duly depressing *Werther's Younger Brother* (1930), all publicized through his own Carrefour Press. Miller, who befriended Fraenkel out of a genuine interest in his ideas and not only for the free food and lodging that came with them, was elated after reading his work: 'I felt that I had made a great discovery,' he wrote to Fraenkel, 'You are saying what no one in America is saying – that I would dearly love to say myself.'[92]

Throughout the 1930s Fraenkel and Miller collaborated on several projects (most notably, the monumental *Hamlet Correspondence* published through Fraenkel's Carrefour Press in the years 1939–41). Fraenkel would call Miller the godfather of his own tract *Bastard Death: The Autobiography of an Idea*,[93] while echoes of Fraenkel's teachings filled Miller's letters, essays, and other texts. Miller, who caricatured Fraenkel in *Tropic of Cancer* as Boris the dreary Weather Prophet ('the weather will continue bad, he says. There will be more calamities, more death, more despair ... There is no escape'),[94] would even worry that he had '"plagiarized" Fraenkel's death philosophy in *Tropic of Cancer* in the passages that spoke of death and decay.'[95] Fraenkel's most significant contribution to Miller's own philosophy, however, had to do with his connection of the death of civilization and the death of literature. Miller developed this notion further: according to him, if contemporary literature was part of the death process that civilization was undergoing, then literature itself should be discarded as a thing dead and useless.

Significantly, both Fraenkel and Miller believed that the last great writer of vibrant and intensely 'alive' literature was none other than Dostoevsky (Miller maintained that in Dostoevsky's novels 'there is an intensity and acuity almost superhuman').[96] Dostoevsky was reacting in his novels to the disintegration of the world around him but he was writing at the time, Miller believed, when the decay of civilization had not yet reached its nadir, as it had in the world in which Miller himself lived. The idea that literature was dead and the belief that Dostoevsky was the last writer of living literature contributed to the development of Miller's single most creative insight into Dostoevsky's work: his belief that Dostoevsky's novels were both the culmination and the termination of literature, an idea that would dramatically alter his own path as a writer and, subsequently, have a major impact on the other writers of the Villa Seurat Circle. Miller related his views on the subject in an essay titled 'Reflections on Writing' (1941), explaining that he began his writing career with 'dreams of rivalling Dostoevsky' as a novelist but that he eventually realized that both society and the individual 'had evolved to a point far beyond that of Dostoevsky – *beyond* in the sense of degeneration.' Dostoevsky could still use the novelistic form to reflect upon and to capture his own epoch, but Miller felt that '[i]t was quite impossible for me ... to think of writing novels.'[97] Dostoevsky, according to Miller, had exhausted the possibilities of the novel and indeed of literature itself: a new and revolutionary form of writing had to be devised to express the absurdities and shocking incongruities of modern life.

Paradoxically, however, Miller felt that in order to go beyond the constraints of literature and to create a new prose form he still had to return to Dostoevsky's novels as his starting place. The kernel of this idea was already found in some of the Dostoevsky criticism with which Miller would have been familiar in the 1930s; for example, Middleton Murry, one of the main proponents of the Dostoevsky cult, saw Dostoevsky as 'stand[ing] upon the furthest edge of the old, which is the threshold of the new.'[98] Miller took this concept much further, however, by declaring that literature itself was the threshold of the 'old' that had to be crossed by going beyond Dostoevsky's achievements. These ideas are dramatized by Miller in a lengthy parodic passage in *The Rosy Crucifixion*, when the narrator is approached by a grotesque would-be writer who proposes that the two of them leave America, go to a foreign country, and put their energies together to create a new kind of book. Miller's narrator, who is aspiring to be a writer himself, is intrigued and wants to hear more on the subject. The man explains that despite all of Dostoevsky's literary achievements, Dostoevsky is not only 'finished with'[99] but that he took everyone to 'to the end of the road.'[100] Since, however, 'with Dostoevsky's death the world entered upon a complete new phase of existence,'[101] a new kind of writing is required. In order to create that new kind of writing one has to go back to Dostoevsky's novels: 'that's where we start. From Dostoevsky.'[102]

This is where the question of what it is, precisely, that Dostoevsky achieved in his novels artistically, and how he achieved what he did, became vitally important to Miller. If Dostoevsky really was the last visionary of the novel who took literature to its final frontier, then to break through the limits of literature in their own visionary new prose the Villa Seurat writers had to go beyond Dostoevsky's own achievements. It was one thing for Villa Seurat writers to rave about Dostoevsky's style in vague, obscure, and ultimately meaningless terms (according to Fraenkel, for instance, Dostoevsky was the only novelist who approached a style 'that is at once full and empty, consistent and contradictory, certain and uncertain, hard and gentle, comprehensible and incomprehensible, cold and passionate'),[103] but it was an altogether different matter to be able to define the most important elements of Dostoevsky's style and to determine how one could potentially go beyond that which Dostoevsky managed to achieve in his own novels. Miller, who always believed that he understood Dostoevsky and his literary mastery, which included the vexing question of his literary style, better than anyone else, felt that the main key to solving this dilemma lay in that very concept of the textual breakdown that he had associated with Dostoevsky's prose from the very beginning.

Explosive Texts

Miller held that the Villa Seurat writers could advance beyond Dostoevsky's own achievements by increasing and intensifying the moments
of textual breakdown that occur in Dostoevsky's novels. In one of his
later pieces Miller wrote, 'Dostoevsky hadn't gone quite far enough. I
was for straight gibberish. One should go cuckoo!'[104] The revolutionary
new prose that the Villa Seurat writers strove to create called for a relinquishing of all control. In *The Rosy Crucifixion* a short passage suggests
the importance Miller had come to place on the release of controls within
the text: the narrator (the 'Henry Miller' persona) reads a chaotic and
'crazy' passage from his own writings to Reb, a mad philosopher, who is
amazed and delighted, despite his initial reservations: 'It was one of
those crazy passages which I myself couldn't make head nor tail of ...
'*Miller!*' He shouted. "*Miller*, that's just marvellous! You sound like a
Russian. I don't know what it means but it makes music."'[105] Brassaï –
the famous photographer of Paris who befriended Miller and became a
regular at Villa Seurat – reports that he once reproached Miller for the
chaotic prose style and that Miller explained to him that 'his chaos was
completely deliberate, that what he was looking for was neither logic nor
order, but something like the overflow of the Mississippi ... sweeping
away everything in its path, its muddy waters carrying a million odds
and ends: uprooted trees, furniture, cadavers.'[106] While it is probably
coincidental that this very image of a mighty river in flood was used by
Sherwood Anderson to praise Dostoevsky's style (although Anderson
was one of the writers Miller knew personally),[107] it is precisely this spilling over and relinquishing of all control over the text that the Villa Seurat
writers strove to implement in their writing.

Miller's usual shorthand for his notion of extreme textual chaos was
not a flood, however, but an explosion, which would acquire a number
of layered meanings for the Villa Seurat writers. According to Miller,
the Villa Seurat writers had to aim textually for the kind of shock and
violent disintegration that only an explosion can bring about. Reminiscing about his conception of *Tropic of Cancer*, Miller wrote: 'in the
middle of the book I would explode. Why not? There were plenty of
writers who could drag a thing out to the end without letting go of the
reins; what we needed was a man, like myself for instance, who didn't
give a fuck what happened.'[108] In a self-reflexive passage the narrator
of *Tropic of Cancer* insists that 'Art consists in going the full length. If
you start with the drums you have to end with dynamite, or TNT.'[109]

Practically, of course, this textual 'explosion' was difficult if not impossible to achieve. At the very least, a surrender of all controls presupposed that there would be no subsequent editing of the text, something that Miller claimed for his own writing, explaining that he did not edit his manuscripts at all, but instead 'br[oke] new ground until I reach the level of exact expression, leaving all the trials and gropings there.'[110] In reality, it is well documented that Miller, Nin, and Durrell were inveterate editors of their own and each other's texts. Miller wrote countless drafts of *Tropic of Cancer* and Nin helped him to further cut and edit the final draft of the book. Durrell admitted to rewriting *The Black Book* many times, and when he sent his manuscript to Miller and Nin in Paris, the two provided him with further suggestions for revisions. Even Nin, who claimed to write in a 'white heat' without subsequent rewriting, was always editing and reconfiguring her text. In the second volume of the first published set of the *Diary* (1967) Nin gives this insight into her writing habits in the 1930s: 'Back to work. Rewriting volume 45 (New York, Rank, Henry). There are in the diary so many flowers like the Japanese paper-flowers, which need to be placed in water to achieve their flowering. So I am putting all the closed buds in water. What a bloom.'[111] Nonetheless, the concept of surrendering all controls and creating a textual explosion, a violent blasting apart of narrative, remained an ideal at Villa Seurat, viewed as an opportunity to break through the boundaries circumscribed by Dostoevsky.

Nin encouraged young Durrell to achieve this textual explosion in his book, saying that she hoped she would be 'the one to give [him] the courage of [his] strength, of exploding.'[112] She felt that she herself had reached this goal in the *Diaries*: 'In the diary,' she said, 'I did explode.'[113] Miller describes Durrell's *Black Book* as a 'bag of dynamite'[114] and advises him to let the future books 'explode inside you.'[115] Miller also comments elsewhere that his writing breakthrough came when 'finally I decided to explode – and I did explode.'[116] Both Miller and Durrell felt that they reached this goal in *Tropic of Cancer* and *The Black Book*, respectively.

Autobiographical Prose and Higher Realism

The correlation between the exploded text and the exploded 'self' acquired a particular resonance for Miller and the other writers of Villa Seurat, who came to believe that the new revolutionary prose had to be fashioned out of the individual identity of the author, a process which called for a ruthless and violent evisceration of the psyche. Once again, this idea was connected to their attempts to surpass Dostoevsky's literary achievements and, once again, the explosion of the self acquired a set of deeper meanings at Villa Seurat.

Like many American readers of his time, Miller placed a special emphasis on the supposed autobiographicity of Dostoevsky's novels, identifying him with his characters and deciding that he wrote through and of his own experiences of suffering. According to the Villa Seurat writers Dostoevsky's characters, from Stavrogin to Zosima, were really self-portraits, depictions of his inner self. In *Tropic of Cancer* Dostoevsky appears as one of those 'divine monsters' who empty themselves into their art, 'rip[ping] out his entrails ... and flinging to us his torn bowels,'[117] Dostoevsky's text becoming a public record of a personal evisceration or soul revelation. In *Tropic of Capricorn* the narrator calls Dostoevsky the first man to 'reveal his soul to me.'[118] Predictably then, the Villa Seurat writers' attempt to surpass Dostoevsky's literary attainments included an amplification of the autobiographical element – a more explicit soul-baring and a more violent self-disembowelment – in their own transliterary texts.

Miller believed, however, that there was another important reason for post-Dostoevskian writers to write predominately autobiographical texts. In 'Reflections on Writing' Miller says that when he realized that the world 'had evolved to a point far beyond that of Dostoevsky – beyond in the sense of degeneration,' he decided that the only thing left for a writer to do was to use his 'own shattered and dispersed ego as heartlessly and recklessly as [he] would the flotsam and jetsam of the surrounding phenomenal world.'[119] Elsewhere, he argues that humanity is 'facing an absolutely new condition of life. An entirely new cosmos must be created, and it must be created out our separate, isolate, living parts.'[120]

Further, if both the novel and literature were exhausted by Dostoevsky, and if society and its individual members had degenerated to the point where they could not sustain the focus of an artist's or a writer's inquiry (in *Tropic of Cancer* the narrator laments the impossibilities of depicting that 'world of men and women whose last drop of juice has been squeezed out by the machine – the martyrs of modern progress ... [a] mass of bones and collar buttons which the painter find so difficult to put flesh on'),[121] then the only subject the new writer could draw on was his own life experience. In Durrell's first letter to Miller, written after reading *Tropic of Cancer*, he announces that it is one of the few books that 'really gets down on paper the blood and bowels of our times,' mainly because it has been 'built out of [the author's] own guts.'[122]

Notably, autobiographicity became strongly associated with the work of both Miller and Nin, an association that they encouraged. In the many statements Miller made about his own work he usually claimed that his writing is wholly autobiographical, that he is 'a man telling the story of his life,'[123] and that 'all my characters have been real, taken from life, my own life.[124] Fittingly, the narrator and central persona of Miller's books is named Henry Miller, and the characters within his texts are all supposedly 'real people' with just their names altered. Miller's most explicit statement on this account is found in the already cited 'Open Letter to Surrealists Everywhere' 'The naive English critics, in their polite, asinine way, talk about the "hero" of my book (*Tropic of Cancer*) as though he were a character I had invented. I made it as plain as could be that I was talking in that book about myself. I used my own name throughout. I didn't write a piece of fiction: I wrote an autobiographical document, a *human* book ... At a certain point in my life I decided that henceforth I would write about myself, my friends, my experiences, what I knew and what I had seen with my own eyes.'[125] Nin's writings have an even stronger aura of the autobiographical about them, since they all emanate from, or are a part of, her famous diary, where she purported to record her day-to-day life. She would suggest when lecturing that her writings represented a gift she was making to the readers: her own life, a perfect record.[126]

Durrell, considered to be the least autobiographical writer of the Villa Seurat trinity, confided to Miller that he wrote *The Black Book* as an autobiographical text: 'I tried to say what I was: but of course with my talent for covering myself in confetti made out a hell of an epic. I wanted to write myself so miserable and wormy and frightened as I was: NUMB, really – that terrible english provincial numbness: the english death infecting my poor little colonial soul and so on.'[127] Interestingly, Durrell would explore the interrelation between autobiographical fact and invention in literary text most persistently of all the writers at Villa Seurat. *The Black Book*, particularly, is filled with lengthy metafictional and self-conscious discussions on the writing of fictional texts versus the writing of journals and other autobiographical texts. Thus, Durrell's Herbert Gregory, the diarist whose secret diary, 'the little black book,' provides the title of Durrell's text, interrupts his description of the events of his life by exclaiming in disgust, 'literature! literature!'[128] and argues that 'Books should be built of one's tissue or not at all. The struggle is not to record experience but to record oneself ... There is only my tissue, my guilt, transmuted by God knows what alchemy, into a few pints of green ink and handmade paper. Understand me well.'[129] Durrell's later writings, including *The Alexandria Quartet* (1957–60) and *The Avignon Quintet* (1974–85), include more elaborate variations on the interplay between life and text, as various characters write diaries or even novels about themselves and their friends, reinventing their lives in the process; the theme reaches an apogee in *The Avignon Quintet*, where Blanford and Sutcliffe (both novelists, but the second invented by the first, or the first, perhaps, by the second) continuously argue about who has a greater claim on reality and is more true to life.

Clearly, it would be dangerous to assume that any of the works produced by the Villa Seurat writers represent an unadulterated setting down of events as they actually occurred. Even without the famous omissions of Nin's diary (the revelation of which was a shock to many when the unexpurgated versions of the *Diary* began coming out in the mid-1980s), she rewrote and re-formed the text of her diary as she saw fit, with little regard for factual detail. Similarly, Miller warns his readers repeatedly that not everything that he puts down into what he sometimes calls his 'autobiographical romances' is factual.[130] He problematizes the nature of truth, authenticity, and, by extension, autobiographical writing, by commenting in one of his pieces that 'there are no solid facts to get hold of. Thus, in writing, even if my distortions and deformations be deliberate, they are not necessarily less near to the truth of things. One can be absolutely truthful and sincere even though admittedly the most outrageous liar.'[131] In the revealing Coda passage in *Tropic of Capricorn*, where the narrator broods upon the book he is writing, he asks, 'Will this book be the truth, the whole truth, and nothing but the truth, so help me God?' He answers himself: 'I have always told the truth. But the truth can also be a lie ... Truth is only the core of a totality which is inexhaustible.'[132]

If the writers of Villa Seurat looked down upon mere factual reporting, they did think highly of capturing a deeper reality in their prose. Notably, their views echo Dostoevsky's famous statement on the subject, about being a realist not in the sense of depicting everyday trivialities, but in the higher sense of depicting the depths of the human soul (27:65), which was first published by Nikolai Strakhov in his 1883 biographical sketch of Dostoevsky and quoted by almost every Dostoevsky scholar at one time or another, including Janko Lavrin (with whom Miller would develop a personal connection). When some critics called Miller a realist he replied that his realism was different from that of 'the journalistic writers, so-called hard-boiled writers.'[133] Miller elaborated his position in a passage that closely paralleled Dostoevsky's own views: 'what people call reality is not reality in my mind. I am not only telling the truth; I am telling the whole truth, which is in your whole being and not just the surface truth ... There's the inner force, which is so much more important.'[134]

To reveal this 'inner force,' or the springs of psychological motivation, which roughly corresponded to Dostoevsky's 'depths of the human soul,' Miller says, 'I employ every device. I use dream sequences frequently, and fantasy and humor and surrealistic things, everything and anything which will deepen and heighten this thing called reality.'[135] Durrell follows Miller's suit when he explains that the 'phantasmagoria' of The Black Book is used to disclose 'real problems of the anglo-saxon psyche.'[136] In a 1938 attempt to write a blurb for The Black Book, Durrell writes that it depicts 'the private inferno of the human being' as opposed to the 'formal display of the façade in literature.'[137] Nin interprets Dostoevsky's 'realism in a higher sense' in a similar way to Miller and Durrell. In the essay 'Realism and Reality' (1946), she argues that a writer should depict a 'deeper world' of psychological stimuli, the 'inner drama,' as opposed to detailing merely 'the opaque quality of our external world which is used in most novels as a defense against a disturbing inner world ... with all evasions of the essential inner drama practiced by the so-called realistic novel in which we are actually being constantly cheated of reality and experience.'[138] The writer should attempt to reveal 'layers not uncovered' in the novel, Nin asserts, adding immediately that her comment about the novel 'does not apply ... to the Dostoevskian novels in which people act by the impulses of the unconcsious.'[139] Her solution for disclosing the inner reality, particularly in a world which has disintegrated to the point 'where people's acts no longer correspond to their inner impulses,' is to use symbols and associations, and to write about her own experience, where the link between the act and the impulse is clearer to her.[140] A remark she makes in another essay once again links the fragmented psyche and the explosive text, since the contemporary writer should 'face the fact that this new psychological reality can be explored and dealt with only under conditions of tremendously high atmospheric pressures, temperatures, and speed.'[141]

The writer's need to faithfully represent the 'essential inner drama' of the psyche, however, was further complicated by the fact that it is a dynamic and continuous process which unfolds over time and whose only physical boundaries are birth and death. How could a writer represent that kind of dynamism and continuity? Once again, the Villa Seurat writers located the answer to this dilemma in Dostoevsky's body of work.

(Mis)Reading Dostoevsky Critics and Creating Serial Texts

The critical commentary on Dostoevsky's novels that Miller cited most often was the already mentioned book by André Gide, based on a series of lectures given in 1922. Gide's book quickly became not only Miller's but most of the Villa Seurat writers' all-time favourite critical study of Dostoevsky's work (Nin would even write Miller that she 'like[d] Gide's explanation of Dostoevsky almost as much as [she] like[d] Dostoevsky').[142] At one point, Gide remarks on what he perceives as the links between the novels of Dostoevsky: 'I was fascinated by Dostoevsky's manner of passing from one book to another. Undoubtedly it was natural that after *The House of the Dead* he should write Raskolnikov's story in *Crime and Punishment*, the story of the crime that sent the latter to Siberia. More absorbing still to watch how the last pages of the novel lead up to *The Idiot*.'[143] Miller refers to this passage in a 1933 letter to Nin, where he discusses the path their own writing must take. Miller explains to Nin that 'Since it has been made so clear to us, through Gide's words on Dostoevsky, that each book contains the germ of the next, let us take advantage consciously of this condition of creation. The author is like a tree in the midst of his creations; his creations are the atmosphere in which he bathes; as he grows he sends down roots and it is from the roots that the future trees grow, not from the blossoms and the acorns. Or think of a snake: a snake does not shed the old skin until he has grown a new one. The book you write is the old skin that you are shedding. The important book, the new skin, is always the one that is unborn, or, if not unborn, unseen ... the great author is like a monster who produces not a single prodigy, but a whole litter!'[144] Miller then tells Nin that he is planning to write a series of interlinked books and urges her to do the same.

Miller's commentary on the Gide passage is interesting for two reasons. First, Miller's gloss on Gide illustrates his typically idiosyncratic (mis)interpretation of Dostoevsky criticism. Whereas Gide suggests that the links between Dostoevsky's novels occur on profoundly socio-historical, psychological, and philosophical levels (that is, the rebirth of

Raskolnikov as a Christian at the end of *Crime and Punishment* leads to the question of whether a true Christian *can* exist in the corrupt and materialistic Russian society of the 1800s, which, in turn, is the subject of *The Idiot*), Miller argues that the novels are interconnected as a result of their reflection of the author's personal and creative growth. Each written text, in fact, is a record of the author's previous life experience: a cast-off skin of the same snake. The present life and day-to-day experiences of the author will become the next written text.

Miller's injunction to write in series, as Dostoevsky ostensibly did, becomes especially significant when it is recalled that Miller, Nin, and Durrell all wrote and regarded their books as a vast series of interlinked texts. In fact, the interconnected books that the three produced and became famous for were all begun during the Villa Seurat period. Miller's own *Tropic of Cancer*, *Tropic of Capricorn*, and *Sexus*, *Plexus*, and *Nexus* of *The Rosy Crucifixion* trilogy of 1949–60 are all conceptually part of a single set of books (the last four books are a depiction of Miller's life with June before his arrival in Paris and his breakthrough as a writer, which is dealt with in *Tropic of Cancer*). Nin's entire body of work (including the *Diary*) is one long interconnected series, with the same characters and events figuring again and again in different texts (on the backcover blurb of *A Spy in the House of Love* [1959] five of her books are called a 'continuous novel'). Finally, Durrell is probably best known for his *Alexandria Quartet*, a set of four interlinked books about a set of eccentric characters leading interconnected lives in the city of Alexandria, which he published in 1957–60. His award-winning *Quartet* was followed by a series of five interlinked books about a set of even more eccentric and intertwined characters mostly centred on France, and titled *The Avignon Quintet* (1974–85). Notably, the *Quartet* evolved from *The Book of the Dead*, which Durrell intended to be part of a set that included *The Black Book* and that was meant to be a tribute to Miller. 'I have planned AN AGON, A PATHOS, AN ANAGNORISIS,' Durrell wrote to Miller in 1937, 'If I write them they should be: The Black Book, The Book of Miracles, The Book of the Dead.'[145] Durrell would later say that he had accomplished this goal, making the following connections: an Agon=*The Black Book*; a Pathos=*The Alexandria Quartet*; and an Anagnorisis=*The Avignon Quintet*.[146]

Dostoevskian Signposts

In a quest to find their own unique identities and voices as writers, the members of the Villa Seurat circle rejected the writing produced by their contemporaries and began looking for alternative models to reflect their own experience and to revolutionize prose. Miller and, subsequently, the other writers of Villa Seurat, chose Dostoevsky as their pathway towards a new kind of prose.

Miller's choice of Dostoevsky as his inspiration and his interpretation of Dostoevsky's prose was significantly affected by his American reception but, ultimately, it was the result of a unique vision of his significance that Miller developed during his Paris years. Miller came to view such commonly acknowledged features of Dostoevsky's literary prose as the supposed formlessness of his novels and their depressing if useful autobiographicity as the real virtues of Dostoevsky's work. His most creatively stimulating insight into Dostoevsky's novels, however, proved to be his vision of Dostoevsky as the last great writer who managed to capture his own epoch, society, and problems of the individual within the boundaries of the novel. His books, according to Miller, represented the greatest of what could be achieved in a novel form, but by their very greatness they also terminated the novel, hastened the death of literature itself, and made necessary a different kind of writing.

According to Miller, there was no sense in merely emulating Dostoevsky's novels. He postulated that the contemporary world had become too decayed to be contained in a novel form, which could neither adequately reflect the frenzied and disjointed twentieth-century reality nor convincingly expose the conflicts and chaos facing contemporary society. Dostoevsky's novels were liminal expressions of what was possible in literature, but literature no longer sufficed. Beyond Dostoevsky's accomplishments, on the other side of the boundary of literary text, as it were, existed a new, still unknown form of text, a transliterary text, freed from the literary conventions of a plot, clearly defined fictional provenance, three-dimensional fictional characters, and contrived style, that could be achieved by carefully considering Dostoevsky's own achievements and then pushing beyond them beyond. When Miller and other Villa Seurat writers read Dostoevsky's novels they were actually searching for signposts of the direction in which they had to travel in order to create a new transliterary post-Dostoevskian prose.

Such characteristics of the texts produced by the Villa Seurat writers as extreme autobiographicity, attempts to represent inner reality and states of consciousness, the interconnectedness or serialism of their texts, and stylistic chaos are all related in whole or in part to their attempt to go beyond what Dostoevsky accomplished in his novels. While the Villa Seurat writers' identification of some of these textual features with Dostoevsky's novels represents a blatant misreadings of his work and, occasionally, of the work of his critics, what is important here is the creative breakthroughs that they achieved in their own texts as a result of attempting to surpass Dostoevsky in their own writing. If it is questionable whether Miller, Nin, and Durrell actually succeeded in transcending Dostoevsky and creating the utopian transliterary prose that they attempted to achieve, their own creative achievements are undisputed. Each of them, in fact, has been praised for creating a new kind of writing. Miller, for example, has been celebrated for 'invent[ing] a new style of writing, a style as revolutionary in its own way as Joyce's or Hemingway's or Stein's.'[147] Nin has been lauded for creating, through her 'diaries,' a 'breakthrough in literary form, a form that transcends both the art of the "confessions" and the art of the novel itself.'[148] Durrell has been called the inventor of a new genre of writing.[149] Furthermore, through engaging with Dostoevsky's texts, the writers of Villa Seurat derived a sense of personal and literary freedom that allowed them to strive for their creative breakthroughs in the first place. This freedom is what Nin had in mind when she noted, after discussing Dostoevsky's The Idiot with Miller, that 'Dostoevsky's language has released both of us.'[150] This is also the freedom celebrated by Miller in Black Spring, when he wrote that after Dostoevsky 'every door of the cage is open and whichever way you walk is a straight line toward infinity.'[151]

6 Understanding Dostoevsky's 'Philosophy' at Villa Seurat

Dostoevsky ... it is a pity that we shall never again have the opportunity to see a man placed at the very core of the mystery and, by his flashes, illuminating for us the depth and immensity of the darkness.

Henry Miller, *Tropic of Cancer*, 255

A recent phenomenon in the field of Dostoevsky publishing in post-Soviet Russia is the emergence of book-length compilations of quotations culled from Dostoevsky's novels, essays, letters, and notebooks and organized into a variety of subjects, from immortality to education.[1] There are many reasons for the popularity of these books, some of the chief ones being the frustration experienced by Russian readers after being force-fed a censored and distorted account of Dostoevsky's belief system for many decades and their desire to know what he really thought about various topics. Their frustration is easily understood by readers outside of Russia, who were also given highly curtailed and tendentious accounts of Dostoevsky's beliefs over the course of the twentieth century, as symbolists, surrealists, existentialists, Freudians, Marxists, and others reframed Dostoevsky's ideas in ways that suited their own agendas.

James Scanlan, whose insightful and well-documented study, *Dostoevsky the Thinker* (2002), is itself in many ways a reaction to the historically widespread obfuscation of Dostoevsky's ideas, poses the question of whether it is even possible to determine what Dostoevsky's 'philosophical convictions really were,' given that his novels teem with conflicting but persuasive voices, leading some to question the existence of an 'overarching authorial position.'[2] Scanlan answers his own question

by pointing out that 'if we had no independent monological evidence
allowing us to identify the author's convictions and helping us to dis-
criminate between authorial and nonauthorial positions as they come
forth in the fictional context,' we could possibly be persuaded by those
who 'erect [the novels'] dynamic interplay of ideas and convictions into
a philosophical doctrine of the "unfinalizable" nature of truth, based on
a supposed irreducible ambivalence in the writer's thinking.'[3] Because,
however, we have a 'mountain' of 'independent monological evidence'
in the form of Dostoevsky's personal letters, nonfiction articles, his
Writer's Diary, and his notebooks, which 'provide unambiguous indications of which side he was on,' we can easily reconstruct Dostoevsky's
own perspective on a number of issues. Borrowing Mikhail Bakhtin's
terminology, Scanlan demonstrates that if 'Dostoevsky's philosophizing
[is] dialogical in style,' it is clearly 'monological in substance.'[4]

Despite the fact that a vast amount of 'independent monological evidence' of Dostoevsky's own credo is available to readers (even to those
who have to read Dostoevsky in translation), extreme misinterpretations and distortions of Dostoevsky's beliefs and ideas are a constant
in Dostoevsky's reception worldwide. One of the most striking features of that reception is the fact that those who claim to be followers
of Dostoevsky frequently hold beliefs diametrically opposite to those
espoused by the novelist himself. What is more, upon examining what
actually lies behind many claims of being influenced by Dostoevsky's
philosophy, one often encounters a cluster of loosely related philosophical or vaguely metaphysical concepts associated more with
Dostoevsky's characters than with Dostoevsky himself, and even these
are often based on a misreading of Dostoevsky's text, a misunderstanding of some biographical circumstance of his life, or a misinterpretation
of an argument made by a Dostoevsky critic.

It is well known, for instance, that despite Dostoevsky's early interest
in Western-style social reform, by the time he returned from exile for his
involvement in the Petrashevsky affair and resumed his writing career,
he was fervently committed to the postulates of Russian Orthodoxy,
autocracy, and nationhood (*pravoslavie, samoderzhavie, narodnost'*), largely
contemptuous of foreigners, disdainful of Russia's nascent women's
rights movement, and wary of any kind of 'free thinking.' None of this
would seem to make Dostoevsky a likely choice of ideologue for a group
of Bohemian cosmopolites living in Paris between the two world wars.
Yet if the iconoclasts at Villa Seurat, with Miller at the helm, chose
Dostoevsky as their guide in matters literary, they also turned to him as

an ultimate authority in questions of philosophical, metaphysical, and sociological import. In one of his essays Miller stated that Dostoevsky 'was infinitely more than a novelist' for him,[5] while in shorter fictional texts and essays he wrote that Dostoevsky's ideas had a transformative impact on his life. In the concluding section of Miller's *Rosy Crucifixion* trilogy his narrator calls Dostoevsky one of the 'horsemen of [his] own private Apocalypse,'[6] a thinker whose work lies at the very foundation of his own thought and belief system. Moreover, unlikely as it may seem, Miller, Nin, and Durrell, the three Musketeers of Villa Seurat, whose interest in religion was esoteric rather than mainstream, whose political views approached anarchism, and whose personal lives were highly unconventional, believed that they were following Dostoevsky's own credo both in their texts and their lives.

Miller, Nin, and Durrell's readiness to ignore the seemingly unbridgeable gulf between their own beliefs and those of Dostoevsky cannot be written off as the result of an ignorance of Dostoevsky's corpus of writings and belief system. They were all well-read in Dostoevsky's canon, absorbing his fictional and nonfictional 'monological' writings as well as his biography and many of the critical monographs written about his work. There is also overwhelming evidence that Miller, Nin, and Durrell were interested and well read in contemporary philosophy, metaphysics, and sociology and were themselves inveterate armchair philosophers. Miller, for example, spent countless hours in philosophical duels with Michael Fraenkel, expostulating at length on Keyserling, Spengler, Spinoza, Wittgenstein, Nietzsche, Berdiaev, Kant, Schopenhauer, Lao Tse, and Chuang-Tse, along with more obscure and esoteric thinkers, and speculated in his own writings about the meaning of life, death, and creativity. Nin theorized about the nature of cruelty, sexuality, and gender. The youngest of the three Musketeers, Durrell, even came up with a new and somewhat fuzzy philosophic model of the world, which he called the 'heraldic universe.'

Philosophical and metaphysical discourse, serious or playfully subversive, permeated Villa Seurat. Here, for instance, is a note Durrell wrote to Miller upon his arrival to Villa Seurat in 1937: 'Dear Miller: Two questions: (1) What do you do with the garbage? AND (TWO) (2) When you say 'to be with God' do you identify yourself with God: or do you regard the God-stuff reality as something *extraneous* towards which we yearn?'[7] Miller's note informed Durrell that the garbage is put in a little can under the sink, and that 'as to the second question, being rather pressed for time, and slightly jocund at the moment I should say blithely – sometimes you approach and sometimes you become! Gottfried Benn answers it nicely (via Storch) in an issue of *transition* which I will dig up for you and show you. I could discuss it better over the table.'[8]

Despite the Villa Seurat writers' interest in ideas in general, and despite their claims to being influenced by Dostoevsky's ideas specifically, it is apparent that the corpus of ideas that the Villa Seurat writers associated with Dostoevsky and professed to be influenced by were not necessarily those that Dostoevsky would have recognized as his own. In fact, an examination of Miller and the other Villa Seurat writers' reaction to Dostoevsky's philosophy from the perspective of his reception studies appears at first to be a wasted effort, if only because Dostoevsky himself is so prominently absent, the philosophic ideas are so nebulous and ill-defined, and their understanding of these ideas, frequently based on passages decontextualized and sometimes blatantly misread, or on critics' misinterpretation of these same passages, is so idiosyncratic. Paradoxically, however, it is because of all these factors that the Villa Seurat writers' response to Dostoevsky's 'philosophy' is valuable: their readings are often so obviously warped – if invariably creative – their interpretations frequently so transparently narrow and tendentious, that they provide a clearer insight into the mechanics of the distortion of Dostoevsky's ideas than many of the more sophisticated but, ultimately, similarly flawed interpretations of Dostoevsky's thought.

Dostoevsky as the Anti-Intellectual's Intellectual

During the Villa Seurat period, Miller, Nin, and – to a lesser extent – Durrell, liked to represent themselves as uneducated anti-intellectuals. Miller identified most with the stance of a crude 'natural man,' an unschooled product of the New York jungle, writing to Durrell, 'I am ignorant. Even about English literature,'[9] and claiming to be 'almost an illiterate.'[10] Not to be outdone, the almost excessively erudite Durrell confessed to Miller that he was 'hopelessly ill-read.'[11] Nin, who wrote a critical monograph on D.H. Lawrence, subtitled it 'An Unprofessional Study' and subsequently denied any critical or literary expertise on her part, disingenuously explaining to Miller that her conscious mind had no part in the project, because she wrote it 'a bit like a medium, if you wish, a bit in a trance ... I am not lucidly responsible for this.'[12]

There was some truth to the Villa Seurat writers' claims. Due to various personal circumstances, none of the three writers received a higher education: Miller left the City College of New York after failing to make it through Spenser's *Faerie Queene*, Nin dropped out of high school, and Durrell failed university entrance exams. Nonetheless, all three, especially Miller, were voracious readers and committed autodidacts. There is overwhelming evidence that Miller, Nin, and Durrell were interested and well read in philosophy, sociology, psychology, and a number of other fields. Why then would they take such pains to present themselves as anti-intellectuals?

The anti-intellectual stance of the Villa Seurat writers is partly a product of their vision of life itself as the measure of all things, and their celebration of spontaneity over ponderous reasoning. In a letter to Miller, for instance, Nin writes that she trying to live 'by impulse, by emotion, by white heat,' and that, consequently, she is in 'full rebellion against [her] own mind.'[13] The attitude was a common one in the Villa Seurat circle's Parisian milieu. Parallels can be traced with the surrealists, for instance, who tried to circumvent the mind's conscious control over their art. Distrust of the conscious mind, with its boundless capacity for self-deception, is also a given in psychoanalysis, and while Durrell only dabbled in psychoanalysis, using his family and friends as subjects, Miller and Nin practised it professionally (despite questionable qualifications to do so). Significantly, however, the explanation that the Villa Seurat writers themselves most often cited for their anti-intellectual credo is based on their understanding of Dostoevsky as both an anti-intellectual and a 'bad' thinker, one of the ideas which they borrowed from André Gide, their favourite Dostoevsky critic.

In Gide's book on Dostoevsky (the 1925 translation that Miller most likely read first), he explains that Dostoevsky distrusts the intellect, 'whence proceed the worst temptations ... [and wherein] dwells, according to Dostoevsky, the treacherous demonic element.'[14] Even more importantly (as far as the Villa Seurat writers were concerned), Gide announces that the view of Dostoevsky as an intellectual writer is a 'grave misconception': '[In the *Diary of a Writer*] Dostoevsky sets forth his ideas. It would seem the simplest and most natural thing in the world to make constant reference to this book; but I may as well admit at once that it is profoundly disappointing ... In a word, Dostoevsky is not, strictly speaking, a thinker; he is a novelist.'[15] Gide reiterates his views a number of times in the book, explaining that 'in theoretical or critical articles [Dostoevsky] never rises above mediocrity';[16] '[a]s soon as Dostoevsky begins to theorize, he disappoints us ... he becomes stale and unprofitable';[17] and '[he is] painfully awkward when speaking in his own name.'[18]

Gide's words found an enthusiastic response among the writers of Villa Seurat. In a characteristic twist, however, that which was a deficiency in Gide's eyes (he candidly admits to being disappointed that Dostoevsky is 'not a thinker'), becomes something to celebrate for the writers of Villa Seurat. Miller explained to Nin, somewhat cryptically, that 'Gide has mind, Dostoevsky has the other thing, and it is what Dostoevsky has that really matters,' and she enthusiastically responded: 'For you and me, the highest moment, the keenest joy is not when our minds dominate but when we *lose* our mind.'[19] In another letter to Miller, Nin exclaims: 'Oh, God, today I pray [to] you on my knees for Dostoevsky's obscurity, blindness, the most sacred and precious of all things.'[20] When Nin writes to Miller about her inability to analyse her position on the writings of D.H. Lawrence she cites Gide's views on Dostoevsky: 'Remember Gide on Dostoevsky – "when he began to explain himself he showed himself a bad thinker."'[21] Significantly, in a Parisian interview given later in life, Miller justifies his staunchly anti-intellectual position by pointing to the example of Dostoevsky and citing Gide's passage, which he professes to have just discovered: 'l'autre soir, relisant les pages d'André Gide sur Dostoïevski, j'ai été frappé en voyant que Dostoïevski, lui aussi, a toujours méprisé l'intellect. Il dit même que c'est cela, le diable ... la grande tentation dans laquelle le diable essaie de nous induire. Les héros de Dostoïevski, ses personnages essentiels, comme le prince [Myshkin], sont tous des êtres qui placent le sentiment plus haut que la tête, la grande tentation.'[22]

Gide's statement that Dostoevsky 'sets forth his ideas' in the *Diary of a Writer*, with the implication that he does not do so in his novels, where the 'thinker' is somehow absent, is deeply ironic. As we have seen, Dostoevsky himself viewed his novels if not as propaganda, artistically handled, then at the very least as a setting forth of his beliefs on the subjects of primary concern to him. Gide's argument (whether intentionally or not) encouraged some of his readers to divorce Dostoevsky's own expressed beliefs from his novels and to ignore his novels' ideological thrust, which, in turn, made it easier for them to impose their own ideological perspectives, no matter how far removed from the Dostoevsky's own, on his fictional texts. Gide's strategy of separating Dostoevsky's novels from his ideology, combined with D.H. Lawrence's famous adage to 'trust not the teller but the tale' (also well known to the writers of Villa Seurat), became a tactic used in some of the more outrageous misinterpretations of Dostoevsky's novels, including those practised by Miller and his circle.

Engaging Dostoevsky

The idea that Dostoevsky was not 'strictly speaking, a thinker' and the fact that the writers of Villa Seurat professed to be anti-intellectuals did not prevent them from turning to Dostoevsky for answers to questions primarily philosophical and metaphysical in import. Miller, for instance, includes an emblematic passage in *The Rosy Crucifixion* where Dostoevsky is given a seat of honour next to the chairman of the 'Holy Philarmonic Synod,' which is considering the question 'If there were no God would we be here?' and has the chairman solicit his opinion especially.[23] It would seem that Miller's and the other Villa Seurat writers' condemnation of intellectualism and philosophizing only applied if they found these to be abstract and removed from life, which apparently did not apply to Dostoevsky, in keeping with Gide's maxim that the 'questions' addressed by Dostoevsky in his novels are 'never ... from the abstract.'[24] In Miller's essay 'The Philosopher who Philosophizes' (1940) he explains that as long as philosophy is separated from life, it 'bore[s] [him] to death,' and evokes the image of 'a net [lying] above the surface of human activity.'[25] On the other hand, Miller writes, when there is no artificial separation of the two realms as, presumably, in Dostoevsky's novels, and when philosophy is a part of life, it 'excites me, much as good wine does: I accept it not only as a legitimate part of life but as a *sine qua non*, a [sic] without which no life.'[26]

In a letter to Trygve Hirsch, the attorney defending Miller's books on obscenity charges in the Norwegian Supreme Court, Miller explains that it is his need to 'get at the nature of this reality which pervades all life, and which *is* life,' that leads him 'to grapple with the metaphysical aspects of suffering, freedom, experience,' and cites Berdiaev's views on Dostoevsky in support of his own ideas.[27] Dostoevsky, according to the Villa Seurat writers, was not an ivory tower thinker advancing abstract philosophical theories, but instead wrote from and of his own experience, in an effort to understand his own reality.

The idea of Dostoevsky being an autobiographical writer, particularly emphasized in American readings of Dostoevsky, was further amplified by the writers of Villa Seurat, who considered his philosophical insights important precisely because they believed that he was always writing about himself (an insight they found confirmed in Gide), recording that which was 'true' rather than 'logical,' plotting the parameters of his own personal experience in order to get to the truth and to demonstrate it to his readers. As we have already seen, in *Tropic of Capricorn* Dostoevsky figures as 'the first man to reveal his soul'[28] to the narrator. In *Plexus*, Dostoevsky becomes one of those great writers who 'reveal ... the depths of the human soul in a manner and to a degree never before heard of.'[29] In *Tropic of Cancer*, Dostoevsky appears as a man 'placed at the very core of mystery and, by his flashes, illuminating for us the depths and immensity of the darkness.'[30] Nin fervently agrees with Miller's vision of Dostoevsky, citing the 'man placed in the very core of mystery' passage in a 1932 letter to Miller and writing about 'how much it meant to [her].'[31]

All this effusive talk about Dostoevsky being placed at core of the mystery, revealing his soul to his readers, and so forth, was, of course, cliché by the 1930s; a quick glance at the writings produced by the Dostoevsky cult critics will reveal similar claims even more extravagantly expressed. The mystery that the Villa Seurat writers were particularly interested in, however, was not the mystery of the psyche per se, but the mystery of creativity. As Miller suggests, it was through the process of trying to find out how, practically speaking, Dostoevsky became a great writer that the writers of Villa Seurat found themselves having to engage with the various philosophic, theological, and sociological issues addressed in Dostoevsky's texts, including his ideas regarding the state of Western civilization, the meaning of happiness, and the nature of good and evil.

Miller and the other Villa Seurat writers came to believe that the explanation for Dostoevsky's achievements as a writer lay in his ability to accurately perceive and honestly depict his own inner world, which was in turn rooted in his suffering during his Siberian experience. The emphasis on Dostoevsky's imprisonment as a key to his character was a common feature of Dostoevsky reception both in Europe and America, along with the vague notion connected not only with Dostoevsky but more generally with the lingering Romantic conception of a tormented genius that a writer had to suffer before he could produce anything of real worth. The Villa Seurat writers, however, added a different twist to the idea when they insisted that not only was Dostoevsky's suffering the sole important feature of his biography and the experience that made him a real writer, but that he willingly (if perhaps unconsciously) brought it upon himself in order to become a great novelist.

Miller, who revisited this issue many times, was especially persistent in his claim that Siberian imprisonment was not only Dostoevsky's first real experience of life but enabled his discovery of his essential self and was the true source of his writing ability. Miller called Siberia 'un riche désastre ... un trésor' for Dostoevsky in a French interview, explaining that it allowed Dostoevsky to be really born as an artist.[32] Nin agreed, writing that 'the Siberia of Dostoevsky contributed to [his] compassion for humanity' and that his '[s]uffering became transmuted into works of literature.'[33] In one of his essays, Miller suggests that it was Dostoevsky's 'excessive suffering and deprivation' that allowed him 'to give us glimpses of worlds ... unseen, unknown'[34] as a writer.

While Miller allowed that Dostoevsky may not have consciously chosen the misery of Siberian imprisonment, he insisted that he did it subconsciously, 'creat[ing] the special conditions relating to [his] cruel experience, *and* condition[ing] [himself] to transmute and ennoble the experience.'[35] In *Tropic of Capricorn* Miller's narrator says that although the intellect resists the choice of suffering over comfort, this is what an artist must do: 'Suffering is futile, my intelligence told me over and over, but I went on suffering *voluntarily*.'[36] In the same book another character tells the narrator that he is destined for greatness as a writer, warning him that 'first you'll have to suffer a bit. I mean *really* suffer.'[37] One of Miller's shorter texts dating from his 1940 trip across America includes an account of his meeting with a visionary drunk who tells him, 'I don't know what kind of stuff you write, but ... the thing to do is to learn what it is to suffer. No writer is any good unless he's suffered.'[38]

Miller admits that suffering is potentially dangerous and that only 'budding geniuses' can effect the 'transmutation of suffering permitting us a work of art,' while others end up 'insan[e] ... or psycho[tic],'[39] but he still sees it as the prerequisite to gaining the freedom necessary to become a great writer. In his *Rosy Crucifixion* trilogy Miller's narrator argues paradoxically that 'Suffering *is* unnecessary. But one has to suffer before he is able to realize that this is so.'[40] Miller closes the final book of the trilogy with another meditation on transformative nature of suffering that includes an allusion to Dostoevsky via his *Raw Youth* [*Podrostok*], where Versilov, a high-born Russian, observes that Europeans are never free and that 'in Europe I alone with my Russian yearning was free' (8:377): 'It is only then, moreover, that the true significance of human suffering becomes clear. At the last desperate moment – when one can suffer no more! – something happens which is in the nature of a miracle ... One is 'free' at last, and not 'with a yearning for Russia,' but with a yearning for ever more freedom, ever more bliss ... '[41] According to the Villa Seurat writers, it is because of his suffering that Dostoevsky became liberated to write works of genius; correspondingly, 'the horrible wound' that Miller's narrator experiences, his emotional and psychological suffering, finally frees him 'to write this book.'[42]

Suffering, of course, is one of the key concepts popularly connected both with Dostoevsky (going back as far as Vogüé's essay) and his characters. Dostoevsky himself included discussions about the nature and value of suffering in many of his books, including, prominently, *Brothers Karamazov*. It is clear, however, that the writers of Villa Seurat interpret the value of suffering in a way that is very different from Dostoevsky's interpretation. James Scanlan, who explores the role suffering plays in Dostoevsky's belief system, writes that his 'conception of the moral value of suffering ... is dominated by the figure of Christ as the supreme ethical ideal ... [it] serves to counter egoism, humbling the individual and enlivening conscience ... [and therefore] promoting observance of the moral law ... [and even more so] when, in Christlike fashion, it is freely accepted for the good of others.'[43] Miller was well aware of the accepted critical perspective on suffering in Dostoevsky's novels. In that same letter to Trygve Hirsch, for example, he comments, 'As Berdiaev so well puts it, when treating of Dostoevsky, "Suffering is not only profoundly inherent in man, but it is the sole cause of the wakening of conscious thought."'[44] He himself, however, assigned a somewhat different value to its meaning and value. First of all, Miller repeatedly suggested that suffering is valuable because it expanded rather than humbled his ego; secondly, in Miller's books suffering does not encourage the protagonist to accept the moral law, rather the opposite; finally, if Miller did write about taking on suffering on behalf others, he connected it not with the imitation of Christ but the awakening of creativity.

Suffering and Relations Between the Genders

The idea that personal suffering can lead to the creation of great art informs the Villa Seurat writers' fascination with another aspect of Dostoevsky's novels: his depiction of tortured relationships between women and men, the greatest and most productive source of suffering, according to Miller. We have already noted that Miller and June turned to Dostoevsky's characters as both behavioural and interpretive models back in New York. The same trend continued at Villa Seurat. When Nin first went into psychoanalysis she decided that the clue to her psyche was that she was 'more like a Dostoevskian character than a Latin';[45] when a psychoanalyst asked her whether there were 'fiction heroines ... literary models you sought to emulate,' she responded that in the past 'June, Henry, and [she] were all Dostoevskian characters.'[46] Although Nin does not specify which Dostoevskian characters they emulated or were closest to, the two character types in Dostoevsky's novels that exerted a particular fascination over Miller, Nin, and Durrell were the tormented beautiful woman and her counterpart, the man obsessed with her. One of the more immediate reasons for their interest in both lay in the fact that June, the dark muse of both Henry Miller and Anaïs Nin, was using Dostoevsky's tragic beauties as a model for her own behaviour, to the point of changing her appearance and biography to match that of her favourite Dostoevskian heroines.

The character type that June was particularly attracted to in Dostoevsky's novels was that of the fantastic or infernal woman [*fantasticheskaia zhenshchina* or *infernal'nitsa*], characterized as a woman of great personal beauty who had been abused and mistreated but who still retained a purity of soul and an innocence of sorts. Dostoevsky's fantastic woman might be the cause of all kinds of havoc but she suffers most because of it; she is torn by the love of men who are, in turn, irresistibly attracted to her and destroyed by her. A prominent example of this type is Nastasia Fillipovna of *The Idiot*, who is called a 'fantastic woman' by both her seducer Totsky and the narrator (8:9, 170), while her beauty is described as 'fantastic and demonic' (8:482).

June found Nastasia Fillipovna to be particularly inspiring as a role model, and this link was repeatedly emphasized by both Henry Miller and Nin. Miller saw June as a version of Nastasia Filippovna, 'angelic vampire[s]' both,[47] writing at the impressive age of eighty-six to his last love interest that Nastasia Filippovna and June were both 'extraordinary female[s] ... Unique.'[48] Nin, who consciously set out to imitate June (she writes in her diaries, 'I want to be June'[49] and proceeds to copy her dress, make-up, and mannerisms), also links her with Nastasia Filippovna. When meditating on her own simultaneous relationships, for instance, Nin cites the example of June's many love affairs and then connects this to *The Idiot*: Nastasia Filippovna is unable to chose between Prince Myshkin and Parfen Rogozhin, while Prince Myshkin is unable to chose between Nastasia Filippovna and Aglaia. Asked whether he wishes to love *both* Nastasia Filippovna and Aglaia, Prince Myshkin responds that he does, shocking his interlocutor, who exclaims, 'Prince, what are you saying, come to your senses!' [8:484]). Nin writes: 'like June I have infinite possibilities for all experience ... [Prince Myshkin] and Nastasia [Filippovna] are more important to me than the self-denial of Abélard and Héloïse. The love of only one man or one woman is a limitation.'[50]

In Dostoevsky's novels, the counterpart of the fantastic woman is the man who cannot live without her and who is tormented by his love for her. For Miller, this character type was best represented not by the tragic figures of Parfen Rogozhin or Prince Myshkin of *The Idiot*, but by the tragicomic Pavel Pavlovich Trusotsky of the novella *Eternal Husband* [*Vechnyi muzh*] (1869), a work that Miller particularly admired as one of 'only a few books which I can read over and over,'[51] and as his 'favourite of all Dostoevsky's works.'[52] Trusotsky's wife, who comfortably fits the type of the fantastic woman, has the 'gift of attracting, enslaving, and dominating' (9:26) and dies young of consumption after several extramarital affairs, of which her husband was blissfully unaware. Trusotsky, already broken by his beloved wife's death, becomes unhinged when undisputable evidence of her unfaithfulness is found after her death, upon which his jealousy and suffering overwhelm his sense of reason and lead him to seek vengeance. He fails, however, to enact his revenge and eventually marries another beautiful woman who is also unfaithful to him, a fact of which he is once again oblivious. Miller's relationship with June promoted his identification with Trusotsky; his marriage placed him in a position where he constantly oscillated between jealous suspicion that she is betraying him with others and trust in her loyalty.

The fantastic woman and her tormented partner in Dostoevsky's novels and novellas are involved in a painful relationship which ultimately brings them much suffering and usually ends in tragedy. Miller, however, saw the suffering generated by these kinds of relationships as the best impetus to creativity and infinitely desirable for that very reason. Nin wrote in her diary that Miller sought out painful relationships on purpose and that she found herself having to play the role that June played for him: 'I can give him back a little anguish, jealousy, fear, because he wants them, Henry, the Eternal Husband. He loved his suffering with June.'[53] Miller himself suggested as much in a series of interviews given in 1970, pointing to Dostoevsky as the source for this kind of relationship and, by extension, this kind of reasoning: 'Quelle bonne relation [i.e., his marriage with June], hein? ... Un mariage où tout est harmonie n'est *pas encore* un mariage, à mon avis. Il faut ce conflit et cette torture entre deux êtres ... Mais voilà que je parle très subjectivement, très personnellement ... C'est un peu comme chez Dostoïevski. Oui, je trouve la même chose chez lui.'[54]

Tormented relationships are enshrined in the texts produced not only by Miller but also by Nin and Durrell. In Miller's texts, the relationship between the 'Henry Miller' persona and the Mona/Mara figure is depicted in precise terms, with the implication being that 'Henry Miller' could become a writer only because he went through the suffering generated by this relationship. In Durrell's *Black Book*, Herbert 'Death' Gregory exhibits profoundly sadomasochistic qualities in his relationship with Grace, a former street girl. At one point in the text Grace confesses to Gregory that her friendship with another character is turning into an affair, which she, however, is not really interested in consummating. Gregory realizes that 'she was just Plasticine. I could have convinced her in a half-minute [not to go],'[55] but he sends her to the other man anyway, literally pushing her out of the room. He comments: 'That half-second's pause after I asked whether she really wanted to go was enough to outrage the *professional husband* in me ... This you see, begins my perverse business of torturing myself ... It was a delicious sensation, like standing on the edge of a cliff [emphasis added],'[56] and he goes to write the experience down in his diary, his only creative outlet.

Similarly, in Nin's *Cities of the Interior* series of texts, Jay, an artist based on Miller, has a tormented relationship with Sabina, a character based on June, who complains that Jay is absurdly jealous and spies on her constantly. Their love affair is a difficult one; Jay hates Sabina when he first meets her, and the hate lingers even through his love for her. All the same, the love/hate and tortures that Jay imposes on himself and others help him create.

Interestingly, in Nin's diary of the 1930s she criticizes psychoanalysis for ignoring the redeeming quality of unhealthy relationships, couching her words of criticism in recognizably Dostoevskian terms: 'Another truth overlooked by psychoanalysis is that after they have classified a relationship as masochistic they never consider that what may seem to be the seeking of suffering may in some cases be one's spiritual salvation. They completely forget the fact of the soul's salvation.'[57] She then turns to consider her relationship with Miller, noting her 'frustration' but also suggesting that it is not the soul's salvation that interests her but becoming a better artist. She believes that her suffering 'deepened [her] own [insight] and humanized [her]' and rhetorically concludes, 'Who is to say what is destructive and what is creative?'[58]

Creativity, however, was never a goal in itself for the writers of Villa Seurat. Once the artists/writers were liberated by the suffering they went through they could then embark on their real mission: bringing about the apocalypse.

Dostoevsky and Apocalypse

One of the key beliefs espoused by Miller and the other members of Villa Seurat circle was that apocalypse was just around the corner. Miller describes his age as one of cataclysms and eschatological portents, when old reality slowly collapses unto itself. According to Miller (via Fraenkel, Spengler, and others) the world and society has finally achieved its nadir, after declining for millenia. A new reality would replace it: 'This is the Apocalyptic Era,' he intones in one essay, 'when all things will be made manifest unto us ... The death which had been rotting away in us secretly and disgracefully must be made manifest, and to a degree never before heard of ... we are moving into a new realm of being.'[59] Miller's narrator in *Plexus* observes that 'A grey, neutral world is our natural habitat, it would seem ... But that world, that condition of things, is passing ... we stand on the threshold of a new world.'[60] The narrator of *Plexus* laments that he, an American, found out about this apocalyptic 'reality' much too late, in contrast to the Russians, who have been working on ushering in a new consciousness for mankind: 'A whole century of Russian thought (the nineteenth) was preoccupied with this question of 'the end,' of the establishment on earth of the Kingdom of God. But in North America it was as if that century, those thinkers and searchers after the true reality of life, had never existed.'[61]

Dostoevsky, according to Miller, ranks first among the Russian searchers of apocalyptic realities. In Miller's essay about Balzac's mystical novel *Seraphita* he calls Dostoevsky 'the Apocalyptic writer of the century ... [who] saw the end of Europe ... [and] had also a vision of the world to come.'[62] In another epistolary essay Miller asserts that Dostoevsky 'is eschatological.'[63]

But if a new world was imminent, the problem, according to the writers of Villa Seurat, was that the end of the present world and, therefore, the birth of a new one was taking far too long. Michael Fraenkel's idea of cultural death was that of a continuous dying process, a festering life-in-death, which went on indefinitely. Miller's narrator in *Tropic of Cancer* argues that this process has to be stopped by a complete destruction of the old world: 'for a hundred years or more the world, *our* world, has been dying ... The world is rotting away, dying piecemeal. But it needs the *coup de grâce*, it needs to be blown to smithereens.'[64] It is in this context that the narrator of *Tropic of Capricorn* wants to 'annihilate the whole earth.'[65] Similarly, in *Art and Outrage*, written when Miller was sixty-six, he writes that the whole world 'must be razed ... Nothing less will satisfy.'[66]

But what means do the writer and artist have to actually destroy the old world, according to the writers of Villa Seurat? Miller, with uncharacteristic idealism, believed that the destruction of the world was tied to the destruction of old forms, which could be accomplished through new revolutionary art and writing. The books of the writers of Villa Seurat were meant to be exploding texts; they were a 'vessel in which to pour the vital fluid, a bomb which, when we throw it, will set off the world.'[67] The 'self' of the writer and the artist, no matter how badly fragmented and mangled, provided the vital fluid channelled into the explosive books released upon the unsuspecting world, shocking it and altering it thereby. The narrator of *Tropic of Cancer* explains that when a man dares 'to translate all that is in his heart, to put down what is really his experience, what is truly his truth ... the world would go smash ... it would be blown to smithereens.'[68] Lawrence Lucifer, Durrell's autobiographical narrator of *The Black Book*, echoes this idea: 'I have the sensation of being a bomb ... I am on the point of exploding.'[69]

The artist and writer destroy not only the old vehicles but themselves (or their old selves) by the act of metaphorically ripping themselves open in their texts or paintings. In *Tropic of Cancer* the narrator proposes that 'Side by side with the human race there runs another race of beings, the inhuman ones, the race of artists ... slaying everything within reach ... A man who belongs to this race must stand up on the high place with gibberish in his mouth and rip out his entrails.'[70] In fact, one of the reasons for Miller's later fascination and identification with Yukio Mishima's suicide, committed by ritually disembowelling himself after his failed coup attempt, was that Mishima's seppuku, regarded by the Japanese as the act of ultimate sincerity and a restoration of honour, was also the literal embodiment of Miller's own textual ideal, the metaphor made flesh.[71] The writer's self-evisceration, his merciless exposure of the self, is devastating but it is also a breakthrough into a new mode of existence for himself and others, as Miller comments in one interview: 'When a man is crucified, when he dies to himself, the heart opens up like a flower ... you only reach a new level of vision, a new realm of consciousness, a new unknown world.'[72] The self-sacrifice of the writer/artist leads not only to a personal rebirth but to the liberation of those around them from the prison of cultural death. Writing of Dostoevsky and Whitman, Miller argues that their efforts lay in precisely that direction: 'They were no longer "men of letters," no, not even artists any more, but deliverers. We know only too well how their respective messages bust the frames of the old vehicles ... Their concern with art was of a different order from that of other celebrated revolutionaries. It was a movement from the center of man's being outward.'[73]

In Miller's interpretation it is this state of grace, wherein everything is permitted to the artist as a means of destroying old exhausted forms and bringing about apocalyptic revelations, that equates the writer with the criminal, the saint, and the mentally ill – the extreme positions at which common codes of conduct cease to function. Meditating on this subject in his notes on D.H. Lawrence in the 1930s, Miller writes that 'the man of genius is a monster, a traitor and a criminal, among other things ... the more abnormal he is – the more monstrous, the more criminal – the more fecundating his spirit.'[74] A character in *Plexus* to whom the narrator gives a Dostoevsky novel is puzzled to discover that 'the criminal, the idiot, the saint are not so very far apart.'[75] The writer, who combines the features of saint, criminal, and idiot (also in the sense of a *iurodivyi* or divinely inspired holy fool), must try to shock his readers into a new awareness for their own good, despite the possibility of being declared a criminal and having his work banned.

If Villa Seurat writers were accused of producing criminally explicit texts that were banned as result, they themselves claimed that they were actually attempting to bring in a new state of awareness by shocking their readership and by breaking down old literary forms. Nin often calls Miller 'the master destroyer,'[76] while Miller praises Durrell's *Black Book* as 'the most violent act of destruction' and concludes that now Durrell can be considered 'an apocalyptic writer.'[77] Durrell must have been pleased with Miller's description, because he would often say that he had begun his literary journey as an aspiring commercial novelist with 'premonitions of facility, mediocrity and, perhaps later, prosperity,'[78] and it was only after he read Miller's *Tropic of Cancer* that he realized these no longer sufficed. Durrell, in fact, wrote to Miller that he was one of those shocked and liberated into a new state of being by *Tropic of Cancer*: 'the damn book has rocked the scales like a quake and muddled up all my normal weights and measures';[79] '*Tropic* opened a pit in my brain. It freed me immediately.'[80] After his liberation by Miller Durrell was ready to assemble his own bomb – the shocking *Black Book* – discarding his earlier ambitions of becoming a commercial author willing to 'take a self-deprecating stance, somewhere between faith hope and charity, and speak in loud treacly tones. If you cover your head with a tea-cosy so much the better. The voice is muffled, and the indeterminate buzzing MIGHT be an author speaking – and it might be just gnats.'[81]

A year after his original contact with Miller and during the writing of *The Black Book*, Durrell came up with his own model of the 'heraldic' but really apocalyptic universe, influenced by *Tropic of Cancer*'s depiction of a timeless world 'unfurl[ing] its drama simultaneously along a meridian which had no axis,'[82] as well as by new advances in physics with Einstein's relativity theory. Durrell explains to Miller that in his new vision of the world '[there are]only three dimensions. Time, that old appendix, I've lopped off.'[83] Durrell's other source for the idea may have been Book of Revelation 10:6, where the Angel of the Apocalypse swears that 'there should be time no longer,' a passage also cited in *The Devils* (10:188).

Shocking Gestures: Kirillov's Suicide

It comes as little surprise that the heralds of the apocalypse at Villa Seurat were not only fascinated with Dostoevsky's femme fatales and the men who are tortured by them, but also with those of his characters who operate on the premise that ordinary rules do not apply to them and who attempt to destroy old forms with their actions and lives. Their appreciation of the characters in *The Devils* is a case in point. Miller discussed the novel many times with Nin and Durrell and identified with many of its characters (because the Villa Seurat writers read the novel in the Garnett translation, they refer to it as *The Possessed*). Nin tried to gain insights into the people in her own life by correlating them with the characters in the novel; she also titled two of her diaries written in the early 1930s 'The Possessed' and 'Journal of a Possessed.' Durrell's autobiographical poem 'Cities, Plains and People' (1943), which describes his travels in Europe with his first wife Nancy, proposes as their alter egos Dostoevsky and his wife, whom he calls '*the possessed*/Fëdor and Anna' (emphasis added).

The characters in *The Devils* who interested Miller, Nin, and Durrell particularly, however, are Aleksey Kirillov and Nikolai Stavrogin. Kirillov, an engineer by profession, is known for his eccentric ways, his ill-fated visit to America, and his inability to speak proper Russian, even though it is his native tongue. He becomes involved with an underground Socialist group, develops a peculiar theory of man's mission on earth, and commits suicide by shooting himself with a revolver. Stavrogin is an enigmatic young aristocrat who returns to the Russian provinces from St Petersburg, where he led a life of dissolution and crime; he becomes involved with the same underground Socialist group as Kirillov and ultimately commits suicide by hanging himself. Together with the saintly Zosima from *Brothers Karamazov* – who likewise fascinated the Villa Seurat writers – these characters are interpreted by Miller and friends in a way that supports their thesis about the closeness of the idiot, the criminal, and the saint.

The part of Kirillov's life that attracted the attention of the writers of Villa Seurat is his suicide or, more accurately, the reason for his suicide. Kirillov's decision to kill himself is predicated by his ideology. Although his beliefs are somewhat hazy and he has difficulty articulating, let alone explaining them (he has a problem communicating on simpler topics), he says that he is shooting himself to prove that if there is no God, man himself is God. His suicide is his ultimate 'assertion of self-will' [*svoevolie*] as that new Man-God (10:470). Miller and, subsequently, other Villa Seurat writers interpreted Kirillov's suicide as an example of a deliberately shocking gesture, meant to bring humanity closer to apocalyptic renewal. Interestingly, however, Miller decided that the real reason Kirillov committed suicide was because he was happy. Although this interpretation requires turning a blind eye both to Kirillov's terror in the face of death and his own expressed ideas about why he is killing himself, Miller repeatedly linked his suicide with the idea of discovering happiness. In *Hamlet Correspondence* Miller calls Kirillov 'one of those blessed men who bumped himself off out of sheer ecstasy.'[84] In 'The Enormous Womb' Miller asserts, 'When one really understands what happiness is one goes out like a light. (Vide Kirillov!)'[85] In 'First Impressions of Greece' he writes that 'in the *Possessed* Kirillov kills himself because he has discovered the secret of happiness.'[86]

Although Kirillov talks about finding happiness, he does not connect the idea to his impending death. The Dostoevsky character who does explicitly link suicide with happiness or rapture [*vostorg*] is Dmitry Karamazov, who explains in *Brothers Karamazov* that he once wanted to kill himself 'because of the rapture … from some types of rapture you can kill yourself.'[87] Miller, however, insists on interpreting Kirillov's suicide as being committed in a state of ecstasy, decontextualizing it in the *Hamlet Correspondence* (he cites the entire speech Kirillov makes about happiness but does not include the lines where Kirillov explains that he discovered he was happy only several days earlier, whereas his suicide had been planned for several years), and perpetuating this misreading in his other texts.

Miller's narrator identifies with Kirillov 'sho[oting] or hang[ing] himself because he was too happy ... That was me all over.'[88] The happiness that Miller seems to have in mind, however, is an ecstasy achieved when one is at the end of one's rope, and when the old self can be more easily dismissed and destroyed. The narrator of *Tropic of Cancer* declares, 'I have no money, no resources, no hopes. I am the happiest man alive.'[89] According to Miller, it is this state of liminal happiness that allows the writer to stand on a high place and vivisect himself, as it were, spilling his soul into his prose, and his prose onto the readers, shocking his readers into an awareness of themselves and their time, and bringing the apocalypse a step closer. 'To be permanently happy,' the narrator explains in *Sexus*, is 'to set the world on fire.'[90]

Shocking Gestures: Stavrogin's Bite

If the act that attracted Villa Seurat writers to Kirillov was his most significant gesture in the novel, what fascinated them most about Stavrogin was a relatively minor episode. According to some of Miller's favourite critics, Stavrogin was 'the strangest perhaps and the most terrifying of Dostoevsky's creations'[91] and 'the most puzzling figure ever created by the author.'[92] Miller proclaimed Stavrogin 'the supreme test' for Dostoevsky[93] and was particularly impressed by Stavrogin's extraordinary presence and his destructive ability. Comparing Stavrogin to Marcel Proust's Baron de Charlus in his 'The Universe of Death,' Miller writes that Stavrogin 'permeates and dominates the atmosphere when off the scene ... the poison of his being shoots its virus into the other characters, the other scenes, the other dramas, so that from the moment of his entry, or even before, the atmosphere is saturated with his noxious gases.'[94] Of all the events involving Stavrogin in the novel, however, the one that Miller found especially fascinating was the minor incident during which Stavrogin unexpectedly bit the ear of the town's governor (10:42–3).

Interestingly, Stavrogin's bite attracted the attention of a number of writers, including Miller's beloved John Cowper Powys and D.H. Lawrence. Powys, like Miller, refused to accept the immediate explanation offered for the bite in the novel: namely, that Stavrogin was on the verge of delirium and did not know what he was doing. Powys interpreted the act as a 'wild, unexpected, crazy gesture [breaking] the superficial coating of the propriety of life,' and commented on Stavrogin's 'diabolical life-zest and ... love of spitting in the face of common decency by doing something totally ridiculous like *biting the ear* of the leading official of the town.'[95] D.H. Lawrence, for his part, has nothing positive to say about Stavrogin's bite, but in his novel *Aaron's Rod* (1922) a character refers to several others as 'a lot of little Stavrogins coming up to whisper affectionately, and biting one's ear.'[96]

When Miller reread *Aaron's Rod* for his projected Lawrence study in the early 1930s he became indignant about this offhand and derisive reference to Stavrogin. In his notes, Miller observes that Lawrence keeps returning to Stavrogin again and again, and explains it by saying that Lawrence is jealous of him: 'Stavrogin ... wielded a tremendous power – for evil perhaps. And Lawrence can't stand that. And so he tries to make a petty, malevolent little devil of Stavrogin – *biting people's ears*. Why does he *distort* the way that Stavrogin bit people's ears?'[97] Miller suggests that there is more to Stavrogin's bite than is first apparent, that it is, in fact, a gesture both creative and apocalyptic, and he goes on to argue that 'Dostoevsky was obsessed with the *idea* of a Stavrogin. He *had* to create him.'[98] In *Tropic of Cancer* Stavrogin is described as a 'divine monster standing on a high place and flinging to us his torn bowels,'[99] a violent image favoured by Miller to symbolize a writer's own agon of rending his very self in order to create his books. Miller's narrator suggests that Stavrogin is not simply an 'imaginative individual' who experiences a catastrophe, but one who manages to bring the apocalypse closer, initiating 'a cataclysm in which a large portion of humanity is buried, wiped out forever.'[100] According to this perspective Stavrogin, like his creator, is trying to shake up the indifferent world, which allows the narrator to come to the conclusion that 'Stavrogin was Dostoevsky.'[101] In 'The Universe of Death' Miller elaborates: 'Stavrogin was the ideal image of himself which Dostoevsky jealously preserved. More than that – Stavrogin was the God in him, the fullest portrait of God which Dostoevsky could give.'[102]

Shocking Gestures: Zosima's Love

If Villa Seurat writers believed, following Miller's lead, that Stavrogin was Dostoevsky, they felt that Zosima of *Brothers Karamazov* represented another face of Dostoevsky, a conclusion to which Miller arrived after considering the question of evil in Dostoevsky's novels. Miller tried to reconstruct Dostoevsky's approach to evil in a long essay that appears in

The Books in My Life: '*And what of Evil?* Suddenly it is Dostoevsky's voice I hear. If there be evil, there can be no God. Was that not the thought which plagued Dostoevsky? Whoever knows Dostoevsky knows the torments he endured because of this conflict. But the rebel and the doubter is silenced towards the end, silenced by a magnificent affirmation' (230). Miller then turns to saintly Zosima's teachings in *Brothers Karamazov*, where this affirmation can be located. He cites from the 'Discourses and Teachings of the Elder Zosima' in Book Six of the novel – 'Love all God's creation and every grain of sand in it. Love every leaf, every ray of God's light. If you love everything, you will preserve the divine mystery of things' – adding a short note of his own as a commentary: 'Father Zosima, alias the real Dostoevsky.'[103]

The distortion that Miller introduces here becomes obvious when one examines the Dostoevskian passage in context. Zosima never advises anyone to love evil, of course. His acceptance and love of creation includes love of the less-than-perfect mankind ('Brothers, do not be afraid of the sins of mankind, love man even in his sin,' Zosima says right before the words quoted by Miller [14:289]), but Miller sets the passage up in such a way as to suggest that Zosima's exhortation to love the world includes an instruction to love evil, and turns Zosima's very proper Christian credo into a shocking gesture.

Even though the idea that Zosima approved of evil is as misleading as the idea that Dostoevsky was exclusively interested in it, the writers of Villa Seurat began to identify Dostoevsky with a special focus on evil and eventually concluded that Dostoevsky accepted it, an attitude that they themselves came to adopt. In a diary entry made in the early 1930s Nin quotes Miller as telling her that he is 'inspired by evil. It preoccupies me, as it did Dostoevsky ... It is evil which fascinates me.'[104] In *Plexus*, a young man explains to the narrator that since he was 'the one who urged me to read Dostoevsky ... [he] know[s] what it is, then, to be dragged into a world of unmitigated evil.'[105] In *Art and Outrage* Miller rails against the 'false religious attitude which desires only the good.'[106] Nin begins with a rejection of evil but ends by accepting and celebrating it. In a diary entry made in March of 1932 she quotes Stavrogin's words from the excised chapter nine of *The Devils*, containing his confession of the rape of an adolescent girl: '"I found as much pleasure doing evil ..." said Stavrogin,' and then concludes, 'To me, an unknown pleasure' (ellipsis in the original).[107] But already in April 1932, after many conversations with Miller on the subject, Nin writes these words in her diary: 'I am going to make a new beginning. I want ... all evil,'[108] deciding eventually that she will achieve this evil mainly through her writing: 'the evil I do not act out, I write out.'[109]

In this way Zosima, Stavrogin, and Kirillov – three characters who could not be more different from one another – become almost interchangeable in the Villa Seurat reading of Dostoevsky's novels, all becoming stand-ins for 'the real' Dostoevsky and supporting the thesis that the saint, the criminal, and the idiot 'are not so very far apart,' at least in their capacity to embrace shocking beliefs or commit shocking gestures.

Shocking Gestures at Villa Seurat

It is interesting to note, in connection with the importance the Villa Seurat writers assigned to the shocking gestures in Dostoevsky's novels, that Miller advocated and practised similarly shocking gestures, designed to break through 'the superficial coating of the propriety of life' during his life in Villa Seurat. Together with Alfred Perlès, the Austrian-born French avant-garde writer who was his look-alike and 'boon companion' at Villa Seurat, Miller continually engaged in deliberate *épatage* of those around him. On one occasion, Miller and Perlès invited Roger Pelorson, a journalist with whom Miller was on friendly terms, and his wife to Villa Seurat for dinner. With Miller's encouragement and full approval, Perlès climbed up on the table with his bare feet in the middle of dinner, and began imitating Hitler's speeches and insulting the guests, breaking a couple of glasses and bloodying his feet in the process.

The love of the shocking gesture was dear to the heart of many of The Villa Seurat circle's contemporaries in Paris in the 1930s, of course, including the surrealists and the futurists. What sets the Villa Seurat circle's love of shock apart from that of their contemporaries is that the former understood their own gestures in the context of an apocalyptic model, where they were not only breaking through the façade of social convention but actually destroying old forms to help prepare ground for the emergence of the new.

Even the audaciously explicit treatment of sexuality in the texts produced by Villa Seurat writers (a feature most commonly associated with their work) has been explained by them as another attempt at a shocking textual gesture, meant to liberate the reader. Miller claimed that explicit passages describing sex in his writings were meant to be obscene rather than pornographic. In a short text specifically dedicated to the obscene in art and writing, 'Obscenity and the Law of Reflection' (1947), Miller explains that he views obscenity as a way 'to awaken, to usher in a sense of reality.'[110] After sending Nin a draft of a text peppered with swear words, Miller explains that his 'idea was to use the nasty words in their strongest form ... not to make people lascivious.'[111] In an interview given, ironically enough, to *Playboy*, Miller commented that obscenity was there to shock rather than to arouse: 'Pornography is a titillating thing, and the other is cleansing; it gives you a catharsis.'[112] Miller and, following his suit, Durrell and Nin, argued that explicit depictions of sex in their texts were meant to function as liberating, taboo-breaking acts of self-exposure that would shock readers into destroying their perception of the world. In Nin's preface to *Tropic of Cancer* she suggests that the 'violence and obscenity are ... manifestations of the mystery and pain of creation' and that the real intention is 'to shock, to startle the lifeless ones.'[113] Durrell, for his part, would write in his introduction to a 1960 edition of *The Black Book* that the graphic passages that made it practically unpublishable in the 1930s were an attempt to 'break through the mummy wrappings – the cultural swaddling clothes' of Western civilization.[114]

Particularly revealing in this respect is the correspondence that Miller and Durrell exchanged after the completion of *The Black Book*. Miller raved to Durrell, 'You have written things in this book which nobody has dared to write ... it's an onslaught ... No English or American publisher would dare print it.'[115] Durrell's response, after some of the initial euphoria wears off, is to muse, 'Was I a monster? I tried to say what I was.'[116] In an interview given in 1966 Miller explains that he introduced explicit sexual content into his books 'to get at the truth of one man: myself ... It just happened that this was the part that had shock value.'[117] Similarly, when Nin reflected on her diary in the 1940s (when she was still considering publishing it with little expurgation), she writes that she includes the explicitly sexual passages because they were those of 'revelation ... when the real self rises to the surface, shatters its false roles, erupts and assumes reality.'[118]

The connection of all of these ideas with Dostoevsky's own belief system is, obviously, a very slender one. The writers of Villa Seurat were picking out various unrelated concepts in Dostoevsky's novels, decontextualizing them, misinterpreting them, and then including them in their own reading of Dostoevsky's 'philosophy.' The comments of their favourite critics on Dostoevsky, some of them highly unreliable readers of his novels, were also frequently misread and misinterpreted.

A number of characters from novels were said to be stand-ins for Dostoevsky himself and quoted at length, although their words and actions were also decontextualized and misread, sometimes, it would seem, on purpose, in order to support a particular contention of the Villa Seurat writers. All of these elements were then combined into the Villa Seurat's own version of Dostoevsky's belief system and included as such in their own writings. Even though that version is crude and in some cases even comic, the mechanics of how their misreadings were enacted and perpetuated are not different from the way other writers and readers misinterpreted Dostoevsky. What is more, it becomes evident that the enormous gap that often exists between Dostoevsky's personal beliefs and those of his readers makes little difference. The readers of Villa Seurat picked, *à la carte*, those ideas Dostoevsky's books that bolstered their own perspectives and furthered their own agendas. As long as Dostoevsky retained his place of importance in major cultural discourses, invoking him in their writings was a good strategy, and did not prevent them from believing the composite they put together. It was this composite, their own 'Dostoevsky,' that they followed in their own texts and lives.

7 Writing the Underground

My understanding of the meaning of a book is that the book itself disappears from sight, that it is chewed alive, digested and incorporated into the system as flesh and blood which in turn creates new spirit and reshapes the world.

Henry Miller, *Tropic of Capricorn*, 221

Scholars, critics, writers, and cultural mavens all concur that *Notes from Underground*, written by Dostoevsky in the early 1860s and virtually ignored upon publication, has become one of the most important and influential literary texts of the twentieth century. Joseph Frank writes, 'Few works in modern literature are more widely read than Dostoevsky's *Notes from Underground* or so often cited as a key text revelatory of the hidden depths of the sensibility of our time. The term "underground man" has become part of the vocabulary of contemporary culture, and this character has now achieved – like Hamlet, Don Quixote, and Faust the stature of one of the great archetypal literary creations ... Most important cultural developments of the present century – Nietzscheanism, Freudianism, Expressionism, Surrealism, Crisis Theology, Existentialism – have claimed the underground man as their own or have been linked with him by zealous interpreters.[1] The book's impact on American literature has been particularly powerful, leading one scholar writing almost a century after the book's publication to conclude that 'recent American fiction ... does not stem only, as Hemingway claimed, from a book by Mark Twain called *Huckleberry Finn* but also from another ... by Dostoevsky called *Notes from Underground*,'[2] an observation that rings true for a host of American texts that have become canonic or even cult classics in their own right. From Saul Bellow's *The Dangling Man* (1944) to

Richard Wright's *The Man Who Lived Underground* (1945), from Jack Kerouac's *The Subterraneans* (1958) to Bret Easton Ellis's *American Psycho* (1991), countless American novels and novellas testify to the fascination that *Notes from Underground* exerted upon their authors. When an interviewer suggested to Ralph Ellison that his novel *Invisible Man* (1952) owed much to 'the American vernacular tradition' and contained many parallels with *Moby Dick*, Ellison countered by reading aloud the opening lines of Dostoevsky's *Notes from Underground* and triumphantly concluding, 'That ain't Melville.'[3]

Notes from Underground occupies a special place in the works of Miller, Durrell, and Nin – a connection that was, for the most part, acknowledged, if never actually explored by their professional readers. It is clear, for instance, that the persona created by Dostoevsky as the nameless narrator of the book, along with his dissident stance against the dominant cultural forces of his time and the tortured philosophy that he expounds, became a major focal point for the writers of Villa Seurat. Texts produced by Miller, Nin, and Durrell during the period of their close literary association adopt so many of Dostoevsky's strategies and techniques in *Notes* with regard to the persona of the narrator, plot, setting, imagery, and style that their lineage is unmistakable. Miller's *Tropic of Cancer* and *Tropic of Capricorn*, Nin's diaries and other writings of those years, and Durrell's *Black Book* all incorporate key features of Dostoevsky's *Notes from Underground*, albeit transposed into a different linguistic, temporal, and cultural matrix and reworked to suit their own particular needs. An examination of their texts through the lens of *Notes from Underground* simultaneously illustrates their authors' continuous efforts to engage with Dostoevsky on his own territory and reveals subtle differences in their individual interpretations of Dostoevsky's work.

Dostoevsky's Underground

Dostoevsky uses the term 'underground man,' or even 'underground people,' in a number of his texts. In the *Eternal Husband*, for instance, both the ex-lover and the distraught husband of the dead woman are called 'underground ... people' (9:87). In *Brothers Karamazov*, Dmitry Karamazov calls himself one of the 'underground people' (15:31). Dostoevsky repeatedly refers to 'underground types' within his novels and stories, calling, for example, Goliadkin of *The Double [Dvoinik]* (1846) his 'chief underground type' (1:489). In a draft for an introduction to his novel *Raw Youth [Podrostok]* (1875), Dostoevsky asserts that the happy families in the novels of Lev Tolstoy and Ivan Goncharov represent the exception rather than the norm, and that he alone faithfully depicts the tragic underground life of the majority (17:329): 'The satirists keep saying – the underground, the underground, *a poet of the underground*, as if it is something of which I ought to be ashamed. Fools. That is my glory, because therein lies the truth' (17:330). In the same notebook, Dostoevsky jots down, 'The underground man – [is] the most important man' (17:420). There is no dispute, however, that if Dostoevsky himself identified a number of his characters as belonging to the underground type in his novels, the designation 'Underground Man' has become permanently affixed to his nameless narrator of *Notes from Underground*.

Much has been written about *Notes from Underground* and the influence exerted by the text and its narrator upon writers worldwide. Probably the best-known works of literary scholarship on the subject are Robert Louis Jackson's *Dostoevsky's Underground Man in Modern Russian Literature* (1958) and Edward F. Abood's *Underground Man* (1973), both of which focus on the persona of the narrator of the *Notes* and demonstrate how this 'classic literary figure, Dostoevsky's immortal neurotic,' spawned 'a multitude of famous descendants.'[4] Although the persona of the Underground Man – his philosophical outlook, his anger, and his alienation – has attracted most attention and critical comment, the book's structure, plot, setting, imagery, and style have also proved to be important to subsequent generations of writers. Both Abood and Jackson show that subsequent writers responded 'to the whole complex of "underground" psychology, philosophy, imagery … mak[ing] it possible to speak of a body of prose works as literature of the "underground",'[5] and both studies suggest that the problems raised in the text 'have lost none of their relevance today, not only in Russia but also the West.'[6]

Dostoevsky's letters and published journal notices of the time indicate that he originally intended to write a large novel titled *Confession* [*Ispoved'*]. The existing two parts of *Notes from Underground* were evidently meant to be the first two sections of a much longer work. His plans changed, however, and he ended *Notes* on the second section. It was almost totally ignored by the press upon publication and began to attract the attention of readers and critics only after Dostoevsky's death.

The best concise description of *Notes* was provided by Dostoevsky himself. In a rare, if not the only, instance of such a disclaimer in his entire body of work, Dostoevsky attempts to disassociate himself from his narrator, explaining in a short signed statement included as a footnote to the opening of the *Notes* that the 'author of the notes' and the *Notes* themselves are 'obviously fictional' but were created to exhibit 'more clearly than usual' a social type existing in contemporary Russian society as representative of an older generation. Dostoevsky writes that in the first part of his text (titled 'The Underground') this character introduces 'himself and his outlook' and 'desires, as it were, to understand the reasons why he appeared and was bound to appear in our midst.' The second part of the text (titled 'On the Occasion of Wet Snow'), Dostoevsky continues, will 'already consist of the actual "notes" of this individual concerning some events in his life' (5:99).

As his footnote indicates, Dostoevsky wanted to ensure that readers perceive *Notes from Underground* as a fictional text and his narrator as an incarnated social phenomenon separate from its creator.[7] Dostoevsky's original aim in writing *Notes from Underground* is suggested in an outraged letter he wrote to his brother Mikhail Dostoevsky after seeing the changes that the government censors wrought on the first part of his text ('The Underground'): 'Are the censors conspiring against the government, or what? ... It would have been better not publish the penultimate chapter [of Part One] at all, (the most important one, where the whole idea [of the work] is expressed) than to publish it in the way it appears, [as a series of] disconnected phrases and contradicting itself. But what can you do! The censors are swine: [the places] where I mock everything and at times blaspheme *for show* have been left in, but [the places] where I deduce from all of it the necessity of faith and of Christ have been cut out' (28/II:73). At the time, Dostoevsky was still writing the second part of his text ('On the Occasion of Wet Snow'). It remains a matter of conjecture whether he concluded the *Notes* instead of expanding it into a full-sized novel because of his personal circumstances (his first wife died; he became very ill; his financial situation hit another low) or because the changes introduced by the censors in 'the most important' penultimate section of Part One altered his original plan to such an extent that he could not continue with the novel, which he envisioned originally as a polemic proving 'the necessity of faith and Christ.'

The original version of *Notes from Underground* as Dostoevsky intended it to be read has not survived. The existing version of the text does not include a defence of Russian Orthodoxy or Christianity in general (at least, not explicitly). When Dostoevsky brought out *Notes from Underground* again in 1865 – the last time that it would be published in his lifetime – he retained all the changes that the censors had introduced. This censored and distorted text became the definitive version of *Notes from Underground*, translated into English as well as into other languages and read by the writers of Villa Seurat.

Dostoevsky's Underground Man and His Notes

There were so many influential interpretations of *Notes from Underground* in the twentieth century that it is now difficult to read the book without being affected by its famous readers' perspectives. Nevertheless, a close reading of Dostoevsky's text allows us to construct a reasonably objective description of the Underground Man and the text he narrates, which we can then use as a reference point when we consider the Villa Seurat writers' responses to Dostoevsky's text.

Notes from Underground is set in Dostoevsky's contemporary Russia of the 1860s, in St Petersburg, the nation's capital. It is narrated in the first person by the 'writer' of the *Notes*, a narrator who gleefully acknowledges his own unreliability and contradictions. While he is 'writing' the *Notes* as a private document, he still imagines a readership whom he loathes and taunts, but whose responses he anticipates and counters throughout the text. In the opening of the *Notes* we learn that the Underground Man is forty years old. He is a former civil servant who lives alone in a squalid apartment and has practically no human contacts. He no longer works and has no active pursuits of any sort. He despises himself for his failure to achieve anything either great or humble, and for his failure to become 'neither a hero nor an insect' (5:100).

In Part One, the Underground Man addresses his imaginary readers and proposes to explain to them why it is that he has failed to become anything – 'not even an insect' (5:101). His immediate explanation is that his personal failures originate in his 'constant awareness of the many-many contradictory ... elements' within himself (5:100) and that his 'excessive consciousness' results in a 'fever of vacillation' (5:105) that ultimately prevents him from doing anything at all. He contrasts himself with a typical 'man of action' who is single- or simple-minded enough to bullishly pursue his goals, backing off only where he is stopped by 'impossibility – meaning a stone wall' (5:105), in the form of the laws of nature, the sciences, or mathematics, all symbolized for the Underground Man by the simple, logical, and incontrovertible arithmetical equation of 2+2=4.

This subject makes the Underground Man digress into a critique of the 'naive' idea that human beings make their life choices rationally, based on what is personally good for them. He attacks it first on the grounds that many if not most people base their choices not on what is good for them but on the psychological need to exercise their capacity for free choice, no matter how quirky, destructive, or irrational. Further, he claims that 'personal good' is a subjective category, and that while one person might want health, wealth, and happiness, another might actually want to suffer, as a means, for instance, of reaching that consciousness which the Underground Man sees as 'the greatest misfortune' but which mankind 'loves and will not trade for any satisfactions' (5:119). Finally, he attacks this idea as the foundation of the belief that rational self-interest will one day – together with the rapidly advancing sciences and mathematics – lead mankind to a social utopia, symbolized for the Underground Man by a Crystal Palace, where there will no longer be room for 'suffering, which is doubt and denial' (5:119) and where the individual will be a single part in a huge instrument of progressive humanity. (The image of a Crystal Palace would probably have been recognized by Dostoevsky's original Russian readers as connected to the futuristic building constructed in London for the Great Exhibition of 1851 and to the use made of it in Nikolai Chernyshevsky's utopian novel *What is to be Done? [Chto Delat'?]* [1863].)

According to the Underground Man, social utopians do not take into consideration the fact that an individual will insist on affirming his free will or his 'whim' even to his own detriment and even contrary to logic, because 'the law of logic might not be the law of humanity' (5:118). For an individual then, the Underground Man insists, the idea that two plus two is equal to five might also sound like 'a lovely thing, occasionally' (5:119). He provides another criticism of social utopias in the penultimate section of Part One (the section originally containing Dostoevsky's defence of Christianity, ultimately excised by the censors), where he says that a human being needs a real ideal and that the goal of social utopians falls short of that, being reducible to a well-designed 'rental building, with apartments for impoverished tenants leased for one thousand years' (5:120). In the final section of Part One the Underground Man concludes that because of all of this he chose 'conscious inertia' and ended up in the underground: 'Even though I said that I envy a normal man to the very last drop of my bile, I do not want to be him under the conditions in which I find him' (5:121).

The Underground Man finally halts his diatribe to turn to an episode from his earlier life that continues to haunt him. He again warns his 'readers' that he does not want to exercise any 'restrain … in my …

notes. I will not set up an order or a system. Whatever I will recall, I will write down' (5:122). He relates the actual episode in Part Two of his notes, prefacing it with an epigraph out of Nikolai Nekrasov's 1846 poem about a man who helped a woman abandon prostitution by opening her eyes to the misery of her situation and then by nobly marrying her. The entire Part Two serves as a memoir or a flashback to his twenty-fourth year, when he worked as a minor administrative official amidst co-workers who were 'stupid and resembled each other like sheep' (5:125). His personal life was full of 'dark, subterranean, disgusting' periods when he would visit seedy bars and brothels (5:127), followed by periods when he would shut himself up in his room and dream about 'everything beautiful and lofty' (5:132). He illustrates his inner turmoil by depicting his conflict with an officer who insulted him and upon whom he fantasized of revenging himself for years. He then comes to the episode, which is, presumably, the story that continues to haunt him.

At the end of one period of intensive dreaming about the 'beautiful and lofty,' the young Underground Man experiences a need for human contact and goes to see a schoolmate of his, with whom he retains a contact of sorts. The schoolmate is planning a farewell party for another classmate, a successful careerist, whom the Underground Man despises. The Underground Man gets himself invited to the party, manages to behave in a manner which everyone there, himself included, considers scandalous, and is abandoned by everyone as they go off to a popular brothel. He decides to catch up with them to get his own back or to be worshipped by them, but arrives at the brothel too late – they are all gone. Instead, he is offered a prostitute and has emotionless and anonymous sex with her. Afterwards, however, he begins to talk to the young woman, and learns that her name is Liza, that she is twenty years old, and that she had only recently become a prostitute.

The Underground Man is piqued by her unwillingness to open up to him emotionally and pointedly tells her about the squalid funeral of a prostitute whose coffin was lowered into cold water at the bottom of the grave, going on to contrast the life of abuse that a prostitute faces with the life of a married woman, and describing for her tableau after tableau of happy family scenes. Finally, Liza breaks down into tears and opens her heart to him, showing him a letter from a young man of a good family who was respectfully declaring his love for her. The Underground Man gives her his own address and leaves. He spends several days terrified that she might actually come to him and see his own squalid life, but then decides that she will not come and that it is safe to dream about how beautiful it might have been if he had educated her and then made an honest woman of her by marrying her. To his surprise, Liza does come to see him, catching him in the middle of an ugly confrontation with his servant. The Underground Man goes into hysterics and tells her that he is no saviour, that he himself is a 'scoundrel, a lowlife, an egotist' (5:174) and that she should leave. Instead, Liza tries to comfort him, and the two end up having sex again, after which he cruelly insults her by placing some money in her hand and, in effect, dismissing her. She leaves and he follows her after some hesitation, but it is too late and they never meet again.

The Underground Man begins to tell of his remorse and suffering after his encounter with Liza, but finally decides to conclude his notes. 'A novel,' he says, 'requires a hero, and here, *intentionally*, are collected all the traits for an antihero' (5:178). Before he concludes, however, he advances the claim that his contemporaries are deriving their sense of identity, their likes and dislikes, from popular books and not from their own life and experience. 'We are born dead,' he says, 'and for a long time we haven't even been born of living fathers, and we like it more and more' (5:179).

Notes from Underground and Henry Miller

Most twentieth-century critics examining the subject acknowledged the important position occupied by Notes from Underground in Dostoevsky's body of work. Henry Miller's favourite Dostoevsky critics, however, placed Notes from Underground among Dostoevsky's greatest achievements. André Gide, for instance, contends that 'with [Notes from Underground] we reach the height of Dostoevsky's career. I consider this book (and I am not alone in my belief) as the keystone of his entire works.'[8] John Cowper Powys, another favourite, connected to Notes from Underground in a very personal way, calling it one of the greatest of Dostoevsky's works, which shows 'the perversity at the bottom of our troubled hearts'[9] but also reveals 'the power of the lonely, self-existent, unpropitiated human mind.'[10] Powys identified with the narrator of the Notes on many different levels, writing that his personal 'conviction [is] that real "reality" implies a world of four dimensions, in other words a world with a *super-lunary crack* in the cause-and-effect logic that two and two make four. To me however, as to Dostoevsky's weird hero of [Notes from Underground], they have ever since – and doubtless will till I die – *made five.*'[11]

Miller never actually published any material specifically discussing *Notes from Underground*, nor did he single out *Notes* or its narrator in the way that he had, for example, singled out Nastasia Filippovna of the *Idiot* or Kirillov of *The Devils*, repeatedly testifying to the significance that these characters and texts had for him. Several possible references to *Notes* can be located in his writings, but all of them are tenuous at best and none is particularly memorable. In *Colossus of Maroussi* (1941), for example, the narrator refers to the 'sickly subterranean living and lying' that one must renounce if one is to appreciate the pagan glories of Greece.[12] In *Plexus*, the narrator speaks ironically about his '"underground" life.'[13] In *Big Sur and the Oranges of Hieronymus Bosch* (1957), Miller writes about a young correspondent who 'has not yet taken his soul to the underground – but give him time.'[14]

Despite the lack of explicit references to *Notes from Underground*, both texts and 'characters' created by Henry Miller, especially during the Villa Seurat period, have been repeatedly linked to it. Miller's narrator-autobiographical persona has been called 'a descendant of Dostoevsky's Underground Man without his nastiness,'[15] 'a mock Underground Man,'[16] and, in a slightly more extensive comparison, a 'kind of Dostoevskian underground man' who 'has given up the idea of living in any sort of conventional manner and ... [is] prowling though the bottom strata of a civilization in decomposition, recording disasters ... [h]is rage cut[ting] through the lachrymose posturing of his fellow expatriates like a sword.'[17] Durrell even associated Miller himself with the Underground Man, writing to Alfred Perlès that he occasionally saw in Miller 'the frightened man' from *Notes from Underground*; an observation with which Miller apparently agreed, citing his own excessive sensitivity.[18] *Notes from Underground* has been identified as the book that 'influenced ... [Miller] more than any other piece of writing in the past century.'[19]

On the surface, however, there is little connecting Henry Miller's narrators or texts with Dostoevsky's *Notes from Underground*. The 'Henry Miller' persona who narrates both *Tropics* (the most famous works he produced during his Villa Seurat period) keeps emphasizing his health and good spirits ('I keep thinking of my really superb health. When I say "health" I mean optimism, to be truthful. Incurably optimistic!').[20] He is, superficially, a happy-go-lucky American on a escapade in Europe. His only problem is making sure that all his biological needs are met (in *Tropic of Cancer* he rapturously exclaims, 'A meal! That means something to go on – a few solid hours of work, an erection possibly');[21] his prodigious exploits to procure food, sex, and, occasionally, to find a washroom account for much of the action in the plot of the *Tropics*. He seems, in fact, to be the personification of that bullish man of action so envied and despised by Dostoevsky's Underground Man. He knows what he wants and he finds it in the very thick of humanity. A closer look, however, reveals numerous parallels between Miller's narrator and the narrator of the *Notes*, as well as a number of important connections between Miller's texts, most prominently his *Tropics*, and Dostoevsky's *Notes*.

Robert Louis Jackson sees the literary successors of *Notes from Underground* in 'works centered on the problems of the alienated individual, desperately seeking a pivot within himself, desperately trying to formulate a social and philosophical outlook that would buttress his position in a hostile world.'[22] Edward Abood argues that although the literary descendants of Dostoevsky's Underground Man vary in many ways, they still 'retain their essential kinship' with him because they experience 'anguish, estrangement, heightened consciousness turning in upon itself and impotent rage at being reduced to two times two equals four.'[23] He defines the Underground Man's character type as 'generally a rebel against the prevailing norms of the society he lives in and the great forces that perpetuate them ... whatever action he takes ... is always essentially personal ... he is thus ultimately isolated ... He lives in a constant state of tension and anxiety, aggravated by what is perhaps his most distinguishing quality – a keen, often morbid, sensibility.'[24]

Jackson and Abood's observations are readily applicable to the *Tropics* and especially to the 'Henry Miller' persona who narrates them. The most obvious similarity, however, between the Underground Man and Henry Miller's narrator in the *Tropics* is that both are antiheroes. Neither of them is valiant, admirable, nor even particularly likeable, and both of them are shown engaging in all kinds of unsavory activities. In both *Tropics*, the 'Henry Miller' persona is shown lying, cheating, stealing from friends, callously using his acquaintances for his own ends, and caring only about his own creature comforts. Further, contrary to first appearances, the 'Henry Miller' persona is just as isolated and alienated in his own way as the Underground Man. In *Tropic of Cancer* he insists that he is 'utterly alone in the world';[25] after a dizzying tour of Parisian brothels, for instance, he comments, 'I could be no more truly alone than at this very moment.'[26] His alienation stems in large part from his contempt for everyone who surrounds him throughout his life (the Underground Man, of course, shares this perspective). He explains that 'everybody around me was a failure, or if not a failure, ridiculous. Especially the successful ones. The successful ones bored me to tears.'[27]

Another important reason for his sense of isolation, however, is that the face he presents to the world hides a vastly different inner self. He says, for instance, that those people who 'think they know me know nothing about me'[28] and that '[m]ost of us live the greater part of our lives submerged.'[29] His inner life is hidden from view; he says that he made the conscious decision to 'live ... the secret life of the little man in the wilderness.'[30] If it seems that the 'Henry Miller' persona is living in the hub of life, surrounded by people all the time, he is, at the same time, living in his own personal underground, which is hidden from everyone's view. Whatever the outward appearances of his social activities, he says that inside 'secretly I was praying to be left alone, to go back to my little niche, and to stay there.'[31] In fact, he frequently expresses the very same sense of disconnection from life of which the Underground Man complains (in *Tropic of Capricorn* Miller's narrator laments that he has 'lost hold of life completely').[32]

Like the Underground Man, Miller's narrator feels nothing but disgust for himself and his past; in *Tropic of Cancer* he describes himself 'lying there on the iron bed thinking what a zero I have become, what a cipher, what a nullity'[33] and meditates on the 'agonizing gutter of my wretched past.'[34] He is obsessively replaying scenes of personal humiliation in his mind: 'I thought of all the things I might have said and done, which I hadn't said or done, in the bitter, humiliating moments ... I was still smarting from those old insults and injuries.'[35] He dreams up various revenge fantasies involving all those who inflicted suffering upon him, imagining how he might blow up City Hall,[36] but at the same time recalls 'distinctly how I enjoyed my suffering.'[37] He is deeply uncertain of his real identity. Much like the Underground Man, who envisions himself either an insect or a hero, Miller's narrator muses that there was '[n]o knowing whether I was a monster or a saint'[38] and that he was 'either anonymous or the person called Henry Miller raised to the *n*th degree.'[39] Like the Underground Man, who explains his inaction by his constant awareness of his own contradictions, Miller's narrator explains his own lack of viable achievements by citing the same reasons. 'In everything I quickly saw the opposite, the contradictions, and between the real and the unreal the irony, the paradox,' the 'Henry Miller' persona insists, 'I was my own worst enemy. There was nothing I wished to do which I could just as well not do.'[40] He calls himself 'a contradiction in essence'[41] and draws attention to his own 'supersensitive brain.'[42]

Just as the Underground Man, Miller's narrator is highly unreliable, casually informing his readers that 'everything I say is a lie,'[43] but paradoxically insisting that 'even if everything ... is wrong, is prejudiced, spiteful, malevolent, even if I am a liar and a poisoner, it is nevertheless the truth.'[44] Furthermore, the 'Henry Miller' persona's attitude towards his imagined readers closely parallels the scorn and contempt of the Underground Man for the hostile men he envisions as his readers. Miller's narrator announces at the opening of *Tropic of Cancer* that his text will be 'a prolonged insult ... I am going to sing for you ... while you croak, I will dance over your dirty corpse.'[45]

The 'Henry Miller' persona's strategies towards 'his' text are once again similar to those of the Underground Man. The latter explains that he will not change or cross out anything that he writes; Miller's narrator announces, 'I have made a silent compact with myself not to change a line of what I write. I am not interested in perfecting my thoughts, nor my actions' and, notably, cites Dostoevsky as an example of 'perfection.'[46] The Underground Man repeatedly insists that his notes will have no readers. Miller's narrator in *Tropic of Cancer* is ostensibly writing his 'notes' anonymously as part of a contribution to a collectively authored *Last Book*: 'All those who have anything to say will say it here – *anonymously*.'[47]

The Underground Man goes off on digressions (for which he apologizes) and lengthy tirades, which escalate in emotional intensity, stopping only, as he says, to 'catch his breath' (5:101). Miller's narrator delivers prolonged rants on subjects ranging from Parisian prostitutes to Matisse's paintings, reaching an almost hysterical pitch of intensity, and setting off on one digression after another. Even the automatist lists generated by Miller's narrator are prefigured by the Underground Man's descriptions: 'They talked of the Caucuses, of the nature of true passion, of the card game "Galbik", of well-paying positions in the service, of the income of hussar Podkharzhevsky, whom none of them knew personally, and rejoiced that it was so large, about the extraordinary beauty and grace of Princess D., whom none of them had ever seen, finally they talked about Shakespeare's immortality' (5:146). The Underground Man divides 'his' text into two sections, the first containing his 'confessional,' set in the present (1860s St Petersburg), where he introduces himself and describes his outlook on life, and the second consisting of reminiscences of his early years and his narration of various traumatic events which still continue to haunt him and which account for present position in the underground. The 'Henry Miller' persona organizes 'his' text as two sister volumes: *Tropic of Cancer* is his 'confessional' set in the present (in 1930s Paris), where he introduces himself and describes his perspective on his life and his surroundings; *Tropic of Capricorn* is his reminiscences about his early years in the United States and the various traumatic events which transpired there that which ultimately brought him to Paris, where he is writing the books.

Even the biographical circumstances of Dostoevsky and Miller's narrators are similar. The Underground Man is forty years old; he has quit his administrative position and survives on a pittance but he refuses to move out of the urban centre into a cheaper area of the country; he is writing his *Notes*, he says, as a way to entertain himself. Miller's narrator is in his forties; he has quit his administrative position and is nearly destitute; he points out in the very beginning of *Tropic of Cancer* that he is writing not because he has to write in order to be a writer, but simply because he wants to, in the way that a person might sing something to entertain himself, even though it is 'a little off key perhaps.'[48] Interestingly, both narrators blame their early obsessive reading for contributing to their problems. The Underground Man says with deep irony that reading 'helped a great deal, – [it] stirred, delighted, and tormented' (5:127). Miller's narrator conjectures that he may have been 'spoiled in the bud by the books I read ... the taint is still there.'[49]

Like the Underground Man, Miller's narrator is very much an urban dweller who needs 'that world which is peculiar to the big cities.'[50] Suggestively, his descriptions of both Paris and New York evoke Underground Man's St Petersburg. His Paris, for instance, like St Petersburg, is 'a northern city ... erected over a swamp filled in with skulls and bones.'[51] It is just as sinister as the darker side of St Petersburg's frequented by the Underground Man; Miller's narrator, for example, talks about his attraction towards 'certain leprous streets which only revealed their sinister splendor when the light of day had oozed away.'[52] If the Underground Man's St Petersburg is 'the most abstract and intentional city on the whole planet' (5:101), Paris of the *Tropics* is a 'melange of all the cities of Europe and Central America.'[53] New York of the *Tropics* is also 'cold, glittering, malign ... erected over a hollow pit of nothingness';[54] it has its skyscrapers and the broad streets, which the 'Henry Miller' persona associates with 'the thaws of St Petersburg,'[55] but it is most notable for its darker and seedier sections, its speakeasies and dives, where the narrator lives 'permanently in the zenith of the underworld.'[56] Both cities, like

Underground Man's St Petersburg, are populated by all kinds of physical and moral grotesques, as well as by legions of prostitutes.

Notably, the encounters with these prostitutes in the *Tropics* (containing the naturalistic sexual scenes for which Miller's books were censored and banned for decades), once again parallel the treatment of sexual transactions in *Notes*. After the Underground Man's first sexual encounter with Liza, which is graphologically represented by the two sets of ellipses and a break between sections (which, incidentally, was quite *risqué* for the times and the place where it was published), he asks her: 'Just tell me what's so good about it: here you and I ... came together ... Is this how people love? Is this how two people should come together? It's a disgrace, that's what it is!' (5:155). In the *Tropics*, of course, sex is represented graphically in a way that leaves little to the imagination, but its lack of genuine human contact is also highlighted; one has only to turn to the many depictions of the lecherous character Van Norden's comically obscene attempts to have sex with a prostitute in *Tropic of Cancer*, Miller's narrator observing that 'there is no human significance in the performance.'[57] Elsewhere in *Tropic of Cancer*, the Henry Miller persona criticizes modern sexual encounters for the same reasons as the Underground Man: 'Men and women come together like broods of vultures over a stinking carcass, to mate and fly apart again ... Forward without pity, without compassion, without love, without forgiveness.'[58]

The strongest similarity between the two narrators, however, lies in the Underground Man's and the 'Henry Miller' persona's perspectives on their contemporary culture and its dominant paradigms. In Part One of *Notes*, the Underground Man attacks the idea, popular among liberal Russians of his time, that rational self-interest will one day turn mankind into one gloriously united and organized body, in which the individual will be just a tiny complacent component in a smoothly functioning apparatus of unified humanity. In the *Tropics*, the 'Henry Miller' persona attacks the American dream itself, that desire of Americans to have better lives than their parents did, along with the value system that it utilizes and the work ethic that underlies it. Stories about someone starting at the very bottom of society and then, by perseverance and hard work, making his way to the very top, elicit nothing but scorn from Miller's narrator, who sees the whole scenario as absurd: 'the dream of a sick America, mounting higher and higher, first messenger, then operator, then manager, then chief, then superintendent, then vice-president, then president, then trust magnate, then beer baron, then Lord of all the Americas, the money god, the god of gods, the clay of clay, nullity on high, zero with ninety-seven thousand decimals fore and aft.'[59] The idea that achieving a greater social status or accumulating more possessions somehow makes one happier or more worthy than the next person seems preposterous to Miller's narrator. The idea that society's production of more and more objects constitutes progress elicits his scorn: 'Production! More nuts and bolts, more barbed wire, more dog biscuits, more lawn mowers, more ball bearings, more high explosives, more tanks, more poison gas, more soap, more toothpaste ... *Forward!*'[60]

The work ethic itself, as the means through which these possessions are both produced and obtained and the way through which personal survival is secured, horrifies and frightens Miller's narrator, who sees it as the most effective way of suppressing the individual and absorbing him into the social apparatus. 'If you want bread you've got to ... get in lock step,'[61] he says. According to him, 'The gospel of work ... is nothing, at bottom, but the doctrine of inertia,'[62] since it prevents the individual from breaking free of the oppressive socium. Starving in Paris, the narrator thinks that anything is better than going back to America, 'to work the treadmill.'[63] The immense apparatus of organized anonymous humanity envisioned by the Underground Man as the dystopic future has turned into the reality of an American factory where the individual is nothing but a part of the production process. The 'Henry Miller' persona's response to this situation is again similar to that already envisioned by the Underground Man: rebellion even at the expense of both logic and self-interest. 'I want to prevent as many men as possible from pretending that they have to do this or that because they must earn a living,' says Miller's narrator, '*It is not true.* One can starve to death – it is much better. Every man who voluntarily starves to death jams another cog in the automatic process ... I don't want to be a part of this thing, this infernal automatic process.'[64]

Rebellion against 'personal good' (as society sees it) and logic in favour of personal freedom (as foreseen by the Underground Man) is the choice that Miller's narrator makes over and over, calling himself 'the random shot on the white billiard table of logic.'[65] He sees 'logic run[ning] rampant, with bloody cleaver flashing.'[66] According to him, logic, like economics, sciences, and mathematics, is just a weapon of the state against individual behaviour that deviates too much from the mean. Like the Underground Man, who anthropomorphizes the mathematical equation $2+2=4$ into a mocking figure of an obnoxious man who stands in his path, Miller's narrator also develops a personal and distinctly negative set of associations with the same equation. His mentally ill sister is home-schooled by their despotic mother, who brutalizes her for being incapable of solving simple mathematical problems: 'the mother towering over her with a ruler, saying two and two makes how much? and the sister screaming *five*. Bang! *no, seven*, Bang!' (In a Parisian interview given much later in life, Miller reveals that this description was fully autobiographic, adding 'À la fin, elle devenait hystérique, elle lançait n'importe quel nombre. Et, chaque fois, ma mère lui administrait une gifle. Et moi, j'étais là … j'entendais tout. C'était … J'avais la sueur qui coulait.')[67] The narrator is deeply affected by observing the scene, 'accepting the tortures inflicted upon [his sister] and nourishing them with [his] supersensitive brain.'[68] It also demonstrates to him, however, that insistence on the limits set by mathematics and science leads to a totalitarianism of sorts, a tyranny of logic and reason (No! Wrong! Bang!), whose own limitations go unnoticed, and helps him decide early on that he will choose absolute freedom over the tyranny of a strictly regulated logical world: 'I wanted to be free, free to do and to give only as my whims dictated.'[69]

If the Underground Man uses the image of the anthill to suggest the end product of social utopias, in which the individual of the future will be as insignificant as a single ant and where only the collective will have a meaningful identity (5:118), Miller's narrator sees his own society as an impersonal hive, a 'million-footed mob,'[70] announcing, however, that he 'would not be drowned in the hive, like the others.'[71] While the Underground Man chooses the symbol of the Crystal Palace, or the 'crystal edifice, eternally imperishable,' to represent both the crowning glory of collective endeavour as imagined by social utopians and its hollowness (5:120), Miller's narrator employs the image of the skyscraper to represent both the 'very summit of [American] ambition' and its futility: 'From the top of the Empire State Building I looked down one night … [at] the human ants with whom I had crawled … In their fruitless desperation they had reared this colossal edifice which was their pride and boast,'[72] one of the many 'hideous buildings … [which emit] music of such sullen despair and bankruptcy as to make the flesh shrivel.'[73] If Miller has nothing but suspicion for the kind of society that produces such artifacts, impressive as they may seem, it is only one example of his general suspicion of civilization itself. Like the Underground Man who attacks the idea that civilization is a positive force that softens and improves mankind, arguing that it only makes for bloodier and more horrible wars (5:111) as well as for more complex natures open to a greater variety of sensations (5:112), Miller's narrator asks rhetorically, 'At this very moment… was not the earth giddy with crime and distress? Had one single element of man's nature been altered, vitally, fundamentally altered, by the incessant march of history?'[74] commenting elsewhere that a civilized man is merely a man who has 'complicated needs.'[75]

It is not surprising then, that the 'Henry Miller' persona, living in an ultra-civilized society whose horrific twentieth-century present is the Underground Man's nightmarish future, should open 'his' notes where *Notes from Underground* end. The Underground Man, of course, ends the notes with a famous statement that his generation is 'born dead, and for a long time we haven't even been born of living fathers, and we like it more and more' (5:179). *Tropic of Cancer* opens with the words, 'I am living at the Villa Borghese … We are all alone here and we are dead.'[76]

The numerous close parallels between the *Tropics* and *Notes from Underground*, especially between the personas of the narrators and their philosophical outlook on their respective societies, suggest more than a casual intertextuality between the books and provide ample evidence that Dostoevsky's text did indeed serve as a prototype for Miller when he wrote the *Tropics*. Nonetheless, while the *Tropics* and the 'Henry Miller' persona preserve some of the key features of *Notes from Underground* and of the Underground Man (as described by Jackson and Abood), although transposed into a different linguistic, temporal, and cultural matrix, Miller's narrator is not simply a replica of the Underground Man. Despite corresponding internally to the Underground Man, externally he exhibits all the features of his psychological opposite, the man of action. This outer mask is not only convincing but a vital necessity for his survival.

Unlike the Underground Man, who is safely ensconced in his nineteenth-century Russia, living on a tiny but fixed income, and sending out a servant to procure all that he needs for sustenance, Miller and his narrator are barely surviving in the cataclysmic twentieth-century between two world wars, an era of market crashes and social crises of all kinds, an era of ever-expanding and depersonalizing financial conglomerates on the one hand and of ever more repressive and dehumanizing political systems on the other. Edward Abood observes that '[b]y 1920 the cultural chaos that Dostoevsky had predicted was already a reality,'[77] and Miller's narrator, living like his creator in Paris of the 1930s, is caught in the chaos (he says that 'chaos is the score upon which reality is written'),[78] attempting to exploit it for his own ends but most of the time just trying to survive. Like Miller himself at the time, his narrator has no fixed income and is always hovering on the brink of starvation. He cannot send anyone out to do his errands. A dwelling, no matter how squalid, is frequently too great a luxury, and he finds himself walking the streets or sleeping in parks, where the police brutalize him. As a result, he is forced to take his underground where no one can see it – into his mind – and to behave outwardly in a way that does not attract undue attention from the powers that be. The necessity of hiding his inner self is all too clear; when he manages to land a short-lived job in Paris, for instance, he gets 'a letter from the big mogul upstairs ... and between a few sarcastic phrases about my more than ordinary intelligence, he hinted pretty plainly that I'd better learn my place and toe the mark or there'd be what's what to pay ... After that I never used a polysyllabic word in conversation,' he confides, 'in fact, I hardly ever opened my trap ... I played the high-grade moron, which is what they wanted of us.'[79] Finding himself in hostile surroundings in America, 'feel[ing] as though someone's got a gun against [his] back all the time,' his response is to 'try not to seem too intelligent ... [to] try to pretend that [he] [is] vitally interested in the crop, in the weather, in the elections.'[80]

Miller's version of the Underground Man, outwardly just another man in the crowd, inwardly a raging dissenter, is more than a creative metaphor; it is an attempt to address the problem of the individual trying to survive and retain his individuality in the midst of the mass cataclysms of the twentieth century. Like Dostoevsky in *Notes*, Miller is reflecting in the *Tropics* upon the social and historical realities that shaped the 'Henry Miller' persona, who becomes more than a stand-in for his author, an embodiment of a social phenomenon. Like Dostoevsky, Miller is intensely critical of his society and sceptical of the individual's ability to withstand the depersonalizing and suppressing tendency of his age. Unlike Dostoevsky, however, Miller interprets the underground as one of the few ways the individual, especially a creative individual, can retain his uniqueness under the pressure of the state and resist the pull of the hive. Miller's underground man becomes a hero for our times, and the underground becomes one of the few places where personal survival and artistic creation is possible. If Dostoevsky's underground is a place of stagnation and hopelessness, Miller's underground becomes a place of resistance and hope. Miller's twentieth-century Underground Man became an important model for other writers of Villa Seurat, who used his version together with Dostoevsky's original archetype in the construction of their own narrators and texts.

Notes from Underground and Anaïs Nin

Miller's version of the Underground Man, with his seemingly complacent public persona and rebellious private self, proved to be particularly important to the work that Anaïs Nin was producing in the 1930s and to her larger concerns as a woman writer, even though she paid less attention to the philosophy of the Underground Man (a particular concern for Miller) and more to his psychology. Like Miller, Nin had never written about Notes from Underground or its narrator, although there are scattered references to an 'underground' in her diaries and letters. She was certainly well aware of Notes and its importance, if only because of her thorough familiarity with Gide's book on Dostoevsky, in which Notes is placed among Dostoevsky's greatest works (she wrote about her appreciation of 'Gide's explanation of Dostoevsky'[81] a number of times); in fact, she cites some of Gide's words about the Notes in her diary. She was also instrumental in editing Miller's texts, especially the Tropics, where his version of the Underground Man is developed and encapsulated.

An examination of Nin's texts through the lens of Notes from Underground, however, presents special problems. First, Nin's narrators and central characters are almost exclusively women, not men, which goes against the grain of classic analysis of the Underground Man's archetype and of his impact on other writers and texts; both Jackson and Abood, for instance, consider only male characters among the Underground Man's literary descendants, as if being female somehow automatically disqualifies a character from 'retain[ing] an essential kinship'[82] with the Dostoevskian archetype. Second, while it is obvious that both Nin and the majority of her critics believed that the diary represents her real legacy as a writer, her sprawling diaries, which extend into all her other writing (according to Nin and her scholars, her 'novels, short stories and criticism … [are] distillations from the 150 volumes or so of the Diary,'[83] with which they still retain a vital connection) also challenge traditional notions of a self-contained text with definable boundaries, posing a difficulty when they have to be read closely through the prism of another text. The diaries' relationship with the fictional writing is not straightforward either, since characters from the one emerge in the other and it is again not clear where one ends and the other begins. In the 1930s Nin herself saw this as a great handicap, writing despairingly, 'My book [a novel] and my journal step on each other's feet constantly. I can neither divorce nor reconcile them.'[84] Finally, the bibliographic peculiarities of the diaries add another layer of complexity in a comparative analysis of her texts.

On the other hand, there does not appear to be any reason why a character cannot have an affinity with the Dostoevskian archetype just because she is a woman. One scholar who examines this problem as it relates to female characters from a number of different literary texts even proposes that there is an Underground Woman type, directly descended from Dostoevsky's Underground Man. This Underground Woman 'permits no voice other than her own to represent or define her ... [she is] tormented by excessive consciousness, indulging in self-analysis ... [she] is angry at society, which she perceives as an essentially masculine-oriented enterprise, for its systematically indifferent, often callous treatment of her ... she is typically alienated from others ... and spends a good deal of her time imagining alternative configurations of reality ... [b]ut at the same time she longs for fellowship and a place to belong,'[85] a description that has an obvious affinity with Nin's narrators and to which we will return. As far as the provenance and cohesiveness of Nin's texts is concerned, the flexibility and accommodation expected of a scholar who examines her body of work – a fluid composite of the diaries, the fictional writings, and the essays, with 'all the pieces ... working in harmony'[86] – is no greater than that required in an examination of any continuous or multipartite closure-defying text.

The conflict between the autobiographical/factual and the fictional that Nin felt she had to resolve back in the 1930s is no longer perceived as a conflict, a fact that Nin was already becoming aware of in the 1970s, when friendly and not-so-friendly critics argued that her diary itself belongs to two different provenances as a 'journal-novel.'[87] One of Nin's own students and protégés, Tristine Rainer, who became a noted scholar specializing in contemporary journal writing and narrative autobiography, has shown that diary writing can seamlessly blend with the fictional and the literary and that the autobiographical subject is not necessarily different from the construct of the fictional narrator. General attitudes about the nonfiction/fiction divide also changed with time. If James Atlas felt the need to point out that autobiographical writing is not always strictly factual when he proclaimed the last decade of the twentieth century to be the 'Age of the Literary Memoir' in the *New York Times*,[88] in the first decade of the twenty-first century popular 'reality' shows continuously oscillate between the factual/documentary and the fictional/scripted, without anyone so much as raising an eyebrow. Nin's diaries are valuable as a source of biographical information about her circle of friends and herself, but they can certainly also be viewed as carefully constructed creative texts involving a number of carefully delineated characters (Nin, in fact, asked readers in the 1970s to 'notice that I am calling them characters' as opposed to historical personages or biographical portraits).[89]

As far as the circumstances of the diaries' publications are concerned, it is of course important to be aware of the various complexities resulting from the expurgation of the diaries and their different editions. The first publication of the diaries (now referred to as the expurgated edition) occurred in the years 1966–74. Nin opened the series with her diary of the 1930s, when she met Miller for the first time, in the year that marked 'the beginning of [her] life as a writer.'[90] This first publication had three editors, but Nin herself was always closely involved in the editing process.[91] The expurgated edition includes numerous deletions and alterations necessitated by her belief that she should protect the privacy of everyone involved (as well as avoid the revelation of her many affairs). The second publication, referred to as the unexpurgated edition, began nine years after Nin's death under the main editorship of Rupert Pole, Nin's second husband and literary executor (her literary agent Gunther Stuhlmann also contributed to the editing process). It too covered the 1930s. Rupert Pole claimed that this series represents Nin's 'original diaries ... just as she wrote them,'[92] but it is clear that these volumes were heavily edited to focus on different relationships (especially sexual ones). The second series consists of *Henry and June: From the Unexpurgated Diary of Anaïs Nin* (1986); *Incest: From a 'Journal of Love'; The Unexpurgated Diary of Anaïs Nin, 1932–34* (1992); *Fire: From a 'Journal of Love'; The Unexpurgated Diary of Anaïs Nin, 1934–1937* (1995); and *Nearer the Moon: From a 'Journal of Love'; The Unexpurgated Diary of Anaïs Nin, 1937–1939* (1996).

All of these versions and variations present a certain challenge to an examination of Nin's text (few scholars were granted full access to the original diary notebooks before the death of Rupert Pole in July 2006). At the same time, despite the expurgation and the editing, a composite of the texts published to date provides the reader with a reasonable jigsaw-puzzle picture of what the original diaries must be like – some of the pieces are still missing, but the general pattern is clear. Together with her fictional writings of the 1930s (mainly the so-called 'prose-poem' *The House of Incest* [1936] and her 'novelettes,' such as 'Winter of Artifice,' originally written in the mid-1930s),[93] her criticism, and her letters, which she also includes in the diaries, her published diaries constitute her body of literary work during the most important period of her life in Paris, when she was feverishly searching for her own literary voice as a woman writer.

Nin's autobiographical, fictional, and critical writings may formally belong to different genres, but they are unified by a single autobiographical subject, which is especially true for her work of the 1930s, our primary concern here. Nin repeatedly said that she herself is the narrator of the fictional texts in much the same way as she is the narrator of the diary, a point that was enthusiastically developed by many students of her work; she suggested to one interviewer, for example, that the 'I' in *The House of Incest* is an autobiographical persona: 'My trouble is … seeing too much … I wrote that in *House of Incest*: I see too much.'[94] In the diary she writes that *House of Incest* contains 'the distillation of [her own] experience,' which is recorded in the diary itself in a more direct and expansive manner.[95]

Nin's autobiographical subject of the 1930s, the 'I' that she constructs in her diaries (as seen both in the unexpurgated text and in the so-called first series), her fictional texts like the prose-poem *The House of Incest* (most of her 'novelettes' have a third-person omniscient narrator, but they all focus on the consciousness of a young woman), and her personal essays, does not seem, at first glance, to have much in common with Dostoevsky's Underground Man. The narrator of the diary lovingly describes the many beauties of the village of Louveciennes, her ancient house, and her comfortable and luxurious life.[96] The narrator of *The House of Incest* first appears to be a woman of inner harmony and freedom, who 'loved the ease … [of her] suave voyages … breathing in an ecstasy of dissolution.'[97] The 'narrator' of Nin's essays, as, for instance, of her introduction to Miller's *Tropic of Cancer*, appears to be coolly analytical and confidently intellectual. All of this, however, is quickly revealed to be a front or only a short-lived phase. The narrator of the diaries complains of her sense of being imprisoned[98] and of the lies that she needs 'to cover [her]self,'[99] as if they were 'costumes.'[100] The narrator of the *The House of Incest* is 'choked with anguish.'[101] The 'narrator' of the introduction to *Tropic of Cancer* includes herself in the dramatic description of the 'we' that are 'drowning' in the 'cultural void' and 'fighting with shadows.'[102]

Like Dostoevsky's Underground Man, Nin's narrator/persona exhibits all the characteristics of an antihero. In the diaries, Nin readily depicts her own meddling, obsessiveness, neuroses, and paranoias. Her unexpurgated diaries also document her lies and her manipulations, as well as what she calls her 'disturbed, dangerous, erotic side.'[103] She writes, 'I ... disturb, upset, create tragedy ... I deceive, I cheat, I am lazy ... I make scenes. I fight. I lie.'[104] When critics charged her with narcissism for dwelling on the compliments paid to her by various people in the first published set of the diaries, she responded, 'Anyone who can read through a psychological character knows that I wasn't very pleased with myself,'[105] and her lack of satisfaction with herself readily comes across in all her texts. Nin frequently relates her disgust with herself and her life, replaying scenes of past humiliations in her mind, subjecting herself to what she calls her 'inquisitional self-lacerations'[106] and 'wish[ing] [she] could rid [her]self of [her] whole life.'[107] The young woman whose consciousness forms the focus of 'Winter of Artifice' (the central and longest text in Nin's eponymous book) is deeply dissatisfied with herself and her 'insincerities.'[108] The narrator of the more poetic and allegorical *House of Incest* also talks of being 'enmeshed in [her] lies,' of being cornered by her 'great mounting, choking fear,' and of dreading her own insanity.[109]

Nin's narrators share with the Underground Man their exaggerated consciousness and sensitivity, which makes them aware of their own contradictions and frequently incapable of action. In the diary, the narrator is extremely concerned about how she appears to others, and continuously analyses what others may think of her. At one point she worries that she will see herself 'in caricature.' She asks: 'Why should I care?' and despairingly concludes: 'But I do care. I care about everything. Emotionalism and sensibility are my quicksands.'[110] She notes, 'I have the defect of being hypersensitive,'[111] exclaiming at another point, 'I despise my own hypersensitiveness.'[112] She writes that her 'mind ... is bigger than all the rest of [her], an inexorable conscience' that 'watch[es] her life,'[113] and reflects that it may be 'a greater agony to live this life in which my awareness makes a thousand circles while others' makes only one.'[114]

The young woman of 'Winter of Artifice' also has a heightened consciousness which makes her aware of all her external and internal contradictions and prevents her from acting: 'she pitied herself ... for having expected everything ... At the same time she knew that this was not true. Her mind ran in two directions as she talked, and so did her feelings.'[115] Meanwhile (like the Underground Man who admits to putting on an act when he tells Liza about the horrors of prostitution, but who 'beg[ins] to feel what [he] was saying' [5:155]), she is conscious of lying when she confronts her father for failing her in various ways ('the scene she knew best ... even though it became an utter lie' [94]), but she also begins to genuinely feel what she claims to be feeling, projecting an emotional state for a hypothetical situation ('this statement was untrue only in time ... what would I be feeling now if I had [done what I say I did]').[116]

Similarly, the narrator of *The House of Incest* is acutely aware of the many different contradictions within herself and of the incompleteness of everything she is saying. She says that she is 'a woman ... smiling always behind my gravest words, mocking my own intensity.'[117] It is also noteworthy that another character in the book, Jeanne, who shares a voice with the narrator at several points in the text,[118] delivers a speech which sounds as though it emanated from the Underground Man himself: 'As soon as I utter a phrase my sincerity dies, becomes a lie whose coldness chills me ... I am so utterly lonely, but I also have such a fear that my isolation be broken through, and I no longer be the head and ruler of my universe.'[119]

Interestingly, in *The House of Incest* Nin also picks up two of the metaphors in *Notes from Underground*, specifically those of paralysis (the Underground Man says that 'paralysis was hovering above [him] [5:134]) and of flaying (the Underground Man says, 'I am vain to such an extent it is as if my skin were stripped off my body, and the air itself caused me pain' [5:174]) and turns them into the symbolic figure of the Paralytic who cannot act and into the equally symbolic figure of the 'Modern Christ,' who describes having his skin 'carefully and neatly peeled ... Not an inch of skin left on my body. It was all gently pulled off ... the soft warm air and the perfumes penetrated me like needles through every open bleeding pore ... I shrieked with pain.'[120]

The narrator of the diary reveals that she feels isolated and alienated, 'near death from solitude.'[121] However, unlike the Underground Man, whose inner conflicts are played out in The isolation of his squalid room, she is alone in a life of luxury; she looks at the gate of her estate property and says, 'it takes on the air of a prison gate ... [but] the obstacle lies always within one's self ... I often stand at the window staring at the large closed iron gate, as if hoping to obtain from this contemplation a reflection of my inner obstacles to a full, open life.'[122] She feels completely alienated from the social sphere to which she belongs by marriage to a high-profile banker and feels herself surrounded by '[u]gly, unimaginative, dead people.'[123] She repeatedly expresses her sense of being cut off from real life: 'I feel I am not living';[124] 'You ... believe you are living ... and [then] you discover that you are not living, that you are hibernating.'[125] In her search for real life, she tries to find fellowship but is not successful: 'I was like a stranger in a strange country ... Over and over again I was thrust, and thrust myself, into roomfuls of people with a genuine desire to amalgamate with them, but my fears proved greater than my desire and, after a conflict, I fled. Once alone, I reversed the process and suffered to be locked out and abandoned by those who were talking and laughing in a commonly shared enjoyment and pleasures.'[126]

She looks outside 'proper society' to the quasi-Bohemians but is ultimately disappointed even here, concluding, 'They are as mediocre as the bankers, and I have been so disillusioned by their emptiness, weakness.'[127] She ultimately decides, 'I must learn to stand alone. Nobody can really follow me all the way, understand me completely.'[128] She wants to be with other people and yet, paradoxically, she also 'eludes them all [because] I want to be alone.'[129] At the same time, she is frightened by her inability to communicate with others: 'I can't talk. I can't manifest myself ... It becomes an anxiety ... Communication haunts me.'[130] Her sense of alienation and loneliness suffuses all of her experiences ('Man,' she insists, 'can never know the kind of loneliness a woman knows').[131]

Like the Underground Man, she is a compulsive reader who becomes addicted to reading in her early youth in order to avoid the company of her peers: 'I read avidly, drunkenly ... I rebelled against the rowdy, brutal Public School Number 9';[132] 'the world forced me into fantasy,'[133] she says. Again like the Underground Man, who blames books for providing an irritating and ultimately frustrating stimulus, she blames books for encouraging her escapism (she remembers herself 'from childhood [on] ... living in created dreams as inside a cocoon, dreams born of reading, always reading')[134] and setting up unrealistic expectations of her future life. In an interesting twist, it is Dostoevsky whom she particularly singles out as the author who leads his readers to expect constant high drama in their life, and thus sets them up for ultimate disappointment.[135] She turns to her diary, which becomes her haven and her only real means of self-expression, but which, at the same time, further separates her from life.

Similarly, the young woman of the 'Winter of Artifice' novelette is a compulsive reader from childhood on (significantly, when she grows up she specifically prefers Dostoevsky)[136] and is withdrawn even as a little girl. She too feels alienated, lonely, and secretive. Aware of all kinds of 'subterranean channels' within her,[137] she too keeps a diary that allows her to express herself but also isolates her from life and becomes her underground ('she shut herself up within the walls of her diary. She held long conversations with herself, through the diary';[138] 'This diary ... became ... a secretive thing, another wall between herself and that world which it seemed forbidden her ever to enter').[139] She tries to make contact with others (most notably with her father), but finds that 'all communication [was] paralyzed by the falsity.'[140]

The narrator of *The House of Incest* also talks about her loneliness and the sense of being isolated from others ('I cannot be certain of any event or place, only of my solitude').[141] She tries to connect to life, but fails and ultimately withdraws into her own dreaming: 'Collision with reality blurs my vision and submerges me into the dream ... the distance between the crowd, between the others and me, grows wider.'[142] Evocatively (in view of the Underground Man's identification with a mouse hiding beneath the floor), she imagines herself 'in the cellar where I nibbled at the candles and the incense stored away with the mice.'[143] Like the Underground Man she wants to contact others but is afraid of what might happen if others enter her underground: 'I am so utterly lonely, but I also have such a fear that my isolation be broken through, and I no longer be the head and ruler of my universe.'[144]

All of Nin's narrators are unable to fully participate in life. She writes in the diary that she cannot act because she is 'stopped on [her] course by all kinds of thoughts,'[145] even though she is only too aware of 'the rigidities and the patterns made by the rational mind.'[146] Significantly, she goes on to illustrate her predicament by referring to Gide's words about the Underground Man: 'thought arrests action and being'[147] (Gide's actual words are: '*Notes from Underground*] is the keystone of [Dostoevsky's] whole work, the clue to his thought. "*He who thinks, acts not* ..."'[emphasis and ellipsis in the original]).[148] Again like the Underground Man, who makes so-called excursions into reality after which he returns to his solitary dreams and imaginings, she collides with reality only to withdraw into herself: 'I felt overwhelmed by reality ... When I collide with it ... I seem to experience a sudden break, I feel I swing in space, I go up in the air, I create enormous distance. Then after the collision, I feel submerged into dreams ... And then I cease to live in reality. I feel that I miss it, always. I am living either in a dream or in pure sensuality. No intermediate life. The overtones or the undertones.'[149] Contributing to all this are her deep insecurities about her looks, her talents, her intelligence, and so forth.

Nin's female narrators share many psychological features with Dostoevsky's nineteenth-century Underground Man, closely matching the Underground Woman as described in the outline of the type cited earlier. They exhibit all the signs of an excessive consciousness, they are constantly involved in self-analysis, they are alienated from others around them but long for fellowship, they imagine alternative ways of living her life, and they certainly resent what they view as society's indifferent treatment of them as woman artists, especially as they witness the success that their male colleagues are able to reap. Especially pertinent in light of the claim that the Underground Woman 'tells her own story and permits no voice other than her own to represent or define her'[150] is Nin's narrators' concern with making sure that no one else defines them. The narrator of the diary announces, 'Henry [Miller] cannot impose a pattern on me, because I make my own.'[151] She goes into analysis, but *never* actually permits any of the analysts to have the last word. She says that the psychoanalyst 'does the dissecting and the explorative operations,' but then she continues: 'I bring them home, and sift them to catch impurities and errors in the diary.'[152] In the end, she is the one analysing both herself and her psychoanalysts.

Nin's narrators have an even greater affinity with Miller's version of the twentieth-century Underground Man developed in the *Tropics*, and especially with his notion of an internal underground, a social dissenter hidden behind a socially compliant outward persona. This affinity, however, must be considered within the context of Nin's evergrowing concern with discovering what she called a woman's way of writing – an issue she had already touched upon in her early study of D.H. Lawrence. During the Villa Seurat period, Nin became especially focused on the need to express herself not only as a writer, but specifically as a woman writer, a necessity that she expressed many times to Miller and Durrell, and which they both acknowledged. Nin writes in the diary that at the end of one particularly intense three-way argument at Villa Seurat, where she insisted that she will 'go another, the woman's way' as a writer, both Miller and Durrell respectfully agreed that 'we have a real woman artist before us, the first one.'[153]

While the exact definition of a woman's way of writing eluded Nin to the very end of her life, she repeatedly returned to it in poetically vague language, proposing that 'woman's creation far from being like a man's must be exactly like a creation of children, that is it must come out of her own blood, englobed by her womb, nourished with her own milk. It must be a human creation, of flesh ... the woman artist has to fuse creation and life in her own way, or in her own womb if you prefer ... Woman wants to destroy aloneness, recover the original paradise. The art of woman must be born in the womb-cells of the mind. She must be the link between the synthetic products of man's mind and the elements.'[154] Nin's understanding of what constitutes womanhood rankled countless feminist critics of her work, who labelled it – with considerable justification – 'an alternative form of sexism.'[155] Nin, however, continued to argue publically in her debates, essays, and, subsequently, lectures that a woman is fundamentally different from a man in her need to create harmony, to build bridges, and to avoid destructiveness in her relationships with others. Privately, however (as seen in the sections of the diary that were published after her death), Nin agonized about how to reconcile her own forbidden desires, 'evil' tendencies, and destructive actions, which she identified with her fearless artistic self, with her determination to avoid hurting others, which she identified as her feminine needs. Although she approached a practical solution to this problem as early as her Lawrence study, where she approved of Lawrence's advice to a woman artist to be internally dauntless but externally demure, in other words, to write one way but appear another, as his 'delicate hints to the [female] artist-builder in outward becomingness,'[156] Nin found the real solution to the problem of how to remain true both to her vision of her own 'womanhood' and her artistic identity in Miller's twentieth-century Underground Man.

Miller's version of the Underground Man as a smoldering dissident, a cultural vigilante, whose nonconformist private self was safely hidden behind a seemingly complacent public self, must have made some sense to Nin in her personal dilemma, if only because it was adopted as a strategy by her various narrators and because it became her own strategy for the publication of the diary. To the same underground to which Miller's Underground Man relegated to his soul, away from prying eyes, Nin consigned those sections of the diary that were to be published only after both she and the main players of her personal drama were dead. In the unexpurgated diaries of the 1930s we find a passage in which the narrator meditates on the contradictions in her own personality that make her 'exert her power ... to win men' but '[do] not give [her] joy in destruction' that would have been brought about by an openness about her relationships. She writes, 'what evil I could do ... this evil I do in my journal. My evil will be posthumous – the ruthless truths!'[157] The polished exterior persona of Mrs Anaïs Guiler, banker's wife, gracious hostess, and kind patron of the arts, gives way in the 'secret' diaries to Anaïs Nin, the iconoclastic writer and enraged dissenter, who questions and ultimately discards social mores, revels in her capacity to act fearlessly even if it means doing harm and destroying, and storms against society. Inspired by Dostoevsky's Underground Man and by Miller's twentieth-century version of the same character type, Nin provides her readers with a twentieth-century Underground Woman, whose psychology she traces and examines in all her writings of the 1930s and beyond.

Notes from Underground and Lawrence Durrell

Like Miller and Nin, Durrell paid close attention to Dostoevsky's Notes from Underground and to their narrator. There is considerable evidence testifying to Durrell's heightened interest in Notes from Underground. He cites Notes in the epigraphs to his own works at least twice – once in his novel Tunc (1968) and once in chapter 3 of his Key to Modern British Poetry (1952).[158] Durrell mentions Notes in his correspondence and includes obvious references to them in his own texts. The connection between his work and Notes has never been explored by Durrell's critics, although it has not gone unnoticed. For instance, Richard Pine, author of Lawrence Durrell: The Mindscape (1994) notes the link between the concept of freedom in Durrell's writing and in Notes, suggesting that Durrell might have 'derived inspiration from [the Notes'] closing lines.'[159] The Black Book in particular has been repeatedly linked with Notes. Kenneth Rexroth described Durrell's Black Book in 1960 as 'one of the first and best books of its kind – that long spate of tales of the life and loves of the Underground Man that have become the characteristic literary fad of the last twenty years. It is a tale of a wretched warren of loathsome characters, and like Dostoevsky's manifesto [Notes from the Underground] ... its moral point is that all such people can do is debauch, in rotten frivolity, the ignorant and trusting innocent.'[160] In another article written the same year, Rexroth claims that Dostoevsky's Underground Man is 'the character who forms the pattern for most of the people in The Black Book,' and that both The Black Book and Notes belong to the same 'tradition of "bitter comedy."'[161] Rexroth's interpretation of Notes is problematic (especially his remarks about the 'moral point' of Dostoevsky's text), but his argument about the connection between Durrell's characters and Dostoevsky's Underground Man deserves to be examined more closely.

Durrell's *Black Book* is a complex, intricately constructed, and self-consciously erudite text, written partially in response to Miller's repeated entreaties to see some of Durrell's writings. The bulk of *The Black Book* was written in the period beginning in November 1936 and ending in February 1937, when Durrell was a corresponding member of Villa Seurat and a self-proclaimed disciple of Miller. Durrell regarded *The Black Book* as his first real book; in his introduction to the 1960 edition, he explains that it was his first real attempt at 'self-exploration,' 'to see whether there was anything inside [him] worth expressing.' Despite Durrell's deep admiration for Miller, he wanted to avoid being excessively influenced by him or any of the other writers he admired at the time, and to stand independently as a writer, to 'hea[r] the sound of [his] own voice, lame and halting perhaps, but nevertheless [his] own.'[162] Still, there are many features linking *The Black Book* with Miller's books and with a number of other literary texts and archetypes. Durrell himself recognized both Miller's influence (he wrote in his 1960 introduction to the book that the 'reader will discern the influence of *Tropic of Cancer* in many passages,')[163] and the influence of 'the major Russian writers he had been reading recently ... especially Dostoevsky,'[164] and he attempted to tone down obvious instances of influence or to give them a different twist (he wrote Miller, for instance, that he was trying to 'demillerise' the book as he revised it).[165] All the same, a reading of *The Black Book* through the lens of *Notes from Underground* reveals a number of close correspondences between the two texts as well as several instances where Dostoevsky's plot, imagery, and character psychology, though still recognizable in Durrell's text, appear to undergo ironic reconfigurations, suggesting at the very least that Durrell attempted to engage in *The Black Book* both with Dostoevsky's archetype of the Underground Man and with Miller's interpretation of that archetype in the *Tropics*.

The Black Book is narrated by Lawrence Lucifer, a man in his twenties, writing his first novel. His novel is set in England, where he had lived and taught before deciding to become a writer and moving to Greece. Lawrence Lucifer has been generally identified as Durrell's self-portrait; Ian MacNiven, a noted Durrell scholar and biographer, writes unequivocally that 'Lawrence Lucifer in the book *was* Lawrence Durrell in 1937, as nearly as he could recreate himself.'[166] *The Black Book* has a second narrator, however, Herbert 'Death' Gregory, with whom Lucifer is closely involved, acting as the ego to Gregory's 'tender id.'[167] Gregory is a forty-year-old Englishman whose diary Lucifer discovers in the tiny basement room that he rents in London's seedy Hotel Regina and includes in his novel. He explains, 'I do not pretend to interpret. It would be too much to expect of the interrogative ego ... [rather I will] annotate it, punctuate, edit. Perhaps add a pert little introduction of my own and an apparatus of variants.'[168]

Of the two narrators, it is Gregory who appears at first glance to have the most in common with Dostoevsky's Underground Man as depicted in *Notes*: he is the same age as the Underground Man in part one of *Notes*; he is living on what appears to be a similarly small income in a similarly squalid room (literally underground, this time) on the outskirts of a large urban capital (London, in his case); he despises the way he looks (he examines his reflection in the mirror 'with a loathing that [he is] incapable of communicating to the paper');[169] he does not seem to have any real pursuits (he has been involved in vaguely literary activity but now he mostly reads and broods upon his past and present); finally, he writes his own story in a journal which he purportedly intends to be a private document.

Gregory's psychological profile also resembles that of the Underground Man. Like the Underground Man, whose excessive consciousness makes for constant self-observation, Gregory is constantly observing and analysing himself. He laments this 'eternal consciousness of oneself in substance and in psyche'[170] but feels powerless to change it: 'I am always aware of myself,' he observes, 'as an actor on an empty stage, his only audience the critical self.'[171] Like the Underground Man, he is constantly thinking about the past, revisiting every scene, and hating himself even more: 'Retrospect! Retrospect!' he laments, 'What a hive of memories I have become.'[172] As a result of his constant spying on himself and his obsessive self-analysis, he becomes particularly aware of and disgusted with his 'huge egotism and terror of [him]self.'[173] He admits that he engages in the 'perverse business of torturing [himself]' and that he enjoys his psychological suffering, which becomes 'a delicious sensation, like standing on the edge of a cliff.'[174] His journal becomes an extension of his propensity to torture himself; after rereading it, Gregory becomes 'a little weary and disgusted at the way [he] prey[s] upon [himself],'[175] but he keeps writing, much like the Underground Man who thinks that his own notes may be his 'corrective punishment' (5:178).

Like Dostoevsky's narrator, Gregory is too aware of the many inconsistencies within himself to be able to act. The Underground Man says that 'the direct, lawful, and immediate fruit of consciousness is inertia' (5:108), and Gregory echoes him when he thinks about his own inability to act: 'All my life I have done this – imagined my actions. I have never taken part in them.'[176] Instead, Gregory lives the life of the mind, his 'imagination ... a vast lumber room of ideas. There is no dogma which does not find an echo').[177] He is cut off from life itself and although he consoles himself 'with Pascal's remark about the thinking reed'[178] when he thinks about his lack of actual life experience, he is deeply unsatisfied.

Gregory's sole activity is reading and, as with Underground Man, the books serve as yet another buffer between him and the experience of real life; Lucifer mentions the 'monstrous behaviour of literature which [Gregory] use[s] as a cloak for his terrors and realities.'[179] Interestingly, Gregory's reading list appears to include Dostoevsky's novels, possibly even *Notes from Underground* itself. At one point, talking about his relationship with a street girl named Grace, he writes that it had a 'critical point, as when, in any Russian novel, the Christian protagonist, having speculated for pages on the properties of murder, actually *does* poleax his grandmother.'[180] The Russian novel lampooned here is doubtlessly Dostoevsky's *Crime and Punishment*, where the Christian protagonist, Raskolnikov, after going through endless introspection about whether he can 'cross the boundary' and actually kill someone, and thinking about the implications of murder, finally poleaxes an elderly woman. At a different point in his diary, Gregory recounts a disastrous party that he gave ostensibly for Grace but really to amuse himself with his guests' discomfort. One of his guests tells him that he is not particularly impressed with his behaviour. When Gregory asks him to explain himself, the following exchange takes place:

'This party of yours. An elaborate piece of self-gratification. You must always take it out of somebody mustn't you? Life is one long revenge for your own shortcomings.'
'You've been reading the Russians,' I said. Nothing else. It was furiously annoying.

'That evening,' Gregory continues, 'I took it out on Grace, appeased the rage that [his] little observation had bred in me.'[181] This appears to be another one of Durrell's slyly oblique Dostoevsky references, this time to *Notes from Underground* itself, where the notion of revenging oneself on others for one's own problems is the specialty of the Underground Man (he thinks that the prostitute Liza who walks in on him during his fight with his servant 'will pay me dearly *for all of this*' [5:171] and also says that having sex with her afterwards was 'almost like revenge' [5:175]).

Like Dostoevsky's Underground Man, who is both isolated and alienated from others around him, Gregory is pained by his own profound isolation, which he calls 'six by three. The isolation of a coffin.'[182] Gregory loathes and looks down on people around him for their stupidity or their pretensions (he says that he is 'in the grip of ... slow suppurative hate'[183] and imagines stabbing another resident of the hotel with his pen), but he also envies them because they appear to be more connected to life than he is ('I wander along my private wilderness ... envying everyone. Yes, the butcher, the baker, the nun, and the candlestick maker. The porter who brings me my meals').[184] He wants to be alone but, like the Underground Man, he also feels the need to communicate and to confess, to tell everyone what he has been bottling up inside for all those years – 'at night sometimes I am aware, as of an impending toothache, of the gregarious fiber of me'[185] – which is how his diary comes into being.

As a narrator of his own journal Gregory is just as unreliable as the Underground Man. He freely admits that he lies to others (another character asks him whether he keeps a diary and he 'contemptuously ... tell[s] him, "No"')[186] and he provides accounts of events in the journal that he later contradicts, deliberately misleading his 'readers' but then announcing, 'I am being honest with you for once, I, Death Gregory.'[187] Like the Underground Man, he claims that he is writing events down without editing, as quickly as the memories 'go ... through [him]' so that he 'cannot distinguish the various flavours of incident in their chronological order,' but then admits, 'I am a liar. It is artifice which dictates this form to me.'[188] He insists that his journal is private and will be destroyed (he says that he will burn 'these tedious pages')[189] but he still imagines a readership, whose response he anticipates at every turn ('You yawn?' he asks his 'readers' at one point;[190] 'If you are affected by my tediousness, take heart,' he sneeringly advises them at another, 'This might have been a novel').[191] Notably, he is just as hostile towards his imagined readers as the Underground Man is to the gentlemen whom he continuously addresses as his audience. Towards the end of his diary, Gregory again addresses his 'readers' directly and tells them of the 'terrible thin squealing which I would like to rise from this paper and stifle you. This thin, astringent script of mine – let it be poured into your ears, most delectable of corrosives, until your brains turn green, cancerous, nitric.'[192]

Despite his compulsive self-analysis, or maybe because of it, Gregory is just as unsure of his identity as the Underground Man. He feels that there are 'seventy million I's' within him,[193] and although he adopts the guise of a placid nineteenth-century literary man, wearing a skullcap and sitting with a leather-bound tome of Pascal in an armchair beside the fireplace, he is aware that this is only a façade, and unsuccessful one at that. Gregory knows all too well that the nineteenth-century gentleman of letters persona he adopts is hopelessly outdated in the twentieth century. Like the Crystal Palace, which is mentioned many times in *The Black Book*, where it appears as ugly and incongruous, it no longer impresses. If Dostoevsky's Underground Man positions the Crystal Palace as the embodiment of collective achievement, a futuristic shrine of social utopians, Gregory sees 'the dumb domes of the Crystal Palace' as the 'final assured vulgar mark of Ruskin's world on history.'[194] Like the Crystal Palace, Gregory's gentlemanly façade, which John Ruskin would have surely approved in the nineteenth century, seems quaintly outdated when confronted with the harsh realities of twentieth-century life. Others can see right through it and sarcastically compliment Gregory on the '[g]rand show' he puts on. Gregory is devastated; these comments 'ruin' his already inadequate façade and add to his uncertainty about who he is – he cannot be 'sure of [him]self.'[195]

The solution suggested by Miller and Nin for their own twentieth-century versions of Underground People, an innocuous public persona that allows the hidden inner self to safely express his rage, does not work well for Gregory. He manages to produce a journal – his account of his disgust and anger with himself and with what he calls the 'English death' – but he is both unsatisfied with his work and unable to meaningfully bring it out in the world. Gregory finds that 'what [he] had to offer [he] gave,' but 'it was not enough;'[196] he is simply not gifted enough to produce anything of value, unlike the talented 'darling[s] of the gods.'[197] Gregory is aware that there is something within him that he could have built upon, even 'a work of genius I could write if I put my own principles into practice,'[198] as he says mockingly, which would turn him into a real writer rather than a 'literary gent,' but he announces, 'I shall not bother to fight for it. The struggle is too hideous, the inner extraction of dead selves, like giant festering molars is too painful.'[199]

What is more, Gregory realizes that his 'real' self is slowly deteriorating behind the respectable front that he painstakingly built up over the years. This is to his credit: another character, Tarquin, essentially a caricature of all that Gregory represents, is blind to that process. Tarquin proudly tells Lawrence Lucifer that underneath his own 'façade ... there are enormous reserves of strength ... If there weren't I should be dead by now,'[200] but Lucifer observes that he 'molders away ... nerveless, blanched, waxen, into a kind of pus-drunk senility.'[201]

Gregory is given a chance to resurrect his inner self through his relationship with Grace, a young streetwalker, a relationship that echoes and ironically reconfigures many plot motifs surrounding the Underground Man's relationship with Liza, whom the Underground Man meets in a brothel and who was sold into prostitution by her family. After their initial encounter, he considers helping her escape from the brothel and making her his wife, citing the lines of Nikolai Nekrasov's poem about just such a rehabilitation: 'And into my home, openly and freely,/Enter the absolute mistress of it all!' He fantasizes about how he could have developed her mind and about how they could have both ennobled and resurrected each other into a bright new life. Ultimately, of course, he does not marry her and lets her leave his life forever, something which he regrets for the next twenty years.

In *The Black Book*, Gregory encounters Grace, a street girl whom he buys 'without any bargaining, for the promise of a cup of coffee.'[202] Grace's prostitution is tacitly approved by her family. She tells Gregory: 'When I don't go back they don't worry. Glad to be free of me. Not earning me keep any more, see?'[203] Liza in *Notes* cherishes and shows the Underground Man a letter from a respectful young man who would possibly like to begin a relationship with her; Grace similarly cherishes and shows Gregory a letter from her first lover, who seduced and used her and then wrote to her ending the relationship. Where the Underground Man considers educating Liza ('I develop her mind, I educate her' [5:166]), Grace actually suggests that Gregory give her books to read so that she could 'get improvement,' but he finds the thought of her reading Gibbon, Voltaire, or Butler unnerving and does not do as she asks.[204] In another reversal of the situation in *Notes* Gregory eventually marries Grace (though outsiders are 'shocked by the knife edge of cruelty that cut down into our social relations')[205] and she really does become the 'absolute mistress' of his home.

Grace's 'rebirth' and transformation into a 'respectable woman,' however, turns her into an embodiment of everything Gregory considers vulgar and narrow-minded. Gregory is horrified by the metamorphosis: 'It began almost as soon as the wedding guests left ... "We must get the parlour shipshape," she remarked once or twice, and I recognized a new note in her voice. There was the ring of the Penge matron coming to life in her tones.'[206] Grace becomes tyrannical as well as 'boring and silly' and is impossible to bear. There are 'frightful domestic uproars.'[207] Gregory writes that he 'began to loathe her' and concludes that the 'marriage was not a success.'[208]

There is still a possibility that Gregory might be transformed by the relationship. He himself admits that there were moments of genuine human contact 'when [their] lives seemed to ... twist up into red shapes of real fire and tenderness,'[209] but in another reworking of a motif from *Notes*, the fate that the Underground Man menaces Liza with when he tells her the story of a prostitute who died of tuberculosis and was buried in a water-filled grave becomes Grace's own lot. Grace has tuberculosis and she dies of it in a nursing home (Liza tells the Underground Man that prostitutes do not die at home, but always at a hospital) 'just at the time when [Gregory] had no emotion whatsoever to spend on her' and is buried near the sea under 'the vast reports of the waves against the concrete' as the rain drizzles down into her grave.[210]

With Grace's death Gregory loses his chance for a personal rebirth. When she dies what affects him most is not his loss of her, but 'the loss of the embryo Gregory which was born in her, and which she took away into death with her.'[211] Just as Liza is essentially a pawn in a game the Underground Man decides to play for his own amusement (he says, 'Most of all, I was carried away by the game' [5:156]), so Gregory tells himself that Grace 'is just a pawn in this philosophic game which you are playing.'[212]

After Grace's death, Gregory realizes that he prefers a total and immediate destruction of his inner self to a partial and slow deterioration: a suicide of the individual within him. Gregory embarks upon the path to self-annihilation when he is trod upon (literally) by a barmaid who subsequently 'take[s] [him] in hand.'[213] He realizes that she is 'the most ordinary person [he] could find'[214] and thus the perfect means to achieve the Underground Man's vision of the ant in the anthill or, in this case, the typical middle-aged married suburban man, absolutely indistinguishable from his neighbours. 'It is,' Gregory says, 'the only solution really, the only way out.'[215]

If Dostoevsky's Underground Man despairs of being able to become an insect, because of his hyper-awareness of his own contradictory emotions and ideas, Gregory chances upon the exact way to achieve insecthood through a renunciation of everything that is unique or individual about him. In another ironic transformation of the Underground

Man's vision of the anthill-like society of the future, Gregory embraces the utter insignificance of the individual and the lack of personal responsibility it makes possible: 'Why are we afraid of becoming insects?' he asks, 'I can imagine no lovelier goal. The streets of Paradise are not more lovely than the highways of the ant heap. I shall become a white ant, God willing ... Let the hive take my responsibilities. I am weary of them.'[216]

Lest the reader thinks that Gregory will be able to retain his other, dissident self while he 'lie[s] in secrecy, a prediluvial secrecy' in his new life, Gregory emphasizes that his new underground is a renunciation of the real self, a defeat, a willing 'going down toward the tomb.'[217] Both he and Lawrence Lucifer describe his choice as a 'quaint suicide.'[218] Gregory imagines his 'new' life as an interment, his hands 'folded upon [his] breast ... grass grow[ing] under my tongue.'[219]

It is tempting to interpret Gregory's sad fate as Durrell's commentary on both Dostoevsky's Underground Man and Miller's version of the Underground Man. Dostoevsky's nineteenth-century narrator is incapable of choosing among his many selves, even the least and most insignificant of them, because of his heightened awareness of his internal contradictions and numerous impulses; in contrast, Gregory finds it almost too easy to erase his own personality and to join the hive through a conventional marriage with all its traditional accoutrements of a little house in the suburbs, 'slippers, the gas fire, the paper, the dripping, the text on the wall,'[220] the lawnmower, the standard fare of beef with two vegetables, and the bad sex. Miller and Nin created narrators who only pretend to conform to social expectations and use their outward personas as a front, behind which they can both hide and express their rage and dissent. Gregory could not create a convincing façade while holding on to his dissenting inner self, and when he finally managed to hit upon a convincing outward persona it destroyed the raging rebel within.

Gregory's crisis and his end is closely observed by Lawrence Lucifer, who believes – like the Underground Man – that his generation is 'a still birth' but is in denial about it: 'we are trying to wipe away the knowledge of our still birth.'[221] Lawrence Lucifer views himself as Gregory's younger self and is afraid that he will end up as Gregory did. While Dostoevsky's Underground Man is looking back at his past at age twenty-four and examining his road to the underground, Lawrence Lucifer is looking at his possible future in Gregory and thinking about how to avoid it. Although Lucifer sees in himself all the features that could turn him into a Gregory (he writes, 'I sit over my books like an insect these long nights, or walk the long cold streets, shaken with the torment of indecision and mania, whose cause I cannot fathom'),[222] he chooses to leave England, escaping the 'log of that universal death, the English death,'[223] and to become a writer. He exiles himself from the society that formed him and that made the underground necessary and settles in a remote area of rural Greece, which exists in a time warp, where life is still very much as it was thousands of years ago, and where it is still possible to avoid the repressive machinery of the twentieth-century state. Instead of working on the façade, as Gregory did, Lawrence Lucifer will be working on his dissenting inner self, who existed only as an embryo while he was living in England. 'I lie awake,' he writes describing his London state of mind, 'the ... I from whom I expect response to noise ... The other ... the embryo, the white something which lives behind my face in the mirror, is lulled underground, hibernating';[224] in Greece his inner self will come out of hibernation and inner death. Beginning his novel in Greece, Lawrence Lucifer says, 'I am beginning my agony ... I shall not choose as Gregory chose.'[225]

The many connections between Durrell's narrators and Dostoevsky's Underground Man, as well as the recognizable parallels in the plot motifs and the ironic transformations that they undergo, testify to the importance of Dostoevsky's *Notes from Underground* to Durrell. Like Miller and Nin, Durrell paid close attention to Dostoevsky's text and clearly attempted to challenge him on his own territory. The Villa Seurat writers' versions of the Underground Men and Women for the twentieth century became increasingly influential as Miller, Nin, and Durrell's fame grew. In particular, Miller's version of the Underground Man became inscribed into American literature and culture alongside Dostoevsky's original archetype and spawned countless literary descendants. The average man in the crowd who walks the streets of a big city with secret hate and loathing, the Underground hidden deep in his soul and a complacent smile on his lips, became both a favourite metaphor and model for writers and social critics – especially Americans – who came after Miller.

8 Pragmatics of Influence, the Dostoevsky Brand, and Dostoevsky Codes

On the fiftieth anniversary of Dostoevsky's death in 1931, an exiled Russian religious philosopher living in Paris observed in an article written for an émigré newspaper that Dostoevsky was 'without doubt the most popular, beloved, and esteemed Russian writer in the West' and that he was 'the only Russian writer who became a factor in the development of ideas in the western world.' He then asked the perennial question: why is it that Dostoevsky acquired this significance outside Russia? In response, he argued that the world was undergoing a crisis of humanism and that it was Dostoevsky's revelation of 'Christian Humanism for modern man' that made him so attractive to modern readers and, consequently, so prominent.[1] His observation about Dostoevsky's widespread popularity holds just as true today, perhaps even more so, because Dostoevsky's novels have since found enthusiastic readers in more remote corners of the world than Western Europe and America (the geographical provenance he presumably had in mind). His explanation as to why Dostoevsky achieved such prominence, however, is as unconvincing now as it was back in the 1930s, when Dostoevsky was being adopted by writers, artists, and cultural vigilantes who were not in the least interested in the ideals of Christian humanism, as was the case with Henry Miller and his close friends at Villa Seurat.

Miller's path to Dostoevsky began with his first reading of Dostoevsky's novels in New York, in the midst of a society from which he felt totally disenfranchised. Yet whatever Miller felt about American society, he was still reading Dostoevsky in America, and not in a social and cultural vacuum. He was doubtlessly affected by the American understanding of what Dostoevsky signified, without perhaps fully realizing it himself.

The American understanding of Dostoevsky was built upon the way in which he was introduced to American readers at the end of the nineteenth century. At that time, Dostoevsky was packaged and presented to the American public as an autobiographical writer, not a particularly good literary craftsman, whose value lay in accurate descriptions of the horrors that he himself experienced, such as his sensational imprisonment in Siberia (a place of particular interest to Americans); altogether the kind of 'based-on-a-true story' marketing that is still effective in America today. The original image of Dostoevsky as an outcast who underwent extreme experiences and wrote about them made him attractive to Americans after the atrocities of the First World War, the rise of psychoanalysis, and major changes in the American social fabric caused many of the traditional European literary models to appear outdated and irrelevant. Constance Garnett's translations of Dostoevsky's works in the period 1912–20 encouraged American readers, including Miller, to perceive Dostoevsky as a contemporary writer who spoke directly to their own experience.

Interestingly (especially from the perspective of the study of intercultural literary contacts), many American writers, who were feeling marginalized in comparison to the writers of Western Europe who operated within well-established literary traditions, saw Dostoevsky as a useful ally in their attempts to make a mark on the international literary scene. This was not only because Dostoevsky himself was marginalized before he was celebrated as one of the great novelists, but also because of his prominence in a variety of cultural discourses. Dostoevsky's eminence and currency made it fairly certain that incorporating him in a text would, if not generate critical interest, then at least bolster the claim of relevance and importance for that work. Obelisk Press advised Miller to produce a brochure about the novels of D.H. Lawrence so that he himself would be taken more seriously as a writer; a similar rationale lay behind the inclusion of Dostoevsky in the texts of many writers, whether he was present as the main event or side show. Dostoevsky was important to many writers, artists, and creative types not as literary inspiration or a provocative thinker, but as a brand associated with edgy, sophisticated intelligence. This is not to suggest that Miller's initial interest in Dostoevsky was cynically strategic – he genuinely admired Dostoevsky's novels and began his literary career by aspiring to become an American Dostoevsky – but he was also most certainly aware of the pragmatics of engaging with Dostoevsky in his own texts, a fact that many scholars of literary influence as well as scholars who study Dostoevsky's reception outside of Russia forget or ignore.

Harold Bloom, whose theories remain popular among scholars of intercultural literary influence, has argued repeatedly that later writers have little choice in selecting which of their great literary predecessors they will engage in their own work. As Bloom wrote in *The Western Canon* (1994): 'strong writers do not choose their prime precursors; they are chosen by them.'[2] While the Romantic notion of a daemonic ancestor who makes a claim upon a young writer and haunts him for the rest of his life is an attractive one, if only because of its simplicity, the American adoption of Dostoevsky shows that a number of considerations have to be weighed by younger writers or ephebes (to borrow Bloom's terminology), and that the choice of a literary ancestor is frequently the outcome of a host of practical decisions that have little to do with an anxiety of influence but a lot more with the pragmatics of how to attract attention and gain acknowledgment and respect for one's own work. It could be argued, of course, that this dynamic is true only of those American writers who were not 'strong' in the first place, but even though Henry Miller has been called a major minor writer, his books have had an impact on so many American and non-American writers, and his *Tropic of Cancer* was included in so many top-100 books of the century lists (though not Bloom's own list of great books), he surely qualifies as a writer of some strength.

Miller's early reading of Dostoevsky differed little from that of his American contemporaries. Eventually, however, he formulated his own vision of Dostoevsky's novels. The most important difference between Miller's personal understanding of Dostoevsky and that of other American writers was that Miller believed Dostoevsky's novels marked not the beginning of a new epoch of the novel, but the end of the novel. Miller came to believe that Dostoevsky's novels not only represented the ultimate in novelistic achievement but that they also exhausted the possibilities of the novel and of literature itself. Further, Miller believed that the dystopic horrors and the disintegration of society that Dostoevsky foresaw in the nineteenth century had become the reality of twentieth-century life, and that neither the novel nor any other traditional literary form was able adequately to reflect that reality. This understanding of Dostoevsky's significance became the cornerstone of Miller's own mission statement as a twentieth-century writer: Miller decided that he would have to go beyond Dostoevsky's achievements and create a new kind of transliterary writing (transcending such literary conventions as developed plots, fleshed-out characters, clearly defined fictional provenance, cohesive text, or stylistic editing), which could both reflect and reveal the apocalyptic realities of twentieth-century life. Since Dostoevsky's novels represented the liminal expression of what was possible in the novel, they would serve both as a benchmark and a gateway into this new kind of prose.

Miller shared his vision of Dostoevsky with Anaïs Nin and Lawrence Durrell, two younger writers who became his closest associates in Paris of the 1930s. The convergence of these three writers at Villa Seurat had a profound impact on their lives and literary visions. Under Miller's leadership and with his encouragement, the writers of Villa Seurat embarked on a quest to create a revolution in prose, which they believed would lead in turn to a revolution in the consciousness of mankind. Dostoevsky not only played an important part in their dialogue with each other but became their close ally in an attempt to create a new kind of writing and to change the world.

While Dostoevsky's importance to Miller, Nin, and Durrell is undeniable, it is also clear that in their reading of Dostoevsky's writings, his biography, and his critics, the writers of Villa Seurat constructed their own customized Dostoevsky code of interpretations and associations (some of which involved considerable distortions both of Dostoevsky's text and his manifest credo), and it is this personalized code that they were actually responding to, engaging with, and trying to surpass in their own work.

One unusual feature of the Villa Seurat writers' Dostoevsky code was their interest in Dostoevsky's prose style and form. While the bifurcation of a Dostoevsky novel into the two supposedly separate spheres of literary form and philosophic content is common in Dostoevsky's reception both in Russia and outside of it, his literary style and the form of his novels were traditionally ignored or else denigrated by critics and readers in favour of his ideas. The writers of Villa Seurat, on the other hand, attempted to learn from Dostoevsky's style, to emulate it, and to surpass it in their own texts. For instance, they believed that Dostoevsky's novels contained many instances of stylistic breakdowns. Unlike many of Dostoevsky's readers, who criticized him for the so-called sloppiness of his literary prose, however, Miller decided that Dostoevsky was *intentionally* relinquishing control over his prose at these moments, and that the stylistic breakdowns in his prose style were both deliberate and important. In the Villa Seurat writers' attempt to surpass Dostoevsky's achievements and to go beyond the boundaries of literature in their own post-Dostoevskian prose, they tried to increase these breakdowns – which they likened to explosions – in their own texts in order to produce a much more spontaneous and cathartic prose that would also be able to reflect the explosive realities of the twentieth century.

The writers of Villa Seurat viewed Dostoevsky's writing as highly autobiographical and believed that many of his more famous characters (including such antipodes as Stavrogin of *The Devils* and Father Zossima of *Brothers Karamazov*) were Dostoevsky's own alter egos and voiced his personal beliefs. In response, they attempted to write texts that were even more autobiographical, with their own life experience as their primary subject. They also believed that Dostoevsky's novels depicted the drama of his own psyche and that in order to better represent their own inner dramas they were free to use any available stylistic and literary device, from surrealist imagery to naturalist descriptiveness. They felt that all of Dostoevsky's novels are interconnected (originally through a misreading of André Gide's comment on Dostoevsky) and that they represent the chronological phases of his own development. In response, they attempted to create even more obviously interconnected texts that would reflect both their own continued development and the flowing, uncircumscribed nature of the psyche itself.

Miller and the other writers of his inner circle were also interested in Dostoevsky's ideas, which they believed were grounded in his own life experience, and therefore authentic and relevant. It is doubtful, of course, whether Dostoevsky would have recognized many of his own beliefs in the Villa Seurat writers' enthusiastic exegesis, but that is hardly the point. Miller and his friends saw Dostoevsky's ultimate credo in the duty of the writer/creative individual to transform the world. In this way, they interpreted the shocking gestures in his novels (such as Nikolai Stavrogin biting the governor's ear in *The Devils*) as Dostoevsky's attempt to reveal to his readers the apocalyptic chaos that lurks beneath day-to-day platitudes, in order to effect a change in their consciousness. Miller was especially committed to the idea that shocking his readers was the best way to effect their inner liberation, a concept that he attempted to implement in his own texts through the inclusion of sexually explicit and obscene passages, with the well-known result of having his works banned for their explicitness. That ban led to the famous obscenity trials of the 1960s around his *Tropics* and the overturning of various obscenity laws in a number of countries, most prominently the United States.

The Villa Seurat writers' response to Dostoevsky's *Notes from Underground* – a text that proved influential on many literatures in the twentieth century, including American literature – is especially revealing in terms of their continuous attempts to engage with Dostoevsky on his own territory as well as their efforts to go beyond Dostoevsky's own achievements in their writing. Miller's *Tropics*, Nin's writings of the 1930s, and Durrell's *Black Book* contain many connections with Dostoevsky's *Notes*, including the ironic transformation and echoing of the plot, the utilization and variation of certain key imagery, and the adoption of narrative techniques, all transposed onto a different linguistic, temporal, and cultural matrix, but all ultimately recognizable. The Villa Seurat writers' most interesting response to this text, however, involves the persona of the Underground Man himself. Miller, Nin, and Durrell all create narrators who are obviously descended from the Dostoevskian archetype and who exhibit many of his key characteristics (alienation, rebellion against dominant cultural paradigms, intelligence, hyperconsciousness, and so forth), but who also respond to their creators' need to deal with their own anxieties centred on the personal and social problem of the survival of a non-conformist individual amidst the realities of twentieth-century life, with its accelerated consumerism, mass culture, repressive political systems, and apocalyptic wars. Miller's narrator-authorial persona represents his attempt to provide a solution to this problem, appearing in the *Tropics* as a canny cultural vigilante, whose nonconformist rebellious self is safely hidden behind a seemingly complacent public mask, allowing him to wage his acts of resistance and cultural subversion, which most prominently include the creation of iconoclastic texts. Nin and Durrell followed Miller's suit with their own narrators, who make the same decision to wage their cultural rebellion from a personal underground, using their prose as a weapon. This new version of the twentieth-century Underground Man (and Woman) created at Villa Seurat gained significance as the fame of the Villa Seurat writers spread (Miller's narrator became an important model for many American writers, who identified with Miller's antiauthoritarian stance; Nin's narrator became an inspiration to many young women writers, who discovered her work upon the publication of her diaries in the 1960s and who also regarded themselves as waging a personal battle against patriarchal forms and practices).

The Villa Seurat writers' unorthodox interpretation of Dostoevsky, their identification with him, and their dogged attempts to engage with him in their own texts raise many complex issues about the kinds of transfiguration that texts undergo as they are excised from their original cultural, historical, and linguistic milieu and reinscribed within a new context, as well a number of questions about how canons themselves are revised and perpetuated. It is clear that by the time Miller and, subsequently, other Villa Seurat writers chose Dostoevsky as a personal and literary model, the latter was already a well-established figure in both Western European and American understandings of the literary canon, his texts culturally sanctified as 'high-brow' literature. The Villa Seurat writers' decision to align themselves with Dostoevsky as followers and literary descendants could be seen as a strategic one, through which they attempted to gain legitimacy and status for their own texts. At the same time, the numerous creative ways in which they responded to his writing and their persistent turning to Dostoevsky argues for a deeper and much more genuine engagement with his work. Their wrestling with Dostoevsky in their texts created their own version of Dostoevsky's legacy, their own Dostoevsky code which combined features of his autobiography, their favourite passages from his novels, their understanding of his prose style, their reinvention of his literary characters, and their interpretation of his corpus of ideas. The Villa Seurat Dostoevsky code represents a radicalized reading of Dostoevsky, which retains and emphasizes the more extreme features of his texts and his life (including the more radical critical interpretations of these), at the same time as it rejects or ignores those features of his text, his politics, and his religious beliefs that do not support their view of him as a transgressive and rebellious figure within his society and culture.

The writers of Villa Seurat were not the first to construct a radical reading of Dostoevsky. One might argue that Dostoevsky's literary texts are particularly open to such a (mis)reading, because of the force and conviction with which some of their more extreme characters are allowed to express their ideological credos. The writers of Villa Seurat were building upon an earlier tradition of Dostoevsky's reception, particularly strong in the American reception of his work, which emphasized his status of a social outsider and a literary underdog. Because of the prominence that their own work attained, however (especially in the case of Miller and Nin, both of whom became household names in the United States), they were particularly successful in reinscribing their even more radicalized version of Dostoevsky back into their own literary and cultural context, which shifted from Paris of the 1930s to post-1940 America.

The extreme distortions inherent in the Villa Seurat revisionist readings of Dostoevsky were frequently lost upon their wider readership.

For example, the American GIs who bought Miller's *Tropics* in the thousands in Paris of the 1940s were, in most cases, first introduced to Dostoevsky through Miller's books and had little background knowledge about Dostoevsky's life or work; the same is true for many of Miller's American readers who rushed to buy his books in the hundreds of thousands when they finally became legal in the United States. Many of the central figures associated with the Beats movement, including Allen Ginsberg (1926–97), Jack Kerouac (1922–69), and William Burroughs (1914–97) (the last two, incidentally, were also American GIs during the Second World War), hero-worshipped Miller and accepted his version of Dostoevsky without question. Subsequently, they also chose Dostoevsky for a literary ancestor and spiritual guide, a proto-Beat in fact, who would have been delighted with their anarchic counter-culture stance.[3]

This is not to suggest that Dostoevsky's literary transmission in the United States proceeded along the lines of a broken-telephone game, with each successive generation of writers adding another layer of misinterpretation and moving further away from an informed reading of Dostoevsky's text. In fact, some groups of American writers, including such writers associated with the literature of the American South as Flannery O'Connor (1925–64), Carson McCullers (1917–67), and Walker Percy (1916–90), produced a much more balanced reading of Dostoevsky that paid more attention to his own manifest beliefs and to his historical and cultural context.[4] Yet other groups, as for example, writers of African-American descent, including Richard Wright (1908–60), Ralph Ellison (1914–94), and James Baldwin (1924–87), constructed radical readings of Dostoevsky that were conditioned by personal and socio-historical experience and emphasized vastly different aspects of his legacy.[5]

Ultimately, Miller's Dostoevsky code is just one version of many among the ways that Dostoevsky was defined and understood by twentieth-century American writers. Nonetheless, his interpretation of Dostoevsky acquired enormous resonance and proved particularly useful to those writers, artists, and film directors who viewed themselves as part of an underground resistance to the forces of social and cultural conformity overtaking American society. Various representatives of American counterculture adopted a radicalized 'Underground' Dostoevsky as an effective ally in their explorations of extreme states of being and alternative consciousness.

While a scholar of Dostoevsky's work would argue that Miller's reading of Dostoevsky is naive and inaccurate, if only because it ignores Dostoevsky's own manifest credo in religion and politics, disregards the social respectability he attained (becoming a frequent guest of the Russian Royal family, for example), and includes blatant misreadings of his texts and critics, a scholar of comparative literature or intercultural studies, while certainly acknowledging all these observations, would ultimately call them irrelevant. Miller and the other writers of Villa Seurat were unquestionably rewriting Dostoevsky in their own image, but they were never concerned with the accuracy of their interpretations. What interested them was the creative potential inherent in their wrestling with their version of Dostoevsky's legacy. Whether the Villa Seurat writers ultimately managed to surpass Dostoevsky's novels and to create a prose revolution or – even more ambitiously – a revolution in consciousness is debatable, although both of these claims have had influential supporters (especially in the case of Miller and Nin). What is clear is that their engagement with Dostoevsky during the critical years at Villa Seurat allowed them to discover and develop their own unique voices as writers.

An analysis of the Villa Seurat writers' understanding of Dostoevsky offers more food for thought, however, than just a series of insights into their own mindset and literary practices, interesting though these may be. The broader implications of the Villa Seurat writers' Dostoevsky code include the question of what happens to texts as they move across linguistic and cultural boundaries and the question of Dostoevsky's prominence in twentieth-century philosophical, literary, social, and cultural discourses. The Villa Seurat writers' effective appropriation of Dostoevsky as a writer of counterculture (despite the fact that by the 1930s he had been firmly established as a mainstream novelist and despite his own professed and well-publicized political and religious beliefs) demonstrates the ease with which the set of associations connected to a particular writer or text can be stripped and substituted to suit the needs of their new readers and the ease with which they themselves can subsequently be appropriated. This, of course, has already been observed by comparative and intercultural scholars studying the selection, reception, and ultimately transformation of texts across cultural matrixes (one has only to look at the transfiguration that awaited many American writers as their works were translated, critiqued, and adapted in Russia during the Soviet era), but in the extreme case of Dostoevsky's reception by Villa Seurat writers

186 The Making of a Counter-Culture Icon

it becomes particularly transparent. For the writers of Villa Seurat, 'Dostoevsky' clearly acquired a very different set of associations and connotations than he had both for his original Russian readers and the Russian readers of their era. On the other hand, although Dostoevsky's reception in America has not been fully explored, the work that has been done to date shows that the Villa Seurat reading of Dostoevsky was only one of a vast number of Dostoevsky codes championed by various groups of American writers. These different codes, which competed for legitimacy and prominence in American cultural discourse throughout the twentieth century, have contributed to keeping Dostoevsky both current and central, emphasizing his importance and transforming his novels into a site of literary and cultural debate in America that continues to attract much attention in the twenty-first century.

Appendix A

Dostoevsky and America: A Brief Bibliographic Overview

While there can be no doubt that the state of scholarship in the area of Dostoevsky's reception and readership in America has greatly improved since René Wellek concluded more than forty years ago that 'Dostoevsky's influence on American writers has hardly begun to be explored,'[1] it is equally clear that much remains to be done. One of the problems encountered in the study of Dostoevsky's reception is the tendency to overgeneralize the response to Dostoevsky for all non-Russian readers, regardless of language, historical epoch, sociocultural provenance, or system of reference. Georgy Fridlender, one of the patriarchs of Soviet Dostoevsky studies, contends in his *Dostoevsky and World Literature* [*Dostoevskii i mirovaia literatura*] (1979) that 'from the beginning of the twentieth century [Dostoevsky] exerted and continues to exert today an enormous influence on the literature and the spiritual life of humanity.'[2] Although Dostoevsky's impact on many national literatures has, indeed, been very significant, we find out that 'humanity' in this case seems to mean Western Europeans, and that the 'World Literature' of the study's title is actually French and German literature, implying, perhaps, that the response to Dostoevsky is basically similar in all the other literatures of the world.

Victor Terras, a prominent American Dostoevsky scholar, writes that Dostoevsky's 'greatest impact has been on Western readers,'[3] an often made and generally accepted judgment which, nonetheless, raises questions both about the meaning of 'Western readers' (Western-European readers in specific countries? European readers in general? readers in the Western hemisphere? non-Russian readers?) and about the force of Dostoevsky's impact on readers in 'non-Western' countries (the Columbian Gabriel Garcia Marquez, Japanese Haruki Murakami, Egyptian Naguib Mahfouz, and Indian Raja Rao, for example, have all talked of the importance Dostoevsky had for them as readers and writers). Wellek himself, while arguing for the need to examine Dostoevsky's reception in a more precise manner and to differentiate between the many different linguistic, national, cultural, social, and historic contexts in which his readers operate, continues to talk about the 'Western' reception of Dostoevsky at the same time as he points out that there are 'divergences in Dostoevsky criticism in the main Western countries,'[4] which turn out to be France, Germany, and England.

The scholarship that addresses Dostoevsky's impact on American literature and culture has often suffered from the assumption that his reception in America was the same as in all the other Anglophone countries, and that the history of his reception in England is a template that requires little modification to understand Dostoevsky's reception in the United States. To date, the standard first stop for anyone inquiring into the issue of Dostoevsky's reception in America is Helen Muchnic's pioneering study *Dostoevsky's English Reputation: 1881–1936* (1939), even though the author herself explains that her study focuses on Dostoevsky's reception in England, commenting that she interpreted '"English"' ... broadly, including much American comment as well as that of Continental authors whose works have been translated.'[5] Muchnic's research is thorough and invaluable (especially for the period ending with the 1920s), but because her focus is not on the United States, many important American sources are omitted. More problematically, Muchnic bases her study on the assumption that the English and American responses to Dostoevsky are identical and determined by the same cultural and social factors. This is clearly not the case, as indicated, for example, by the different attitudes to Dostoevsky in England and America after the demise of the so-called Dostoevsky cult in the late 1920s, when Dostoevsky lost much of his cultural cachet among British intelligentsia but retained his importance among American literati.

The other well-known and frequently quoted study, which, nonetheless, only partially concerns itself with Dostoevsky's reception in the United States, is Gilbert Phelps's wide-ranging *The Russian Novel in English Fiction* (1956). Again, Phelps's focus is on the English reaction to Dostoevsky rather than on the novelist's American readership.

Phelps writes that his aim 'has been to trace the main outlines of the story of the reception of the Russian Novel in England, and to some extent in America, and of its impact upon some of the English and American writers who welcomed it';[6] practically speaking, however, very few American writers are included in his study. Like Muchnic, Phelps does not differentiate between the American and English receptions of Dostoevsky, further, he devotes little space to Dostoevsky, dwelling more on Turgenev, Tolstoy, and Chekhov. He does, however, makes several interesting observations on Henry James's reaction to Dostoevsky and on Constance Garnett's translation of Dostoevsky's novels, which were, of course, also widely read in America.[7]

A.N. Nikoliukin's *The Interrelations of Russian and American Literatures: Turgenev, Tolstoy, Dostoevsky and America* [*Vzaimosviazi literatur Rossii i SShA: Turgenev, Tolstoi, Dostoevskii i Amerika*] (1987) and Myler Wilkinson's *The Dark Mirror: American Literary Response to Russia* (1996) both focus specifically on the literary reception of Russian writers in the United States. Only one chapter of Nikoliukin's work is wholly devoted to Dostoevsky ('The Legacy of Dostoevsky and American Literature' ['Nasledie Dostoevskogo i amerikanskaia literatura'] [238–84]). Despite the brevity of the Dostoevsky chapter, Nikoliukin manages to provide a number of interesting and important insights into the issue of Dostoevsky's reception by American writers. His pre-Perestroika study is flawed, however, by its restriction of American literature to the so-called socially progressive authors (those who do not fit the bill are either derided, like Norman Mailer, or absent) and the Dostoevsky chapter is most convincing and thorough in its discussion of Dostoevsky's impact on Faulkner (264–84), where he takes issue with J. Weisgerber's *Faulkner et Dostoievski: Confluences et influences* (1968), one of the few book-length studies about Dostoevsky's impact on an American writer. Nikoliukin's other important contribution to the field is his article on Constance Garnett's role in shaping Dostoevsky's legacy for the English and American reader ('Dostoevskii v perevode Konstans Garnet' ['Dostoevsky in the Translation of Constance Garnett'] [1985]).[8]

Myler Wilkinson provides a brief but insightful discussion of Dostoevsky's American treatment as the 'Russian Other' (52–5). He also contributes (112–29) one of the first systemic examinations of Dostoevsky's impact on Sherwood Anderson (the Russian scholar Iu. Sokhriakov broached this subject in his 'Tvorchestvo F. M. Dostoevskogo i realisticheskaia literatura SShA 20-30-kh godov XX veka (T. Draizer,

Sh. Anderson, F. Skott Fitsdzheral'd)' ['Dostoevsky's Work and the
American Realistic Literature of 1920s and 1930s (T. Dreiser, S. Anderson,
F. Scott Fitzgerald)'] [1978]), in which he perceptively analyses Anderson's comments about Dostoevsky and then explores the literary and
philosophical dialogue between the two writers by using Bakhtin's theories of polyphony and the carnivalesque. Wilkinson's focus, however, is
on the American literary response to Russia in general and Dostoevsky's
American reception is a secondary concern.

The most significant study of Dostoevsky's American reception has
been done by two German comparativists: Stefan Klessmann, who wrote
*Deutsche und amerikanische Erfahrungsmuster von Welt. Eine interdiszi-
plinäre, kulturvergleichende Analyse im Spiegel der Dostojewskij-Rezeption
zwischen 1900 und 1945* (1990), and Horst-Jürgen Gerigk, who wrote *Die
Russen in Amerika. Dostojewskij, Tolstoj, Turgenjew und Tschechow in ihrer
Bedeuntung für die Literatur der USA* (1995). Klessmann's ambitious study
addresses Dostoevsky's reception both in Germany and the United States
in the first half of the twentieth century. His book extends across several
mediums and disciplines, but since his focus is on the difference between
the American and German outlooks on the world his treatment of the
American writers' reception of Dostoevsky is far from comprehensive.
Klessmann deserves special credit, however, for being the first scholar to
consider the importance of Dostoevsky for Henry Miller (256–6). This
said, he largely ignores Miller's seminal works of the 1930s and bases his
brief assessment of Miller's reception of Dostoevsky on the *Rosy Crucifixion* trilogy (1949–60).

Horst-Jürgen Gerigk's erudite and accessible study poses many
important questions about how a diverse group of American writers
(from William Faulkner to Kurt Vonnegut) responded to Dostoevsky
and his novels. His work is especially suggestive in its consideration of
how Dostoevsky's *Crime and Punishment* (more specifically, the character of Raskolnikov) and *Brothers Karamazov* (especially the character of
Smerdiakov) became adopted and 'customized' to American reality by
American writers. Because, however, Dostoevsky is only one of the
classical Russian writers considered, and because many important
American writers and poets who claimed to be influenced by Dostoevsky are omitted (the entire group of the Beat writers and poets, for
instance), the study cannot be regarded as – nor does it pretend to be –
a comprehensive account of Dostoevsky's reception in the United
States, although it remains one of the most important contributions in
the field to date.

Apart from these general texts there are a handful of book-length studies about Dostoevsky's reception by a particular American author (foremost among these is the already mentioned work of the Belgian scholar J. Weisgerber, *Faulkner et Dostoievski: Confluences et influences* [1968]), or a group of American authors (such as Michael Lynch's *Creative Revolt: A Study of Wright, Ellison, and Dostoevsky* [1990]), and a number of articles on topic, as well as many more about intertextualities and parallels existing between various of Dostoevsky's novels and the novels of various American writers. See Edward Wasiolek's 'Dostoevsky and *Sanctuary*' (1959); Iu. Sokhriakov's 'Traditsii Dostoevskogo v vospriiatii T. Vul'fa, U. Folknera i D. Steinbeka' ['Traditions of Dostoevsky in the Reception of T. Wolfe, W. Faulkner, and D. Steinbeck'] (1980); Temira Pachmuss's 'Dostoevsky and America's Southern Women Writers: Parallels and Confluences' (1981); Donald Fiene's 'Elements of Dostoevsky in the Novels of Kurt Vonnegut' (1981); Dennis Flynn's 'Farrell and Dostoevsky' (1993); Gary Rosenshield's 'Crime and Redemption, Russian and American Style: Dostoevsky, Buckley, Mailer, Styron and their Wards' (1998); and my own 'Rage and Revolt: Dostoevsky and Three African-American Writers' (2001), 'Dostoevsky and the Beats' (2001), 'Anguish for the Sake of Anguish' – Faulkner and His Dostoevskian Allusion' (2004), and 'Dostoevsky and the Literature of the American South' (2004).

Much remains to be done if we are to understand the reasons for Dostoevsky's continuing appeal for American writers and readers. If, as some would have it, there is no single American Literature but, instead, a number of American literatures, can we detect differences in their reception and responses to Dostoevsky? For example, is there a difference in how Dostoevsky was perceived by writers of such popular 'mid-brow' novels as Patricia Highsmith (best known as author of *The Talented Mr Ripley* [1955]) and Mario Puzo of the *Godfather* fame, both of whom repeatedly said that Dostoevsky was their single most important literary ancestor, and the way he was perceived by such canonized 'high-brow' writers as Saul Bellow, who also talked about the importance of Dostoevsky to his work? Did an American writer's regional, ethnic, or religious allegiances influence the way he or she perceived Dostoevsky? Did political and economic changes in the United States have an impact on how Dostoevsky has been understood? Many questions remain to be answered if we are to have a more complete picture and a better understanding of Dostoevsky's meteoric impact on the literature and culture of the United States in the twentieth century.

Appendix B

Miller and the Villa Seurat Circle: A Brief Bibliographic Overview

The last decade of the twentieth century saw an upsurge of interest in Miller, Nin, and Durrell's life and work. *Henry and June*, a film by Philip Kaufman about the relationship between Miller and Nin based on an eponymous volume of Nin's unexpurgated diaries, came out in 1990 and made American cinematic history by garnering the first ever NC-17 rating (a controversial move by the Motion Picture Association of America designed to replace the stigmatized 'X' rating). Two new biographies of Miller marked his centenary in 1991 (Mary Dearborn's *The Happiest Man Alive; Henry Miller, A Biography* and Robert Ferguson's *Henry Miller: A Life*). These were followed by two biographies of Nin written in English: Noel Riley Fitch's *Anaïs: The Erotic Life of Anaïs Nin* (1993) and Deirdre Bair's much-criticized but extremely well-researched and thorough *Anaïs Nin* (1995). A German biography by Linde Salber, *Tausendundeine Frau: die Geschichte der Anaïs Nin*, came out in 1996. A solid and well-researched unauthorized biography of Durrell was published in 1996 (Gordon Bowker's *Through the Dark Labyrinth: A Biography of Lawrence Durrell*) while an authorized biography by Ian MacNiven, a Durrell scholar and friend, appeared in 1998 (*Lawrence Durrell: A Biography*).

Several important collections of critical essays, old and new, were published on each of the writers: Ronald Gottesman edited *Critical Essays on Henry Miller* (1992); Philip K. Jason edited *The Critical Response to Anaïs Nin* (1996); prominent Nin scholar Suzanne Nalbantian edited *Anaïs Nin: Literary Perspectives* (1993); and Anne Salvatore edited *Anaïs Nin's Narratives* (2001); Julius R. Raper, Melody L. Enscore, and Paige Matthey Bynam edited *Lawrence Durrell: Comprehending the Whole* (1995) and Anna Lillios edited *Lawrence Durrell and the Greek World* (2004). There have also been a number of interesting scholarly monographs discussing different aspects of each writer's work. John Parkin wrote about the connection of Miller with Rabelais (*Henry Miller: The Modern Rabelais* [1991]), Gay Louise Balliet about Miller's link with surrealism (*Henry Miller and Surrealist Metaphor: 'Riding the Ovarian Trolley'* [1996]). Suzanne Nalbantian published a comparative study of Nin's autobiography (*Aesthetic Autobiography: From Life to Art in Marcel Proust, James Joyce, Virginia Woolf, and Anaïs Nin* [1994]), Diane Richard-Allerdyce wrote a study of Nin's work in light of her identity as a woman modernist writer (*Anais Nin and the Remaking of Self: Gender, Modernism, and Narrative Identity* [1998]), and Helen Tookey produced an insightful study of Nin's work (*Anaïs Nin, Fictionality and Femininity: Playing a Thousand Roles* [2003]) in which she also emphasized Nin's place within the feminist-modernist discourse and explored her continued attraction for new generations of readers. Richard Pine published an important study of Durrell's fiction (*Lawrence Durrell: The Mindscape* [1994]) and Stefan Herbrechter produced an interesting monograph re-evaluating Durrell's fiction in the context of postmodernist theory and literature (*Lawrence Durrell: Postmodernism and the Ethics of Alterity* [1998]).

In the world of academia, Miller's *Tropics* (especially his *Tropic of Cancer*) are becoming a more common sight in courses on the twentieth-century novel and American literature, although they are still a rarity, testifying perhaps to academic discomfort with teaching transgressive texts. Although Miller is conspicuously absent from Harold Bloom's Great Western Canon list of important twentieth-century American writers, he is included in many other versions of the list, and his *Tropic of Cancer* is frequently cited as one of the landmarks of the twentieth-century novel. Nin's work is studied primarily within the context of women's studies, included in courses on modernist women's writing and, lately, in courses on journal and autobiographical writing. Durrell's work, especially his *Alexandria Quartet*, is usually studied in the context of twentieth-century British literature, while his travel books are taught in courses on travel writing; his writings have also been included in courses on postcolonial literature.

On the popular front, the books of all three writers remain in print and are frequently reissued (especially those of Durrell and Miller). As I write this in 2006, countless websites provide tributes to Miller, Nin, and Durrell. None of this means, however, that the three writers have been fully accepted. Durrell has been especially difficult to place within a particular literary niche (a definite prerequisite for a writer's absorption by academia, which, in turn, promotes new scholarship on the writer and affects republication of his books), because of his emphatic cosmopolitanism (born in India of English-Irish colonial stock, lived in Greece, chose to spend most of his life in France, etc.) and his literary versatility and prolificacy. His work on behalf of the British government also makes him an uncomfortable fit for many postcolonial studies courses. Some Durrell specialists feel that the 'downward turn in Durrell's critical fortunes' from his fame in the 1960s dates to the publication of his *Tunc* and *Nunquam* and reflects the problems associated with their reception.[1] The problems of Durrell's reception and his place in the literary pantheon are addressed by the Lawrence Durrell Society, which calls itself a non-profit educational organization whose purpose is to promote the study of Durrell's works, to explore Durrell's position in twentieth-century literature, and 'to help establish his place in the canon of world literature.' A similar role is fulfilled by *Nexus, The International Henry Miller Journal*, an annual publication with the stated mission of 'preserving the legacy of Henry Miller and the Villa Seurat Circle.' The Henry Miller Library at Big Sur, California, also announces in its mission statement that it is a 'public benefit, non-profit organization championing the literary, artistic and cultural contributions of the late writer, artist and Big Sur resident Henry Miller.' The Henry Miller Museum of Art in Nagano promotes Miller's artwork (he was an avid watercolourist). Even without the work of these organizations, Miller's position as one of the key writers of American counterculture appears to be increasingly recognized, even though some literary scholars persist in seeing him as merely a literary enfant terrible. Anaïs Nin is not currently attracting the attention she did in the 1970s, when she was a household word. It appears, as she herself predicted, that her diaries rather than her fictional writing will remain her lasting legacy, although her collection of short erotic stories is increasingly recognized as a classic of women's erotic writing. The Anaïs Nin Foundation has become less active since the recent death of Nin's editor Gunther Stuhlmann, and that of her second husband, Rupert Pole, in 2006, but Nin's place in world literature is defended by a devoted group of scholars who are actively publishing on various aspects of her literary legacy.

Although there is reason to believe that the work of Miller, Nin, and Durrell is finding new readers, and that the authors themselves are gradually becoming more accepted by the critical and academic establishment, much remains to be done to contextualize their writing and to understand their literary legacy. Their literary interactions and the way in which they influenced each other's work remains a glaring lacuna in scholarship devoted to their work. Aside from sections of their biographies and a few, mostly biographical, articles on the subject (see George Cleyet's 'The Villa Seurat Circle: Creative Nexus' [1981], Lawrence Shifreen's 'Faction in the Villa Seurat' [1981], Deidre Bair's 'Writing as a Woman: Henry Miller, Lawrence Durrell, and Anaïs Nin in the Villa Seurat' [1994], and Jane Eblen Keller's 'Romantic Love and the New Woman: Differing Notions in the Work of Anais Nin and Lawrence Durrell' [1998]) there have been few attempts to understand how their interactions at Villa Seurat affected their understanding of writing and the common ground, parallels, echoes, and re-visions of each other's work of the period and beyond. The 1998 conference 'On Miracle Ground X: The Paris of Durrell, Miller, and Nin,' organized by the Lawrence Durrell Society, was a response to a need felt by many scholars working on the three writers to examine their work within the context of both each other's writing and their broader Parisian experience. To date, however, surprisingly little has been done in the area. There have been even fewer scholarly enquiries into the question of interactions within the wider Villa Seurat circle, which included many important international writers, poets, artists, and photographers, or the impact of the circle on the expatriate scene of the 1930s, the Parisian 'Bohemian' scene, and various other cultural spheres. (A notable exception is the heroic efforts of Karl Orend who continues to write and publish on the subject of Miller and his friends.) One must conclude that 18 Villa Seurat has yet to assume its rightful place in the history of the important cultural, intellectual, literary, and artistic centres of the twentieth century.

Notes

Chapter 1: Intercultural Readings, Dostoevsky's Twentieth Century, and Henry Miller's Literary Ambitions

1 Cited in Gilbert Phelps's *The Russian Novel in English Fiction* (London: Hutchinson's University Library, 1956), 173.
2 W.J. Leatherbarrow, 'Introduction,' in *Fedor Dostoevsky: A Reference Guide* (Boston, MA: G.K. Hall, 1990), xi–xii.
3 Joseph Frank, *Dostoevsky: The Miraculous Years, 1865–1871* (Princeton, NJ: Princeton University Press, 1995), 500.
4 Also known in English under the title *The Possessed*.
5 (Moscow: Gosudarstvennoe izdatel'stvo, 1922).
6 See, for instance, Yurii Kariakin, *Dostoevskii i kanun XXI veka* [*Dostoevsky and the Beginning of the Twenty-First Century*] (Moscow: Sovetskii pisatel', 1989), 204.
7 Vladimir Seduro, *Dostoevski in Russian Literary Criticism 1846–1956* (New York: Columbia University Press, 1957), 276.
8 Vladimir Etov, 'Po obraztsu i podobiiu' ['After the Pattern and Likeness'], *Dostoevskii i mirovaia kul'tura* 1.1 (1993), 148–9.
9 This summary is provided by V.A. Tunimanov in his post-Perestroika article on Dostoevsky, included in a publication of *The Devils* [*Besy*] (Leningrad: Lenizdat, 1990), 623.
10 B.G. Reizov, 'Vmesto predisloviia' ['Instead of an Introduction'], *Dostoevskii v zarubezhnykh literaturakh* [*Dostoevsky in Foreign Literatures*] (Leningrad: Nauka, 1978), 3–4.
11 Geert H. Hofstede, *Culture's Consequences: Comparing Values, Behaviours, Institutions, and Organizations Across Nations*, 2nd ed. (Thousand Oaks, CA: Sage, 2001), 451–2.

12 O.A. Leontovich, *Rossiia i SShA; vvedenie v mezhkul'turnuiu kommunikatsiiu* [*Russia and the USA; Introduction to Intercultural Communication*] (Volgograd: Peremena, 2003), 275.
13 This practice became disturbingly popular outside of Russia, especially in America and England, where the reading list of many university courses includes the chapter excised from the novel and studied as a separate text.
14 Elena Blavatsky, trans., '"The Grand Inquisitor," an extract from *The Brothers Karamazof*,' *The Theosophist* 3 (November 1881), 38.
15 Attributed to Dostoevsky, 'The Priest and the Devil,' *Mother Earth Bulletin* (January 1910), 360–2.
16 See my article 'Dostoevsky and the Beat Generation,' *Canadian Review of Comparative Literature/Revue Canadienne de Littérature Comparée* 28 (June – September 2001): 218–42.
17 Ginsberg quoted by Peter Manso in *Mailer: His Life and Times* (New York: Viking Penguin, 1985), 258–60.
18 Jack Kerouac, 'To Peter Orlovsky' (24 August 1957), Columbia University, Butler Library, Spec Ms Collection Orlovsky, 1.
19 Jack Kerouac quoted in Michael Schumacher, *Dharma Lion: A Critical Biography of Allen Ginzberg* (New York: St Martin's, 1992), 35.
20 Jack Kerouac, quoted in 'Part II: The Beat papers of Al Aronowitz,' *New York Post* (10 March 1959), 47–8; http://www.bigmagic.com/pages/blackj/column22.html.
21 Allen Ginsberg, 'Author's Preface, Reader's Manual,' *Collected Poems 1947–1980* (New York: Harper and Row, 1984), xix.
22 Theodor Dreiser to Victor Smirnov (5 August 1932), *Letters of Theodore Dreiser: A Selection*, ed. Robert H. Elias (Philadelphia: University of Pennsylvania Press, 1959) 2:594.
23 It was originally published under the title *Problemy tvorchestva Dostoevskogo* [*Problems of Dostoevsky's Art*]; the title was changed for the expanded edition.
24 For an account of Bakhtin's life and work, as well for an analysis of his theories on Dostoevsky, see Caryl Emerson's *The First Hundred Years of Mikhail Bakhtin* (Princeton, NJ: Princeton University Press, 1997), 75–93, 127–61.
25 For a comprehensive and insightful discussion into Bakhtin's notion of polyphony, along with the reaction it provoked, see Emerson's *The First Hundred Years of Mikhail Bakhtin*, 127–61.
26 Mikhail Bakhtin, *Problemy poetiki Dostoevskogo* [*The Problems of Dostoevsky's Poetics*] (1929/1963; repr. Moscow: Izdatel'stvo 'Khudozhestvennaia Literatura,' 1972), 462, 464.

27 There are some categories of characters, however, that are effectively silenced in Dostoevsky's novels; most prominently, these include the Jewish characters

28 James Scanlan, *Dostoevsky the Thinker* (Ithaca, NY: Cornell University Press, 2002), 3–4.

29 Helen Muchnic, *Dostoevsky's English Reputation: 1881–1936* (Northampton, MA: Smith's College, 1939), 111.

30 Colin Crowder, 'The Appropriation of Dostoevsky in the Early Twentieth Century: Cult, Countercult and Incarnation,' in *European Literature and Theology in the Twentieth Century: Ends of Time*, ed. David Jasper and Colin Crowder (Basingstoke: Macmillan, 1990), 22.

31 André Gide, *Dostoevsky*, trans. J.M. Dent (1925; repr. London: Secker and Warburg, 1949), 91–3.

32 Henri Peyre, 'French Literary Imagination and Dostoevsky,' in *French Literary Imagination and Dostoevsky and Other Essays* (Tuscaloosa: University of Alabama Press, 1975), 17.

33 Kerouac quoted by Aronowitz in 'Part II: The Beat Papers of Al Aronowitz.'

34 A.N. Nikoliukin, *Vzaimosviazi literatur Rossii i SShA: Turgenev, Tolstoi, Dostoevskii i Amerika* [*The Interrelations of Russian and American Literatures: Turgenev, Tolstoy, Dostoevsky and America*] (Moscow: Nauka, 1987), 250.

35 William Faulkner, *Faulkner in the University*, ed. Fredrick L. Gwynn and Joseph L. Blotner (1965; repr. Charlottesville: University Press of Virginia, 1977), 69.

36 Jean Weisgerber, *Faulkner and Dostoïévski; Confluences et influences* (Brussels: Presses universitaires de Bruxelles, 1968).

37 See Maria Bloshteyn, 'Anguish for the Sake of Anguish' – Faulkner and His Dostoevskian Allusion,' *Faulkner Journal* 19 (Spring 2004): 69–90.

38 There was an earlier pirated edition in 1940, which earned the publisher a jail sentence.

39 For an expert first-hand account of the trials, see the book written by the lawyer who defended *Tropic of Cancer* in numerous court cases: Charles Rembar, *The End of Obscenity* (New York: Random House, 1968).

40 Erica Jong, *The Devil at Large* (London: Chatto and Windus, 1993), 185.

41 Norman Mailer, 'An Appreciation of Henry Miller' (1966), repr: in Norman Mailer, *Existential Errands* (New York: Signet, 1973), 185.

42 Cited from Miller's letter to Grove Press's Barney Rosset, where the former expresses his concern about what would happen 'if by some freak of fortune *Tropic of Cancer* won over the courts.' The letter is quoted almost in its entirety in Jay Martin's biography of Henry Miller Jay Martin, *Always Merry and Bright: The Life of Henry Miller* (Santa Barbara: Capra, 1979), 63.

43 Mary V. Dearborn, *The Happiest Man Alive: Henry Miller, A Biography* (New York: Simon and Schuster, 1991), 279.
44 James M. Decker, *Henry Miller and Narrative Form: Constructing the Self, Rejecting Modernity* (New York and London: Routledge, 2005), 168, n1.
45 Karl Orend, 'Making a Place for Henry Miller in the American Classroom,' *The Chronicle of Higher Education* 50.18 (2004): 6–8; repr. in *Nexus; The International Henry Miller Journal* 2.1 (2005): 62, 65.
46 'Henry Miller: The Art of Fiction XXVIII,' interviewer George Wickes, *Paris Review* 28 (Summer/Fall 1962): 129–59; repr. in *Conversations With Henry Miller*, ed. Frank L. Kersnowski and Alice Hughes (Jackson: University Press of Mississippi, 1994), 44.
47 Decker, *Henry Miller and Narrative Form*, 155.
48 Henry Miller, 'Henry Miller: The Art of Fiction XXVIII,' 36.
49 Henry Miller, 'Mother, China and the World Beyond,' *Sextet* (Santa Barbara: Capra, 1977), 187.
50 Muchnic, *Dostoevsky's English Reputation*, 156.

Chapter 2: Dostoevsky as American Icon

1 For the history of the Dostoevsky portrait painted by Perov and for some Russian reactions at the time see V.G. Bazanov et al., eds., *F.M. Dostoevskii, novye materialy i issledovaniia* [*F.M. Dostoevsky, New Materials and Research*] (Moscow: Nauka, 1973), 118–24.
2 Carl Naerup quoted in Geir Kjetsaa, *Fyodor Dostoyevsky, A Writer's Life*, trans. Siri Hustvedt and David McDuff (New York: Fawcett Columbine, 1987), 269.
3 Term coined by D. Mirsky in *Intelligentsia of Great Britain* (London: Victor Gollancz, 1935).
4 For a discussion of Constance Garnett's importance as a translator, see Charles A. Moser, 'The Achievement of Constance Garnett,' *The American Scholar* 57.30 (1988): 431–8; for a discussion of Garnett's handling of Dostoevsky's texts see A.N. Nikoliukin's 'Dostoevskii v perevode Konstans Garnet' ['Dostoevsky in the Translation of Constance Garnett'], *Russkaia literatura; istoriko-literaturnyi zhurnal* [*Russian Literature; A Historical-Literary Journal*] 2 (1985): 154–62. (This article is also available in English translation in *Dostoevskii and Britain*, a book of essays edited by W.J. Leatherbarrow [Oxford: Berg, 1995], 207–27.)
5 Henry James, *French Poets and Novelists* (Leipzig: Tauchnitz, 1883), 220.

6 Anonymous reviewer, 'French and German Books; *Littérature Contemporaine en Russie*,' *Scribners Monthly*, 10. 2 (June 1875), 256.

7 D.H. Lawrence, *Studies in Classic American Literature* (1923; repr. New York: Penguin, 1986), 4–7.

8 A.N. Nikoliukin, *Vzaimosviazi literatur Rossii i SshA: Turgenev, Tolstoi, Dostoevskii i Amerika* [*The Interrelations of Russian and American Literatures: Turgenev, Tolstoy, Dostoevsky and America*] (Moscow: Nauka, 1987), 262.

9 Helen Muchnie, *Dostoevsky's English Reputation: 1881–1936* (Northampton, MA: Smiths College, 1939).

10 See Appendix A for an account of scholarship available on the subject.

11 Joseph Frank, *Dostoevsky: The Years of Ordeal* (Princeton, NJ: Princeton University Press, 1983), 159.

12 D.I. Pisarev, 'Pogibshie i pogibaiushchie' ['The Perished and the Perishing'] (1866) in *F. M. Dostoevskii v russkoi kritike, sbornik statei* [*Dostoevsky and Russian Criticism*], ed. A. Dmitrieva (Moscow: Gosudarstvennoe izdatel'stvo khudozhestvennoi literatury, 1956), 97.

13 Serge Wolkonsky, *Pictures of Russian History and Russian Literature* (Boston: Lamson, Wolfee, 1898), 7.

14 An American reviewer in an anonymous untitled article which appeared in *The Critic* in 1887 (11:138).

15 It was translated by Jane Loring Edmands and published as *The Russian Novelists* in Boston in 1887.

16 F.W.J. Hemmings, *The Russian Novel in France, 1884–1914* (Oxford: Oxford University Press, 1950), 41.

17 E.M. Vogüé, *Le roman russe* (Paris: Librairie Plan, 1886), 270.

18 Ibid., 261.

19 E.M. Vogüé, *Journal du vicomte E.-M. de Vogüé, Paris–Saint-Pétersbourg, 1877–1883* (Paris: Grasset, 1932), 164.

20 Vogüé, *Le roman russe*, 270.

21 Vogüé, *Journal du vicomte E.-M. de Vogüé*, 164.

22 Vogüé, *Le roman russe*, 208.

23 Ibid., 241.

24 Ibid., 204.

25 Ibid., 240.

26 Ibid., 207.

27 Ibid., 257.

28 Ibid., 255.

29 Henry James, 'To Hugh Walpole,' 19 May 1912, *The Letters of Henry James*, ed. Percy Lubbock (London: Macmillan, 1920), 2:246.

30 Vogüé, *Le roman russe*, 267.
31 Ibid., 203. Interestingly, Vogüé first applied this description to Tolstoy (in the original essays) but thought better of it when he was revising the essays for publication as a book.
32 Ibid., 267.
33 William Dean Howells, *Criticism and Fiction* (New York: Harper, 1892), 126.
34 Ibid., 128–9. Some American scholars and critics have argued that Howell's optimistic vision of America was already outdated when he was writing it. See, for example, Vernon Parrington, *Main Currents in American Thought: The Beginnings of Critical Realism in America 1860–1920* (New York: Harcourt, Brace, 1934), 3:316.
35 S.E. Morison, H.S. Commager, and W.E. Leuchtenburg, eds., *The Growth of the American Republic*, 7th ed. (New York: Oxford University Press, 1980), 2:281.
36 T.S. Eliot, 'To Eleanor Hinkley,' 23 July 1917, *Letters of T.S. Eliot*, ed. Valerie Eliot (London: Faber and Faber, 1988), 1:189.
37 Nathan H. Dole, 'Contemporary Russian Literature,' *The Chautauquan* 8 (1888), 465.
38 T.S. Eliot's response in 1947 to a scholar who noted the parallels between the character of J. Alfred Prufrock and Raskolnikov and surmised that Eliot read *Crime and Punishment* in the Garnett translations (cited at length in Henri Peyre's *French Literary Imagination and Dostoevsky and Other Essays* [Tuscaloosa: University of Alabama Press, 1975], 22–3).
39 Carol Apollonio Flath, 'Demons of Translation: The Strange Path of Dostoevsky's Novels into the English Translation,' *Dostoevsky Studies, New Series*, 9 (2005), 51.
40 Mirra Ginzburg, 'On The Translation,' *Notes from Underground*, trans. Mirra Ginzburg (New York: Bantam Books, 1992), xxvii.
41 See, for instance, A.N. Nikoliukin's 'Dostoevskii v perevode Konstans Garnet' ['Dostoevsky in the Translation of Constance Garnett'] *Russkaia literatura; istoriko-literaturnyi zhurnal* 2 (1985), 154–62.
42 The names of the lane and the bridge that Dostoevsky had in mind here have been identified as Stoliarnyi Lane and Kokushkin Bridge.
43 Fyodor Dostoevsky, *Crime and Punishment*, trans. by Constance Garnett (1914; repr. Hertfordshire: Wordsworth, 2000), 3.
44 Vladimir Dal', *Tolkovyi slovar' v chetyrekh tomakh* [*Dictionary in Four Volumes*] (Moscow: Russkii iazyk, 1989), 2:82.
45 Peter France, 'The Rhetoric of Translation,' *Modern Language Review Supplement, One Hundred Years of MLR: General and Comparative Studies* (October 2005), 267. http://mhra.org.uk/ojs/index.php/MLR/article/viewFile/3/34.

46 Peter France, 'Peter France on the Art of the Translator,' posted at http://
    www.oup.co.uk/academic/humanities/literature/viewpoint/
    peter_france.
47 Lawrence Venuti in conversation with Robert Wechsler. Robert Wechsler,
    Performing Without a Stage: The Art of Literary Translation (North Haven, CT:
    Catbird Press, 1988), 293.
48 Dostoevsky, *Crime and Punishment*, trans. Garnett, 23.
49 Ibid., 129, 165, 381.
50 Ibid., 284.
51 Ibid., 373.
52 Ibid., 26.
53 France, 'The Rhetoric of Translation,' 264.
54 Floyd Dell, 'The Novels of Dostoevsky,' *The New Review: A Critical Survey of
    International Socialism* 3.6 (15 May 1915), 38.
55 Ibid.
56 Ibid.
57 Matthew Josephson, *Life Among the Surrealists: A Memoir* (New York: Holt,
    Rinehart and Winston, 1962), 23.
58 Sherwood Anderson, 'To Hart Crane,' 4 March 1921, *Letters; Selected and
    Edited with an Introduction and Notes by Howard Mumford Jones, in Association
    with Walter B. Rideout* (Boston: Little, Brown, 1953), 70–1.
59 Hart Crane, 'To Gorham Munson,' 23 December 1920, *The Letters of Hart
    Crane, 1916–1932*, ed. Brom Weber (Berkeley: University of California Press,
    1965), 47.
60 John Dos Passos, *The Fourteenth Chronicle: Letters and Diaries*, ed. T.
    Ludington (Boston: Gambit, 1973), 23.
61 Dell, 'The Novels of Dostoevsky,' 38.
62 Dorothy Brewster and Angus Burrell, *Dead Reckonings in Fiction* (New York:
    Longmans, 1925), 175.
63 Ernest Hemingway, *A Moveable Feast* (New York: Scribner, 1964), 137.
64 Thomas Wolfe, 'To Scott Fitzgerald,' 26 July 1937, *The Letters*, ed. E. Nowell
    (New York: Scribner, 1956), 643.
65 Sherwood Anderson, 'To Eleanor Copenhaver Anderson,' 29 April 1929,
    Sherwood Anderson's Love Letters to Eleanor Copenhaver Anderson, ed. Charles
    E. Modlin (Athens: University of Georgia Press, 1989), 9.
66 Theodore Dreiser, 'To Simon and Schuster,' 26 March 1929, *Letters: A Selec-
    tion*, ed. Robert H. Elias (Philadelphia: University of Philadelphia Press,
    1959), 2:488.
67 Gilbert Phelps, *The Russian Novel in English Fiction* (London: Hutchinson's
    University Library, 1956), 169.

68 Upton Sinclair, *Mammonart: An Essay in Economic Interpretation* (Pasadena, CA: Published by the Author, 1925), 265–7.
69 Hemingway, *A Moveable Feast*, 134–5.
70 Ezra Pound, 'To Robert McAlmon,' 2 February 1934, *The Letters of Ezra Pound 1907–1941*, ed. D.D. Paige (New York: Harcourt, Brace, 1950), 252.
71 Randolph Bourne, 'The Immanence of Dostoevsky,' *The Dial* (28 June 1917): 24–5.
72 Malcolm Cowley, *Exile's Return: A Literary Odyssey of the 1920s* (New York: Norton, 1934), 94–104.
73 Ibid., 104.
74 Phelps, *The Russian Novel in English Fiction*, 172.
75 John Cowper Powys, *Visions and Revisions: A Book of Literary Devotions* (New York: G. Arnold Shaw, 1915), 252.
76 John Cowper Powys, *Autobiography* (1934; repr. London: Macdonald, 1967), 526–7.
77 *The Dial* was a monthly journal of literary criticism originally published in Chicago in 1880; it had moved its headquarters to New York by 1918. It became famous for publishing cutting-edge modern authors and reproducing radical modern graphics. *The Masses* was described as '[t]he originator of radical journalism in America as we know it' (Jack Alan Robbins, 'Editor's Introduction,' *Granville Hicks in the New Masses* [Port Washington, NY: Kennikat, 1974], xi).
78 Floyd Dell, 'Review,' *The Masses* (April 1916), 28.
79 Vladimir Nabokov, *Strong Opinions* (New York: McGraw-Hill, 1973), 42.
80 Muchnic, *Dostoevsky's English Reputation (1881–1936)*, 6.
81 Ibid., 156.
82 Ibid., 175.
83 Phelps, *The Russian Novel in English Fiction*, 173. Subsequent scholars who asked the same question arrived at similar conclusions. See, for instance, Colin Crowder, 'The Appropriation of Dostoevsky in the Early Twentieth Century: Cult, Counter-cult, and Incarnation,' in *European Literature and Theology in the Twentieth Century*, ed. David Jasper and Colin Crowder (Basingstoke: Macmillan, 1990), 22–3.
84 Phelps, *The Russian Novel in English Fiction*, 173.
85 Theodore Dreiser, 'To Victor Smirnov,' 5 August 1932, *Letters: A Selection*, 2:595.
86 Theodore Dreiser, 'To James T. Farrell,' 20 January 1944, *Letters: A Selection*, 3:1002.
87 Henry Miller, *Black Spring* (1936; repr. New York: Grove, 1963), 14.
88 Henry Miller, *The Rosy Crucifixion: Nexus* (1960; repr. New York: Grove, 1965), 19–20.

Chapter 3: Henry Miller's Road to Dostoevsky

1 Henry Miller, *Tropic of Capricorn* (1934; repr. New York: Grove, 1961), 208.
2 Henry Miller, *Joey: A Loving Portrait of Alfred Perlès Together with Some Bizarre Episodes Relating to the Other SexVolume III, Book of Friends* (Santa Barbara, CA: Capra, 1979), 103.
3 Henry Miller, *Black Spring* (1936; repr. New York: Grove, 1963), 15.
4 Ibid., 70.
5 Henry Miller in Malvin Wald 'Living History: Life on Kosciuszko Street,' *Creative Screenwriting* (03/25/05). www.creativescreenwriting.com/csdaily/trenches/03_25_05.html.
6 Henry Miller, *The Rosy Crucifixion: Plexus* (1953; repr. New York: Grove, 1965), 610.
7 Henry Miller, 'Mother, China and the World Beyond,' *Sextet* (Santa Barbara: Capra, 1977) 187.
8 Henry Miller, *Art and Outrage: A Correspondence About Henry Miller Between Alfred Perlès and Lawrence Durrell (With an Intermission by Henry Miller)* (London: Putnam, 1959), 384.
9 Emma Goldman, *Social Significance of Modern Drama* (Boston: Richard and Badger, 1914), 273.
10 Attributed to Dostoevsky, 'The Priest and the Devil,' *Mother Earth Bulletin* (January 1910), 360–2.
11 Emma Goldman, *Anarchism and Other Essays* (New York: Mother Earth Publishing Association, 1917), 117.
12 Emma Goldman, *Living My Life* (1931; repr. New York: Alfred Knopf, 1971), 1:91.
13 Erica Jong, *The Devil at Large* (London: Chatto and Windus, 1993), 78.
14 Herman Spector, 'Liberalism and the Literary Esoterics,' *New Masses* (January 1929), 18.
15 Michael Gold, 'Floyd Dell Resigns,' *New Masses* (July 1929), 10.
16 Alfred Kazin, *On Native Grounds: An Interpretation of Modern American Prose Literature* (New York: Harcourt, Brace and World, 1942), 415.
17 Jack Alan Robbins, 'Editor's Introduction,' *Granville Hicks in the New Masses* (Port Washington, NY: Kennikat, 1974), xiv.
18 W.J. Leatherbarrow, *Fedor Dostoevsky: A Reference Guide* (Boston: G.K. Hall, 1990), xxxvi.
19 Matthew Josephson, *Life Among the Surrealists: A Memoir* (New York: Holt, Rinehart and Winston, 1962), 215.
20 See the chapter 'Dostoevsky in the MKhAT Touring Companies and on the Anglo-American Stage,' in Vladimir Seduro's *Dostoevsky in Russian and*

World Theatre (North Quincy, MA: Christopher Publishing House, 1977), 230–409.

21 Henry Miller to W. Gordon, 26 August 1966, *Writer and Critic: A Correspondence with Henry Miller* (Baton Rouge: Louisiana State University Press, 1968), 40.

22 Henry Miller, *Crazy Cock* (New York: Grove, Weidenfeld, 1991), 192.

23 Henry Miller, 'Henry Miller: The Art of Fiction XXVII,' *Paris Review* 28 (Summer/Fall 1962); repr. in *Conversations with Henry Miller*, ed. Frank L. Kernowski and Alice Hughes (Jackson: University Press of Mississippi, 1994), 19.

24 Josephson, *Life Among the Surrealists*, 23.

25 Henry Miller, *The Rosy Crucifixion: Nexus* (1960; repr. New York: Grove, 1965), 11–12.

26 Miller, *Plexus*, 603

27 Miller, *Nexus*, 11.

28 Ibid., 11.

29 Ibid., 12.

30 Anaïs Nin, *Incest: From 'A Journal of Love,' The Unexpurgated Diary of Anaïs Nin, 1934–1935*. (San Diego: Harcourt Brace Jovanovich, 1992), 5.

31 Anaïs Nin, *The Diary of Anaïs Nin, Volume I: 1931–1934*, ed. Gunther Stuhluam (New York: Harcourt, Brace and World, 1966), 158.

32 Ibid., 158.

33 Henry Miller to Emil Conason, undated and unpublished letters from the summer of 1926, cited by Jay Martin in *Always Merry and Bright: The Life of Henry Miller* (1978; repr. New York: Penguin, 1980), 115. Miller was reading the novel in the Garnett translation, in which the title is rendered as *The Possessed*.

34 Anaïs Nin, *Incest*, 4.

35 Henry Miller, introduction, *Just Wild About Harry: A Melo-Melo in Seven Scenes* (New York: New Directions, 1963), 11.

36 Nin, *Diary*, 1:40.

37 Ibid., 54.

38 Nin, *UD:HJ*, 212. *Henry and June: From the Unexpurgated Diary of Anaïs Nin* (San Diego: Harcourt Brace Jovanovich, 1986), 212.

39 Nina Berberova, *Kursiv moi; avtobiografiia. [The Italics are Mine: Autobiography]*, 2nd rev. ed. (New York: Russica Publishers, 1983), 329.

40 AN to HM, 22 February 1932, *A Literate Passion*, 13.

41 Henry Miller, 'Henry Miller: The Art of Fiction XXVIII,' 53.

42 HM to AN, 29 November 1934, *A Literate Passion*, 235–6.

43 F.W. Hemmings, *The Russian Novel in France, 1884–1914* (London: Oxford University Press, 1950), 236.

44 Ibid., 238–9.

45 See Peyre's discussion of Salavin in the Dostoevskian context. Henri Peyre, *French Literary Imagination and Dostoevsky and Other Essays* (Tuscaloosa: Alabama University Press, 1975), 40–1.

46 Henry Miller to Anaïs Nin, 18 June 1933, *A Literate Passion*, 167.

47 Perlès, in *Art and Outrage*, 47.

48 Miller, *Nexus*, 18.

49 Cited in Annette Baxter, *Henry Miller Expatriate* (Pittsburgh, PA: University of Pittsburgh Press, 1961), 184–5.

50 See Miller's Appendix to *Books in My Life* (1952; repr. London: P. Owen; Norfolk, CT: New Directions, 1969).

51 Henry Miller, *Moloch or This Gentile World* (New York: Grove, 1992), 5.

52 HM to LD, 29 July 1937, *The Durrell-Miller Letters 1935–80*, ed. Ian S. MacNiven (London: Baker and Faber, 1988), 85.

53 HM to AN, 12 February 1932, *A Literate Passion*, 24.

54 Miller, *Plexus*, 151.

55 Alfred Perlès, *My Friend Henry Miller* (New York: John Day, 1956), 17.

56 Henry Miller, *Big Sur and the Oranges of Hieronymus Bosch* (London: Heinemann, 1958), 248.

57 Miller, *Nexus*, 18.

58 Miller, *Tropic of Cancer*, 211–12.

59 Henry Miller, *The World of Lawrence: A Passionate Appreciation*, ed. Evelyn J. Hinz and John J. Teunissen (Santa Barbara, CA: Capra, 1980), 111.

60 Henry Miller, *The Books in My Life* (1957; repr. London: P. Owen; Norfolk, CT: New Directions, 1969), 136.

61 John Cowper Powys, *Visions and Revisions: A Book of Literary Devotions* (New York: G. Arnold Shaw, 1915), 244.

62 John Cowper Powys, *Dostoievsky* (New York: Haskell House, 1946), 7.

63 Miller, *Books in My Life*, 210.

64 Janko Lavrin, *Dostoevsky: A Study* (New York: Macmillan, 1947), 156.

65 See G. Poliak, 'Genri Miller i russkie na zapadeO russkoi versii romana' ['Henry Miller and the Russians in the West; The Russian Version of the Novel'], *Tropic raka* [*Tropic of Cancer*], trans. Egorov (Moscow: Terra, 1994), 313–15, and Berdiaev's own comments about Miller's depiction of the world in *Tsarstvo Dukha i tsarstvo Kesaria*. [*The Kingdom of the Spirit and the Kingdom of Caesar*] (1949; repr. Moscow: Respublika, 1995), 323.

66 HM to LD, 28 August 1966, *The Durrell-Miller Letters 1935–80*, 48.

67 HM to LD, 8 November 1953, ibid., 273.

68 Miller, *Nexus*, 18–19.

69 Nikolai Berdiaev, *Dostoievsky: An Interpretation by Nicholas Berdyaev*, trans. Donald Attwater (London: Sheed and Ward, 1934), 14.
70 Oswald Spengler, *Decline of the West* (1918–1922), ed. Helmut Werner, trans. Charles Francis Atkinson (New York: Alfred A. Knopf, 1962), 273.
71 Ibid., 172.
72 Henry Miller, *Wisdom of the Heart* (New York: New Directions, 1941), 231–2.
73 Miller, *Plexus*, 637.
74 D.H. Lawrence, 'Preface to *The Grand Inquisitor*' (1930), in D.H. Lawrence, *Selected Literary Criticism*, ed. Anthony Beal (London: Mercury Books, 1961), 235. Also see the chapter on D.H. Lawrence in Peter Kaye's *Dostoevsky and English Modernism, 1900–1930* (Cambridge: Cambridge University Press, 1999), 29–65.
75 Martin, *Always Merry and Bright*, 286.
76 Henry Miller to Anaïs Nin, 8 August 1933, S.I.U.'s Morris Library, COLL 78/12/11.
77 Ihab Hassan, *The Literature of Silence: Henry Miller and Samuel Beckett* (New York: Alfred A. Knoff, 1967), 49.
78 Peter Kaye, *Dostoevsky and English Modernism, 1900–1930* (Cambridge: Cambridge University Press, 1999), 192.
79 Miller, *Wisdom of the Heart*, 2.
80 Miller, *The World of Lawrence*, 137–8.
81 D.H. Lawrence, 'Letter to J. M. Murry,' 28 August 1916, in D.H. Lawrence, *Selected Literary Criticism* (London: Mercury, 1961), 232.
82 Nin cites Miller on Gide's interpretation of Dostoevsky in a letter of 22 February 1932 (*A Literate Passion*, 12).
83 André Gide, *Dostoevsky*, trans. J.M. Dent (1925; repr. London: Secker and Warburg, 1949), 146.
84 Ibid., 162.
85 Ibid., 127.
86 Miller's letter quoted in Michael Fraenkel, 'Genesis of the Tropic of Cancer,' *Happy Rock: A Book About Henry Miller* (Berkeley, CA: Bern Porter, 1945), 38–56.
87 Miller, *The Books in My Life*, 146.
88 Mary Dearborn, *The Happiest Man Alive: Henry Miller, A Biography* (New York: Simon and Schuster, 1991), 217.
89 Norman Mailer, *Genius and Lust: A Journey Through the Major Writings of Henry Miller By Norman Mailer* (New York: Grove, 1976), 6–7.
90 John Parkin, *Henry Miller: The Modern Rabelais* (Lewiston, NY: Mellen, 1990), 39–40.

91 Ibid., 65.
92 Miller, 'Living Books,' *The Books in My Life*, 138.
93 Miller, *Tropic of Cancer*, 255.
94 Miller, 'Letter to Pierre Lesdain,' *The Books in My Life*, 221.
95 Miller, *Plexus*, 20–1.
96 Ibid., 21.
97 Miller, *The World of Lawrence*, 51.
98 Henry Miller, 'The Universe of Death from *The World of Lawrence*,' *The Cosmological Eye* (New York: New Directions, 1939), 123.
99 Miller, *Books in My Life*, 230.
100 Henry Miller, epilogue, *Smile at the Foot of the Ladder* (1948; repr. Norfolk, CT: New Directions, 1959), 47.
101 Miller, *Nexus*, 31.
102 J. Middleton Murry, *Fyodor Dostoevsky: A Critical Study* (London: Martin Secker, 1916), 263.
103 D.H. Lawrence, 'Letter to J.M. Murry,' 28 August 1916, in Lawrence, *Selected Literary Criticism*, 232.
104 Miller, *The World of Lawrence*, 138.
105 Miller, *Wisdom of the Heart*, 216.
106 T.S. Eliot, 'Ulysses, Order, and Myth' (1923), in T.S. Eliot, *Selected Prose*, ed. Frank Kermode (New York: Harcourt Brace Jovanovich, 1975), 177.
107 Miller, *Joey*, 53–4.
108 Jong, *The Devil at Large*, 239.

Chapter 4: Henry Miller's Villa Seurat Circle and Dostoevsky

1 Henry Miller to Anaïs Nin, 26 April 1934, in *A Literate Passion: Letters of Anaïs Nin and Henry Miller, 1932–1953*, ed. Gunther Stuhlmann (New York: Harcourt Brace Jovanovich, 1987), 231.
2 Alfred Perlès, 'Henry Miller in Villa Seurat,' *Happy Rock: A Book About Henry Miller* (Berkeley, CA: Bern Porter, 1945), 58.
3 See Appendix B for a brief account of scholarship available on Miller, Nin, and Durrell and their work.
4 Harry T. Moore, biographer and scholar of D.H. Lawrence, wrote an introduction to Nin's study upon its American publication thirty-two years later, praising the book for being 'one of the most valuable books on Lawrence because of its discussion of the *texture* of his work' (Harry T. Moore, 'Introduction,' *D.H. Lawrence: An Unprofessional Study*, by Anaïs Nin (1932; repr. Denver: Alan Swallow, 1964), 10.

5 HM to AN, 12 February 1932, *A Literate Passion*, 6.

6 Anaïs Nin, *Henry and June: From the Unexpurgated Diary of Anaïs Nin* (New York: Harcourt Brace Jovanovich, 1986), 34.

7 Nin, *Nearer the Moon: From 'A Journal of Love,' The Unexpurgated Diary of Anaïs Nin, 1937–1939* (New York: Harcourt Brace & Company, 1996), 315.

8 Deidre Bair, *Anaïs Nin: A Biography* (New York: G.P. Putnam, 1995), 230.

9 Ibid., 157.

10 Nin, *Henry and June*, 150.

11 It is highly suggestive that the bloated *Rosy Crucifixion* trilogy, which was extensively criticized at the time of its publication by Miller's own friends and, subsequently, by many of his biographers and scholars, had little, if any, input from Nin.

12 Anaïs Nin to Henry Miller, *A Literate Passion*, 4–5.

13 Nin, *The Diary of Anaïs Nin. Vol 1: 1931–1934*, ed. Gunther Stuhlmann (New York: Harcourt, Brace and World, 1966), 167.

14 Nin, *The Diary of Anaïs Nin. Vol 2: 1934–1939*, ed. Gunther Stuhlmann (New York: Harcourt, Brace and World, 1967), 149.

15 Robert Ferguson, *Henry Miller: A Life* (London: Hutchinson, 1991), 210.

16 Noël Riley Fitch, *Anaïs: The Erotic Life of Anaïs Nin* (Boston: Little, Brown, 1993), 119.

17 Miller, *Tropic of Cancer* (1934; repr. New York: Grove, 1961), 32.

18 Nin, *Diary*, 2:267.

19 LD to HM, 19 December 1936, *The Durrell-Miller Letters 1935–80*, ed. Ian S. MacNiven (London: Faber and Faber, 1988), 30.

20 LD to HM, February? 1937, ibid., 54.

21 LD to HM, September? 1935, ibid., 4.

22 LD to HM, c. 27 January 1937, ibid., 52.

23 Lawrence Durrell, translated interview, 'Using Diversions to Transmit the Essential' (31 March 1988), *Lawrence Durrell, Conversations*, ed. Earl G. Ingersoll (London: Associated University Presses, 1998), 246.

24 Ian MacNiven, *Lawrence Durrell: A Biography* (London: Faber and Faber, 1998), 124.

25 Miller, *Tropic of Cancer*, 2.

26 LD to HM, late March 1937, *The Durrell-Miller Letters 1935–80*, 65.

27 Nin, *Diary*, 2:226.

28 Ibid., 223.

29 Jay Martin, *Always Merry and Bright: The Life of Henry Miller* (1978; repr. New York: Penguin, 1980), 318.

30 LD to HM, late March 1937, *The Durrell-Miller Letters 1935–80*, 65.

31 HM to LD, 8 March 1937, ibid., 55.

32 HM to LD, early December? 1938, ibid., 109.
33 LD's letter to AN included in Nin, *Diary*, 2:183.
34 LD's letter to AN included in Nin, *Diary*, 2:204.
35 Anaïs Nin's letter to LD included in ibid., 150.
36 Ibid., 223.
37 MacNiven, *Lawrence Durrell*, 167.
38 Bair, *Anaïs Nin*, 235.
39 Nin, *Diary*, 2:233.
40 Nancy Myers (Durrell) Hodgkin, recorded memoir, 2:95–6, cited in Macniven, *Lawrence Durrell*, 185.
41 HM to LD, 29 July 1937, *The Durrell-Miller Letters 1935–80*, 84, 85.
42 Nin, 238.
43 Nin, *Nearer the Moon, From A Journal of Love, The Unexpurgated Diary of Anaïs Nin 1937–1939* (New York: Harcourt, Brace, 1996), 90.
44 Nin cited in Fitch, *Anaïs: The Erotic Life of Anaïs Nin*, 339.
45 LD to HM, c. October 1945, *The Durrell-Miller Letters 1935–80*, 187.
46 LD to HM, 25 December 1937, ibid., 97.
47 LD to HM, c. August 1936, ibid., 17.
48 LD to HM, August 1936, ibid., 20.
49 LD to HM, Fall 1936, ibid., 24.
50 See *Booster* drafts, placards, and typescripts at the Durrell Collection in SIU's Morris Collection at Carbondale.
51 Henry Miller, 'Henry Miller: The Art of Fiction XXVIII' [Interview with George Wickes], *Paris Review* 28 (Summer/Fall 1962): 129–59, repr. in *Conversations with Henry Miller*, ed. Frank L. Kersnowski and Alice Hughes (Jackson: University Press of Mississippi, 1994), 55.
52 Martin, *Always Merry and Bright*, 315.
53 Nin, *Diary*, 2:253.
54 Ibid., 231.
55 Nin, *Nearer the Moon*, 169.
56 Nin, *Diary*, 2:231.
57 Lawrence Durrell, translated interview, 'Using Diversions to Transmit the Essential' (31 March 1988), *Lawrence Durrell: Conversations*, ed. Earl G. Ingersoll (London: Associated University Presses, 1998), 247.
58 Lawrence Durrell, preface, *Dear, Dear Brenda: The Love Letters of Henry Miller to Brenda Venus*, ed. Gerald Seth Sindell (New York: William Morrow, 1986), 9.
59 MacNiven, *Lawrence Durrell, A Biography*, 186–7.
60 HM to LD, 22? December 1936, *The Durrell-Miller Letters 1935–80*, 33.
61 Martin, *Always Merry and Bright*, 326.
62 Nin, *Diary*, 2:267.

63 LD to HM, August 1935, *The Durrell-Miller Letters 1935–80*, 2.

64 LD to HM, February? 1937, ibid., 55.

65 Lawrence Durrell, preface, *The Black Book* (1936; repr. New York: Dutton, 1960), 13.

66 Nin, *Diary,* 2:233.

67 S.I.U.'s Morris Library, Special Collections, MSS 30.

68 Anaïs Nin to HM, 12 February 1932, *A Literate Passion*, 4.

69 Nin, *Henry and June*, 49.

70 HM to LD, 3 May 1937, *The Durrell-Miller Letters 1935–80*, 74.

71 HM to Anaïs Nin, 17 October 1933, *A Literate Passion*, 225.

72 HM to Anaïs Nin, 3 May 1937, *The Durrell-Miller Letters 1935–80*, 74.

73 HM to Anaïs Nin, 3 October 1933, *A Literate Passion*, 122.

74 LD to HM, Early September 1937, *The Durrell-Miller Letters 1935–80*, 94.

75 Miller, *Black Spring*, 49.

76 LD to HM, early November 1936, *The Durrell-Miller Letters 1935–80*, 22–3.

77 LD to HM, August 1935, ibid., 2.

78 Ibid.

79 HM to LD, 1 September 1935, ibid., 3.

80 HM to LD, 15 March 1937, ibid., 60.

81 Nin, *Nearer the Moon*, 131.

82 Nin, *Henry and June*, 126.

83 Henry Miller, 'Reflections on Writing,' *Wisdom of the Heart* (New York: New Directions, 1941), 28.

84 Henry Miller, 'Un Être Etoilique,' *The Cosmological Eye* (1938; repr. New York: New Directions, 1939), 289.

85 HM to LD, 8 March 1937, *The Durrell-Miller Letters 1935–80*, 55–6.

86 HM to LD, December 1938, ibid., 108–9.

87 Henry Miller, *Moloch Or, This Gentile World* (1928; repr. New York: Grove, 1992), 201.

88 Miller, *Tropic of Capricorn* (1939; repr. New York: Grove, 1961), 114.

89 Ibid., 114–16.

90 Miller, *Sexus*, 366–7.

91 Ibid., 366.

92 Miller, *Moloch Or, This Gentile World*, 235.

93 Miller, *Tropic of Capricorn*, 112.

94 Ibid., 84.

95 Ibid., 85.

96 Miller, *Books in My Life* (1957; repr. London: P. Owen; Norfolk, CT: New Directions, 1969), 25.

97 Miller, *Black Spring*, 22.

98 Miller, *Tropic of Capricorn*, 92.
99 In 1932, Rank's book was translated into French as *Don Juan. Une étude sur le double*, trans. S. Lautman (Paris: Denoël and Steele, 1932). This is the version that was read by most members of Villa SeuratNin, of course, was familiar with Rank's ideas through her personal and professional association with him.
100 Durrell, *The Black Book*, 80.
101 Ibid., 34–5.
102 My translation of the word *predstoit* is based not on the word's usage in contemporary Russian but on its nineteenth-century usage, as glossed in the second edition of the classic nineteenth-century Russian dictionary *Tolkovyi slovar' v chetyrekh tomakh* of Vladimir Dal' (Moscow: Russkii iazyk, 1990), 3:389.
103 Lawrence Durrell, *Tunc* (London: Faber and Faber, 1968), 317.
104 *Art and Outrage: A Correspondence About Henry Miller Between Alfred Perlès and Lawrence Durrell (With an Intermission by Henry Miller)* (London: Putnam, 1959), 25.
105 Lawrence Durrell, *Key to Modern British Poetry* (Norman: University of Oklahoma Press, 1952), 49.

Chapter 5: Post-Dostoevskian Prose and the Villa Seurat Circle

1 A.A. Tolstaia, 'Vospominaniia' ['Reminiscences'], *F.M. Dostoevskii v zabytykh i neizvestnykh vospominaniiakh sovremennikov [F.M. Dostoevsky in Forgotten and Unknown Reminiscences of His Contemporaries]*, ed. S.V. Belov (St Petersburg: Andreev i synov'ia, 1993), 257.
2 Cited in F.M. Dostoevsky, *F.M. Dostoevsky: Polnoe sobranie sochinenii, tridtsati tomakh. [Collected Works of Doestoevsky in Thirty Volumes]* Academy of Sciences (Leningrad: Navkà, 1976–90) 17:351.
3 L. Tolstoy, 'Tolstoi o literature i iskusstve' ['Tolstoy on Literature and Art'] *Literaturnoe nasledstvo* 37–8 (1939): 546.
4 Vissarion Belinskii, 'Bednye liudi. Roman Fedora Dostoevskogo' ['*Poor Folk*: A Novel of Fedor Dostoevsky'], (1847) *Polnoe sobranie sochinenii [Full Edition of Collected Works]* (Moscow: Izdatel'stvo Akademii Nauk SSSR, 1956), 363.
5 E.A. Ivanchikova, *Sintaksis khudozhestvennoi prozy Dostoevskogo [The Syntax of Dostoevsky's Literary Prose]* (Moscow: Nauka, 1979), 8.
6 N.A. Dobroliubov, 'Zabitye liudi' ['Downtrodden People'] (1861) *F.M. Dostoevskii v russkoi kritike [F.M. Dostoevsky in Russian Criticism]* (Moscow: Khudozhestvennaia literatura, 1956), 51.

7 N.K. Mikhailovskii, 'Zhestokii talant' ['Cruel Talent'] (Moscow: Khudozhestvennaia literatura, 1956), 372.

8 Victor Terras, 'Dostoevsky's Detractors,' *Dostoevsky Studies* 6 (1985): 165.

9 Anna Dostoevskaia, *Vospominaniia A.G. Dostoevskoi [Reminiscences of A.G. Dostoevsky]* (Moscow: Gosudarstvennoe izdatel'stvo, 1925), 150.

10 Strakhov and Dostoevsky had, to all appearances, a close and cordial relationship during Dostoevsky's lifetime. After Dostoevsky's death, however, Strakhov discovered that Dostoevsky had privately expressed some harshly unflattering opinions about him in his notebooks, after which Strakhov wrote harshly unflattering and, some have claimed, slanderous letters about Dostoevsky to such people as Leo Tolstoy.

11 Cited in Vladimir Lobas, *Vsemirnaia istoriia v litsakh: Dostoevskii* (Moscow: ACT, 2000), 2:162–3.

12 Viacheslav Ivanov, 'Dostoevskii i roman-tragediia,' *Russkaia mysl'* (1911) 5:46–61, 6:1–17.

13 The original title of Bakhtin's study was *Problems of Dostoevsky's Art* [*Problemy Tvorchestva Dostoevskogo*]; it was changed for the 1963 edition.

14   See Leonid Grossman, *Poetika Dostoevskogo [Dostoevsky's Poetics]* (Moscow: Gosudarstvennaia Akademiia Khudezhestvennykh Nauk, 1925); Mikhail Bakhtin, *Problemy poetiki Dostoevskogo [The Problems of Dostoevsky's Poetics]* (1929, 1963; repr. Moscow: Izdatel'stvo Khudozhestvennaia Literatura, 1972); D.S. Likhachev, 'Nebrezhenie slovom' u Dostoevskogo' ['"Contempt for the Word" in Dostoevsky's Works'] *Dostoevskii: materialy i issledovaniia [Dostoevsky: Materials and Research]*, ed. G.M. Fridlender (Leningrad: Nauka, 1976), 30–41.

15 Joseph Brodsky, 'The Power of the Elements,' *Less Than One: Selected Essays* (New York: Penguin, 1987), 160.

16 Joseph Brodsky, 'Interv'iu *Vestnika:* Iosif Brodskii' ['*Vestnik* Interviews Joseph Brodsky'], *Vestnik* (Toronto) (2.11.1994): 7.

17 L.F. Dostoevskaia, *Dostoevskii v izobrazhenii svoei docheri [Dostoevsky in the Depiction of His Daughter]*, ed. S.V. Belov (St Petersburg: Andreev and Sons, 1992), 130.

18 Ibid., 231–66.

19 Dostoevsky's novels were occasionally translated from French and German renderings of the original text, often resulting in a broken-telephone effect, with the mistakes of the first translator reinforced and multiplied by the subsequent translators.

20 Virginia Woolf, *The Common Reader* (London: Hogarth, 1925), 220.

21 Truman Capote, *Conversations with Capote*, ed. Lawrence Grobel (New York: New American Library, 1985), 132.

22 Henry James, 'To Hugh Walpole,' 19 May 1912, *The Letters of Henry James*, ed. Percy Lubbock (London: MacMillan, 1920), 2:246.
23 André Gide, *Dostoevsky*, trans. J.M. Dent (1925; repr. London: Secker and Warburg, 1949), 157.
24 For an account of Dostoevsky's influence on OBERIU group see Bella Ulanovskaia, 'Mozhet li solntse rasserditsia na infusoriiu …' ['Can the Sun Become Angry at an Infusoria …,' (1974) *Dostoevskii v kontse XX veka* [*Dostoevsky at the End of the Twentieth Century*], ed. K. Stepanian (Moscow: Izdatel'stvo 'Klassika plius,' 1996), 604–21.
25 Bakhtin, *Problems of Dostoevsky's Poetics*, 462.
26 Donald Davie, *Russian Literature and Modern English Fiction* (Chicago: University of Chicago Press, 1965), 5; Gilbert Phelps, *The Russian Novel in English Fiction* (London: Hutchinson's University Library, 1956), 174–9.
27 Colin Crowder, 'The Appropriation of Dostoevsky in the Early Twentieth Century: Cult, Counterault and Incarnation,' in *European Literature in the Twentieth Century: Ends of Time*, ed. David Jasper and Colin Crowder (Basingstoke: Macmillan, 1990), 26.
28 Ernest Hemingway, *The Green Hills of Africa* (1935; repr. New York: Scribner, 1963), 26–7.
29 Henry Miller, 'Autobiographical Note,' *The Cosmological Eye* (New York: New Directions, 1964), 370.
30 LD to HM, September-October 1937, *The Durrell-Miller Letters 1935–80*, ed. Ian S. MacHiven (London: Paker and Paker, 1988), 117.
31 LD to HM, May-June 1946, ibid., 225.
32 AN to LD, October 1957, S.I.U.'s Morris Library, Special Collections, COLL 42/6/11.
33 Anaïs Nin, *The Novel of the Future* (New York: Macmillan, 1968), 11.
34 HM to LD, February 1937, S.I.U's Morris Library, Special Collections, COLL 42/5/8.
35 Anaïs Nin, 'Link in the Chain of Feeling: An Interview with Anaïs Nin,' (1976), repr. in *Conversations with Anaïs Nin*, ed. Wendy M. DuBow (Jackson: University Press of Mississippi, 1994), 238.
36 LD to HM, August 1935, *The Durrell-Miller Letters 1935–80*, 2.
37 Anaïs Nin, 'Anaïs Nin: An Interview' (October 1974), repr. in *Conversations with Anaïs Nin*, 212.
38 Anaïs Nin, 'Anaïs Nin: An Interview' (1975), repr. in *Conversations with Anaïs Nin*, ed. Wendy M. DuBow (Jackson: University Press of Mississippi, 1994), 223.
39 Miller, 'Universe of Death,' *The Cosmological Eye*, 133.
40 Ibid., 133.

41 Ibid., 129.
42 Ibid., 131.
43 Ibid., 115.
44 HM to LD, 5 April 1937, *The Durrell-Miller Letters 1935–80*, 69–70.
45 André Breton, 'Limits not Frontiers of Surrealism,' in *Surrealism*, ed. Herbert Read (London: Faber and Faber, 1936), 116.
46 Henry Miller, *Tropic of Cancer* (1934; repr. New York: Grove Press, 1961), 5.
47 George Orwell, 'Inside the Whale' (1945), repr. in *Henry Miller and the Critics*, ed. George Wickes (Carbondale: Southern Illinois University Press, 1963), 34.
48 Henry Miller, *Black Spring* (1936; repr. Paris: Obelisk; New York, Grove, 1963), 151, 165.
49 HM to LD, June 1936, *The Durrell-Miller Letters 1935–80*, 14.
50 Gay Louise Balliet, *Henry Miller and Surrealist Metaphor: 'Riding the Ovarian Trolley,'* (New York: Peter Lang Publishing, 1996), 141.
51 HM to AN, 29 November 1934, *A Literate Passion: Letters of Anaïs Nin and Henry Miller, 1932–1953*, ed. Gunther Stuhlmann (San Diego: Harcourt Brace Jovanovich, 1987), 235–6.
52 HM to LD, August 1936, *The Durrell-Miller Letters 1935–80*, 15–16.
53 Ibid., 15.
54 Lawrence Durrell, *The Black Book* (1938; repr. New York: Dutton, 1960), 23.
55 LD to HM, August 1936, *The Durrell-Miller Letters 1935–80*, 18.
56 Herbert Lyons, 'Surrealist Soap Opera,' (1946), repr. in *The Critical Response to Anais Nin*, ed. Philip K. Jason (Westport, CT: Greenwood, 1996), 105–6.
57 Anaïs Nin, *Novel of the Future* (New York: Macmillan Company, 1968), 2.
58 Anaïs Nin, *The Diary of Anaïs Nin, Vol 1: 1931–1934*, ed. Gunther Stuhlmann (New York: Harcourt, Brace and World, 1966), 77.
59 Anaïs Nin, *Fire: From a Journal of Love: The Unexpurgated Diary of Anaïs Nin* (New York: Harcourt, Brace 1995), 177.
60 Deirdre Bair, *Anaïs Nin: A Biography* (New York: Putnam, 1995), 419.
61 Anaïs Nin, *House of Incest* (1936; repr. Chicago: Swallow, 1958), 52–5.
62 Bair, *Anaïs Nin*, 381–2.
63 Nin, *Fire*, 302.
64 Ibid., 338.
65 HM to LD, 24 September 1936, S.I. U.'s Morris Library, Special Collections, COLL 42/5/7.
66 LD to HM, August 1936, *The Durrell-Miller Letters 1935–80*, 19.
67 HM to LD, 13–15 March 1937, ibid., 58.
68 HM to LD, 15 November 1936, ibid., 26.
69 HM to LD, 6 December 1936, S.I.U.'s Morris Library, Special Collections, COLL 42/5/7.

70 Miller, 'Open Letter to Surrealists Everywhere,' *The Cosmological Eye*, 181.
71 According to Read, for example, the surrealists 'cannot protest against the per-
    versions of a moral code for which they have no respect … [although] they
    despise the kind of people who indulge in perversion' (Herbert Read, Intro-
    duction, *Surrealism*, ed. Herbert Read [London: Faber and Faber, 1936], 85).
72 Ibid., 20.
73 Miller, 'Open Letter to Surrealists Everywhere,' 163–4.
74 Ibid., 178.
75 Ibid., 181.
76 Ibid., 194.
77 Henry Miller, 'Reflections on Writing,' *Wisdom of the Heart* (New York:
    New Directions, 1941), 23.
78 Henry Miller, 'Jean Giono,' *The Books in My Life* (1952; repr. London:
    P. Owen; Norfolk, CT: New Directions, 1969), 111.
79 HM to AN, 12 February 1932, *Henry Miller's Letters to Anaïs Nin*,
    ed. Gunther Stuhlmann (New York: Putnam, 1965), 23.
80 Ibid., 24.
81 HM to AN, 12 February 1932, *Henry Miller's Letters to Anaïs Nin*, 24.
82 Henry Miller, *Tropic of Cancer*, 9.
83 Miller, 'The Universe of Death,' 124.
84 Miller, *Tropic of Cancer*, 248.
85 Henry Miller, 'Letter to Pierre Lesdain,' *Books in My Life*, 223
86 AN to HM, 11 February 1932, *Anaïs, An International Journal* 16 (1998), 55.
87 AN to HM, 13 February 1932, *A Literate Passion*, 8–10.
88 Anaïs Nin, *Diary*, 1:267.
89 Anaïs Nin, *The Diary of Anaïs Nin, Vol 3: 1939–1944*, ed. Gunther Stuhlmann
    (New York: Harcourt, Brace and World, 1969), 138.
90 AN to LD, March 1939, *Anaïs: An International Journal* 5 (1987), 98.
91 HM to Michael Fraenkel, 23 November 1935, *The Michael Fraenkel – Henry
    Miller Correspondence Called Hamlet* (London: Carrefour, 1939), 53.
92 Miller's letter is quoted in its entirety in Fraenkel's 'The Genesis of the
    Tropic of Cancer' *Happy Rock: A Book About Henry Miller* (Berkeley, CA: Bern
    Porter, 1945), 38–56.
93 Michael Fraenkel, *Bastard Death: The Autobiography of an Idea* (Paris:
    Carrefour, 1936), 11.
94 Miller, *Tropic of Cancer*, 1.
95 Mary Dearborn, *The Happiest Man Alive: Henry Miller, A Biography* (New
    York: Simon and Schuster, 1991), 184.
96 Miller, 'Letter to Pierre Lesdain,' *Wisdom of the Heart*, 222.
97 Miller, 'Reflections on Writing,' *Wisdom of the Heart*, 28.

98 J. Middleton Murry, *Fyodor Dostoevsky: A Critical Study* (London: Martin Secker, 1916), 201.

99 Henry Miller, *The Rosy Crucifixion: Nexus* (1960; repr. New York: Grove, 1965), 29.

100 Ibid., 32.

101 Ibid., 31.

102 Ibid., 29.

103 Michael Fraenkel, *The Day Face and the Night Face* (New York: Irving Stettner, 1947), 51.

104 Henry Miller, *Stand Still Like a Hummingbird* (New York: New Directions, 1962), 47.

105 Miller, *Nexus*, 263.

106 Brassai, *Henry Miller: The Paris Years* (New York: Arcade, 1995), 36.

107 In an interview given in 1962, Miller says that he met Anderson later, in America, but that he 'had been in love with his work ... from the beginning' (Henry Miller, 'Henry Miller: The Art of Fiction XXVIII,' inteviewer George Wickes, *Paris Review* 28 [Summer/Fall 1962]; repr. in *Conversations With Henry Miller*, ed. Frank L. Kersnowski and Alice Hughes [Jackson: University Press of Mississippi, 1994] 56).

108 Miller, *Stand Still Like a Hummingbird*, 47.

109 Miller, *Tropic of Cancer*, 76–7.

110 Henry Miller, 'Waters Reglitterized,' *Sextet* (Santa Barbara: Capra, 1977), 103.

111 Anaïs Nin, *The Diary of Anaïs Nin, Vol 2: 1934–1939*, ed. Gunther Stuhlmann (New York: Harcourt, Brace and World, 1967), 262.

112 AN to LD, September 1937, S.I.U.'s Morris Library, Special Collections, COLL 42/6/10.

113 Anaïs Nin, 'Interview for Sweden' (1966), *Conversations with Anaïs Nin*, 16.

114 HM to LD, 13–15 March 1937, *The Durrell-Miller Letters 1935–80*, 61.

115 HM to LD, 29 July 1937, ibid., 85.

116 Miller, 'An Open Letter to Surrealists Everywhere,' 161.

117 Miller, *Tropic of Cancer*, 255.

118 Henry Miller, *Tropic of Capricorn* (1939; repr. New York: Grove, 1961), 209.

119 Miller, *Wisdom of the Heart*, 28.

120 Miller, 'Into the Future,' *The Wisdom of the Heart*, 163.

121 Miller, *Tropic of Cancer*, 162.

122 LD to HM, August 1935, *The Durrell-Miller Letters 1935–80*, 2–3.

123 Miller, 'Reflections on Writing,' 20.

124 Henry Miller, epilogue, *Smile at the Foot of the Ladder*, 46.

125 Henry Miller, 'Open Letter to Surrealists Everywhere,' 161.

126 Bair, *Anaïs Nin*, 493.

127 LD to HM, April 1937, *The Durrell-Miller Letters 1935–80*, 72.

128 Durrell, *The Black Book*, 76.

129 Ibid., 121.

130 Henry Miller, 'Draconian Postscript,' *Henry Miller and the Critics*, ed. George Wickes (Carbondale: Southern Illinois University Press, 1963), 188.

131 Miller, 'Reflections on Writing,' 25.

132 Miller, *Tropic of Capricorn*, 333.

133 Henry Miller, inteview (1956), repr. in *Conversations with Henry Miller*, 6.

134 Ibid.

135 Ibid.

136 Durrell, preface, *The Black Book*, 14.

137 Lawrence Durrell, S.I.U.'s Morris Library, Special Collections, COLL 42/7/2.

138 Anaïs Nin, 'Realism and Reality' (1946), *The Mystic of Sex and Other Writings*, ed. Gunther Stuhlmann (Santa Barbara: Capra, 1995), 26.

139 Ibid., 28–9.

140 Ibid., 26–8.

141 Anaïs Nin, 'On Writing' (1947), *The Mystic of Sex and Other Writings*, 34.

142 AN to HM, 11 February 1932, 'On Proust and Dostoevsky: From an Unpublished Letter to Henry Miller,' *Anaïs: An International Journal* 16 (1998): 6.

143 André Gide, *Dostoevsky*, trans. J.M. Dent (1925; repr. London: Secker and Warburg, 1949), 113.

144 HM to AN, 8 March 1933, S.I.U.'s Morris Library, Special Collections, COLL 78/12/11.

145 LD to HM, late March 1937, *The Durrell-Miller Letters 1935–80*, 65.

146 Cited by James Carley, 'The *Avignon Quintet* and Gnostic Heresy,' *Critical Essays on Lawrence Durrell*, ed. Alan Warren Friedman (Boston: G.K. Hall, 1987), 240.

147 Erica Jong, *The Devil at Large* (London: Random House, 1993), 237.

148 Karl Shapiro, 'The Charmed Circle of Anais Nin,' *The Criterion* 17 (October 1937), 35.

149 Vladimir Volkoff, *Lawrence le Magnifique: essai sur Lawrence Durrell et le roman relativiste* (Paris: Juliard, 1984).

150 Anaïs Nin, *Henry and June: From the Unexpurgated Diary of Anaïs Nin* (San Diego: Harcourt Brace Jovanovich, 1986), 88.

151 Miller, *Black Spring*, 14.

Chapter 6: Understanding Dostoevsky's 'Philosophy' at Villa Seurat

1 See, for instance, *Sobranie myslei Dostoevskogo* [*Dostoevsky's Collected Thoughts*], ed. Mikhail Fyrkin (Moscow: Zvonnitsa-MG, 2003).

2 James Scanlan, *Dostoevsky the Thinker* (Ithaca, NY: Cornell University Press, 2002), 2–3.
3 Ibid., 5.
4 Ibid., 3–4.
5 Henry Miller, *Books in My Life* (1952; repr. London: P. Owen; Norfolk, CT: New Directions, 1969), 221.
6 Henry Miller, *The Rosy Crucifixion: Plexus* (1953; repr. New York: Grove, 1965), 639; the other three 'horsemen' are two philosophers and an essayist-historian, Spengler, Nietzsche, and Elie Faure, respectively.
7 LD to HM, mid-August 1937, *The Durrell-Miller Letters 1935–80*, ed. Ian S. MacNiven (London: Paker and Faber, 1988), 90.
8 HM to LD, mid-August 1937, ibid., 90.
9 HM to LD, 22? December 1936, ibid., 34.
10 HM to LD, June 1936, ibid., 15.
11 LD to HM, February 1937, ibid., 80, 66.
12 AN to HM, 23 July 1932, *A Literate Passion: Letters of Anaïs Nin and Henry Miller, 1932*–1953, ed. Gunther Stuhlmann (San Diego: Harcourt Brace Jovanovich, 1987), 71.
13 AN to HM, 13 February 1932, ibid., 44.
14 André Gide, *Dostoevsky*, trans. J.R. Dent (1925; repr. London: Secker and Warburg, 1949), 113.
15 Ibid., 91–3.
16 Ibid., 93.
17 Ibid., 93.
18 Ibid., 51.
19 Miller's words are quoted by Nin in a letter of 22 February 1932, *Literate Passion*, 11.
20 AN to HM, 29 September 1932, ibid., 111.
21 AN to HM, 23 July 1932, ibid., 71.
22 Henry Miller, *Entretiens de Paris avec Georges Belmont* (1969; repr. Paris: Éditions Stock-O.R.T.F., 1970), 67.
23 Miller, *Plexus*, 610.
24 Gide, *Dostoevsky*, 16.
25 Henry Miller, 'The Philosopher Who Philosophizes,' *Wisdom of the Heart* (New York: New Directions, 1941), 71, 72.
26 Ibid., 71.
27 Henry Miller, 'Letter to Mr. Trygve Hirsch,' 19 Sept 1957, *Henry Miller on Writing*, ed. Thomas H. Moore (New York: New Directions, 1964), 206.
28 Henry Miller, *Tropic of Capricorn* (1939; repr. New York: Grove, 1961), 208–9.
29 Miller, *Plexus*, 612.

30 Henry Miller, *Tropic of Cancer* (1934; repr. New York: Grove, 1961), 255.
31 AN to HM, 22 February 1932, *A Literate Passion*, 11.
32 Miller, *Entretiens de Paris avec Georges Belmont*, 14.
33 Nin, *The Diary of Anaïs Nin, Vol 2: 1934–1939*, ed. Gunther Stuhlmann (New York: Harcourt, Brace and World, 1967), 14.
34 Henry Miller, 'Seraphita,' *Wisdom of the Heart*, 193–4.
35 Miller, *Books in My Life*, 241.
36 Miller, *Tropic of Capricorn*, 325.
37 Ibid., 86.
38 Miller, 'The Alcoholic Veteran With the Washboard Cranium,' *Wisdom of the Heart*, 126.
39 Miller, 'Balzac and His Double,' *Wisdom of the Heart*, 229.
40 Miller, *Plexus*, 640.
41 Ibid.
42 Ibid.
43 Scanlan, *Dostoevsky the Thinker*, 117.
44 Henry Miller, 'Letter to Mr. Trygve Hirsch,' 19 Sept. 1957, *Henry Miller on Writing*, 206.
45 Nin, *Incest: From the Unexpurgated Diary of Anaïs Nin, 1934–1935* (San Diego: Harcourt Brace Jovanovich, 1992), 66.
46 Nin, *The Diary of Anaïs Nin, Vol 1: 1931–1934*, ed. Gunther Stuhlmann (New York: Harcourt, Brace and World, 1967), 293.
47 Henry Miller, 'Reflections on Maurizius Case,' *Sextet* (Santa Barbara: Capra, 1977), 164.
48 HM to Brenda Venus, 22 February 1977, *Dear, Dear Brenda: The Love Letters of Henry Miller to Brenda Venus*, ed. Gerald Seth Sindell (New York: William Morrow, 1986), 91.
49 Nin, *Diary* 1:89.
50 Ibid., 42.
51 Henry Miller, *Colossus of Maroussi* (1941; repr. Harmondsworth, England: Penguin, 1950), 24.
52 Miller, *Books in My Life*, 15.
53 Nin, *Henry and June: From the Unexpurgated Diary of Anaïs Nin* (San Diego: Harcourt Brace Jovanovich, 1986), 202.
54 Miller, *Entretiens de Paris avec Georges Belmont*, 109–10.
55 Lawrence Durrell, *The Black Book* (1938; repr. New York: Dutton, 1960), 85.
56 Ibid.
57 Nin, *Diary*, 2:221.
58 Ibid.
59 Miller, 'The Absolute Collective,' *Wisdom of the Heart*, 91–2.

60 Miller, *Plexus*, 88.
61 Ibid., 634.
62 Miller, 'Seraphita,' *Wisdom of the Heart*, 205.
63 Miller, 'Letter to Pierre Lesdain,' *Books in My Life*, 222.
64 Miller, *Tropic of Cancer*, 26.
65 Miller, *Tropic of Capricorn*, 226.
66 Henry Miller, *Art and Outrage: A Correspondence About Henry Miller Between Alfred Perlès and Lawrence Durrell (With an Intermission by Henry Miller)* (London: Putnam, 1959), 33.
67 Miller, *Tropic of Cancer*, 26.
68 Ibid., 249.
69 Durrell, *The Black Book*, 177.
70 Miller, *Tropic of Cancer*, 254–5.
71 Henry Miller, *Reflections on the Death of Mishima* (Santa Barbara: Capra, 1972).
72 Henry Miller, 'Henry Miller: The Art of Fiction XXVIII' [Interview with George Wickes] (1962), repr. in *Conversations with Henry Miller*, ed. Frank L. Kersnowski and Alice Hughes (Literary Conversations Series. Jackson: University Press of Mississippi, 1994), 64.
73 Miller, *Books in My Life*, 242–3.
74 Henry Miller, *The World of Lawrence: A Passionate Appreciation*, ed. Evelyn J. Hinz and John J. Teunissen (Santa Barbara, CA: Capra, 1980), 51.
75 Miller, *Plexus*, 523.
76 AN to HM, 3 August 1932, *A Literate Passion*, 90.
77 HM to LD, 13–15 March 1937, *The Durrell-Miller Letters 1935–80*, 58.
78 Lawrence Durrell, 'To Henry Miller,' September? 1935, 4.
79 Lawrence Durrell, 'To Henry Miller,' August 1935, ibid., 2.
80 Lawrence Durrell, 'To Henry Miller,' 27 January 1937, ibid., 52.
81 LD to HM, Early April 1937, ibid., 71.
82 Miller, *Tropic of Cancer*, 96.
83 LD to HM, August 1936, *The Durrell-Miller Letters 1935–80*, 19.
84 Henry Miller, *The Michael Fraenkel – Henry Miller Correspondence Called Hamlet* (London: Carrefour, 1939), 286.
85 Miller, 'The Enormous Womb,' *Wisdom of the Heart*, 99.
86 Miller, 'Waters Reglitterized,' *Sextet*, 81.
87 F.M. Dostoevsky, *F.M. Dostoevskii: Polnoe sobranie sochinerii v tridtsatitomakh [Collected Works of Dostoevsky in Thirty Volumes]*, Academy of Sciences (Leningrad: Nauka, 1976–90), XIV:106
88 Henry Miller, *Sexus*, 46–7.
89 Miller, *Tropic of Cancer*, 1.
90 Miller, *Sexus*, 162.

91 Gide, *Dostoevsky*, 142.
92 Janko Lavrin, *Dostoevsky: A Study* (New York: Macmillan, 1947), 97.
93 Henry Miller, 'The Universe of Death,' *The Cosmological Eye* (New York: New Directions, 1939), 122.
94 Ibid.
95 John Cowper Powys, *Dostoievsky* (New York: Haskell House, 1946), 85.
96 D.H. Lawrence, *Aaron's Rod* (1922; repr. New York: Viking Compass, 1961), 92.
97 Henry Miller, *Notes on* Aaron's Rod *And Other Notes on Lawrence From the Paris Notebooks*, ed. Seamus Cooney (Santa Barbara, CA: Black Sparrow, 1980), 26–7.
98 Miller, 'The Universe of Death,' 122.
99 Miller, *Tropic of Cancer*, 255.
100 Ibid.
101 Ibid.
102 Miller, 'The Universe of Death,' 123.
103 Miller, *The Books in My Life*, 230.
104 Anaïs Nin, *Henry and June: From the Unexpurgated Diary of Anaïs Nin* (San Diego: Harcourt Brace Jovanovich, 1986), 135.
105 Miller, *Plexus*, 523.
106 Miller, *Art and Outrage*, 41.
107 Nin, *Henry and June*, 103.
108 Ibid., 142.
109 Nin also quotes Stavrogin's words in a letter to Antonin Artaud of 22 June 1933 (that is, after she admits to herself that she actually likes evil): 'Do you remember Dostoevsky's novel *The Possessed*, which says, "I get as much joy from doing evil as from doing good?" I don't feel that way myself' (the letter is translated from the French and included in the day's entry in Nin's *Incest: From 'A Journal of Love,'* *The Unexpurgated Diary of Anaïs Nin* [San Diego: Harcourt Brace Jovanovich, 1992], 203).
110 Henry Miller, 'Obscenity and the Law of Reflection,' *Remember to Remember: Volume 2 of the Air-Conditioned Nightmare* (New York: New Directions, 1947), 287.
111 I am quoting from the original of Miller's letter which is in the archives of S.I.U.'s Morris Library, Special Collections, COLL 46/1/2, rather than from the published version.
112 Henry Miller, '*Playboy* Interview: Henry Miller,' (1964), repr. in *Conversations With Henry Miller*, 81.
113 Anaïs Nin, 'Preface to the *Tropic of Cancer*' (1934), *Tropic of Cancer* (1934; repr. New York: Grove Widenfeld, 1980), xxxi, xxxiii.
114 Durrell, 'Introduction to *The Black Book*' (1959), *The Black Book*, 13–14.
115 HM to LD, 8 March 1937, *The Durrell-Miller Letters 1935–80*, 55–6.

116 LD to HM, Early April 1937, ibid., 72.
117 Henry Miller, 'Sex Goes Public: A Talk with Henry Miller' (1966), repr. in *Conversations With Henry Miller*, 106.
118 Anaïs Nin, 'On Writing' (1947), *The Mystic of Sex and Other Writings*, ed. Gunther Stuhlmann (Santa Barbara: Capra Press, 1995), 37–8.

Chapter 7: Writing the Underground

1 Joseph Frank, *Dostoevsky: The Years of Ordeal* (Princeton, NJ: Princeton University Press, 1983), 310.
2 Ihab Hassan, *Radical Innocence: Studies in the Contemporary American Novel* (Princeton, NJ: Princeton University Press, 1961), 24.
3 Ralph Ellison, interview, 'Ralph Ellison: Twenty Years After' (1973), repr. in *Conversations with Ralph Ellison*, ed. Maryemma Graham and Amrijit Singh (Jackson: University Press of Mississippi, 1995), 202.
4 Edward F. Abood, *Underground Man* (San Francisco: Chandler & Sharp, 1973), 1.
5 Robert Louis Jackson, *Dostoevsky's Underground Man in Russian Literature's* (Gravenhage: Mouton, 1958), 7.
6 Ibid.
7 Dostoevsky's reasons for emphasizing the 'fictionality' of his narrator become more apparent when *Notes from Underground* is viewed within the context of Dostoevsky's other publications of the same period, such as *Diary of a Writer* and *Winter Notes on Summer Impressions* [*Zimnie zametki o letnikh vpechatleniiakh*] (first published in 1863). His *Notes from the Dead House* was published only a few years previously (1860–2). All these earlier 'notes' were widely seen to reflect Dostoevsky's personal experience, and their narrators were commonly identified with Dostoevsky himself. Further, Dostoevsky's incontestably autobiographical and purportedly nonfictional *Winter Notes on Summer Impressions*, which he published just before *Notes from Underground*, incorporates many of the techniques and images that later became associated almost exclusively with his fictional *Notes from Underground*.
8 André Gide, *Dostoevsky*, trans. J.R. Dent (1925; repr. London: Secker and Warburg, 1949), 115.
9 John Cowper Powys, *Autobiography* (1934; repr. London: Macdonald, 1967), 526.
10 John Cowper Powys, *Dostoievsky* (New York: Haskell House, 1946), 85.
11 Ibid., 19.
12 Henry Miller, *The Colossus of Maroussi* (1941; repr. London: Penguin, 1950), 48.

13 Henry Miller, *The Rosy Crucifixion: Plexus* (1953; repr. New York: Grove, 1965), 628.
14 Henry Miller, *Big Sur and the Oranges of Hieronymus Bosch* (London: Heinemann, 1958), 154.
15 Harry T. Moore, 'Review of *Tropic of Cancer*,' *New York Times Book Review* (18 June 1961): 5.
16 Kingsley Widmer, *Henry Miller* (New York: Twayne, 1963), 76.
17 Leon Lewis, *Henry Miller: The Major Writings* (New York: Shocken, 1986), 76–7.
18 *Art and Outrage: A Correspondence About Henry Miller Between Alfred Perlès and Lawrence Durrell (With an Intermission by Henry Miller)* (London: Putnam, 1959), 25, 28.
19 Ronald Hall, introduction, John Cowper Powys, *Letters to Henry Miller* (London: Village Press, 1975), 12.
20 Henry Miller, *Tropic of Cancer* (1934; repr. New York: Grove, 1964), 49.
21 Ibid.
22 Jackson, *Dostoevsky's Underground Man*, 17.
23 Abood, *Underground Man*, 181.
24 Ibid., 1–2.
25 Miller, *Tropic of Cancer*, 184.
26 Ibid., 98.
27 Henry Miller, *Tropic of Capricorn*, 9.
28 Ibid., 325.
29 Ibid., 49.
30 Ibid., 348.
31 Miller, *Tropic of Cancer*, 171.
32 Miller, *Tropic of Capricorn*, 13.
33 Miller, *Tropic of Cancer*, 78.
34 Ibid., 177.
35 Ibid., 266.
36 Ibid., 265.
37 Ibid., 9.
38 Miller, *Tropic of Capricorn*, 318.
39 Ibid., 49.
40 Ibid., 9.
41 Ibid., 14.
42 Ibid., 328.
43 Ibid., 190.
44 Ibid., 13.
45 Miller, *Tropic of Cancer*, 2.

46 Ibid., 11.
47 Ibid., 26.
48 Ibid., 2.
49 Miller, *Tropic of Capricorn*, 60.
50 Miller, *Tropic of Cancer*, 162.
51 Ibid., 241.
52 Ibid., 42.
53 Ibid., 4.
54 Ibid., 68.
55 Miller, *Tropic of Capricorn*, 154.
56 Ibid., 233.
57 Miller, *Tropic of Cancer*, 144.
58 Ibid., 267.
59 Miller, *Tropic of Capricorn*, 31.
60 Miller, *Tropic of Cancer*, 266.
61 Ibid.
62 Miller, *Tropic of Capricorn*, 11.
63 Miller, *Tropic of Cancer*, 69.
64 Miller, *Tropic of Capricorn*, 307–8.
65 Ibid., 123.
66 Miller, *Tropic of Cancer*, 182.
67 *Entretiens de Paris avec Georges Belmont* (Paris: Éditions Stock-O.R.T.F., 1970), 44.
68 Miller, *Tropic of Capricorn*, 328.
69 Ibid., 10.
70 Ibid., 119.
71 Ibid., 324.
72 Ibid., 69.
73 Ibid., 68.
74 Miller, *Tropic of Cancer*, 98.
75 Miller, *Tropic of Capricorn*, 308.
76 Miller, *Tropic of Cancer*, 2.
77 Abood, *Underground Man*, 53.
78 Miller, *Tropic of Cancer*, 2.
79 Ibid., 175–6.
80 Miller, *Tropic of Capricorn*, 310.
81 Anaïs Nin, 'On Proust and Dostoevsky, From an Unpublished Letter to Henry Miller [11 February 1932],' *Anaïs, An International Journal* 16 (1998): 6.
82 Abood, *Underground Man*, 181.
83 Karl Shapiro, 'The Charmed Circle of Anais Nin' (1966), *The Critical Response to Anais Nin*, ed. Philip K. Jason (Westport, CT: Greenwood, 1996), 155.

84 Nin, *Incest: From 'A Journal of Love,' The Unexpurgated Diary of Anaïs Nin, 1934–1935* (San Diego: Harcourt Brace Jovanovich, 1992), 28.

85 Delbert Doughty, 'True Confessions? The Underground Hero in Modern World Literature' (PhD dissertation, Pennsylvania State University, 1995), 26–7.

86 Anaïs Nin, interview, 'A Conversation with Anaïs Nin,' interviewer Keith Berwick (1970), *Conversations with Anaïs Nin*, ed. Wendy M. DuBow (Jackson: University Press of Mississippi, 1994), 64.

87 Duane Schneider, 'Anais Nin in the *Diary*: The Creation and Development of a Persona,' *Mosaic* 11.2 (1978): 10.

88 James Atlas, 'The Age of the Literary Memoir is Now,' *New York Times Magazine*, 12 May 1996, 25–7.

89 Anaïs Nin, *A Woman Speaks: The Lectures, Seminars, and Interviews of Anaïs Nin*, ed. Evelyn J. Hinz (Chicago: Swallow, 1975), 234.

90 Anaïs Nin, interview, 'Writers at Work: Anaïs Nin Talks with Frank Roberts,' interviewer Frank Roberts (1965), *Conversations with Anaïs Nin*, 4.

91 The editors were: Hiram Haydn of Harcourt Brace Publishers; Gunther Stuhlmann, Nin's literary agent, and for the last volume of the *Diaries*, Rupert Pole, Nin's second husband and literary executor.

92 Rupert Pole, preface, Anaïs Nin, *Nearer the Moon, From a Journal of Love; The Unexpurgated Diary of Anaïs Nin, 1937–1939* (New York: Harcourt Brace, 1996), xi.

93 Nin's 'Winter of Artifice' story underwent a number of changes over the years. Originally, it was titled 'The Father Story' and then 'The Double' (Durrell read it first as 'The Father Story' in 1937 and rated it highly; see LD to HM and AN, 22 July 1937, *The Durrell-Miller Letters 1935–80*, ed. Ian S. MacHiven (London: Paker and Paker, 1987, 82). In 1939 it was published by Obelisk press as 'Lilith' (*Winter of Artifice* was the title of the entire collection); in 1942 it was published without a title by Nin's own Gemor press (the narration was changed from first person to third person). The story was first titled 'Winter of Artifice' in a 1961 edition of the book published by Swallow Press All references here are to the 1961 edition.

94 Anaïs Nin, interview, 'Anaïs Nin: An Interview,' interviewer William McBrien (1974), *Conversations with Anaïs Nin*, 206.

95 Nin, *The Diary of Anaïs Nin, Vol 2: 1934–1939*, ed. Gunther Stuhlmann (New York: Harcourt, Brace & World, 1967), 319.

96 Nin, *The Diary of Anaïs Nin, Vol 1: 1931–1934*, ed. Gunther Stuhlmann (New York: Harcourt, Brace & World, 1966), 3–4.

97 Anaïs Nin, *House of Incest* (1936; repr. Chicago: Swallow, 1958), 16–17.

98 Nin, *Diary*, 1:4.

99 Nin, *Incest*, 179.
100 Ibid., 308.
101 Nin, *House of Incest*, 72.
102 Anaïs Nin, Preface to *Tropic of Cancer* (1934), Henry Miller, *Tropic of Cancer*, xxxii, xxxiii.
103 Anaïs Nin, *Henry and June: From the Unexpurgated Diary of Anaïs Nin* (San Diego: Harcourt Brace Jovanovich, 1986), 266.
104 Nin, *Fire: From A Journal of Love; The Unexpurgated Diary of Anaïs Nin* (New York: Harcourt Brace & Company, 1995), 19.
105 Anaïs Nin, interview, 'Link in the Chain of Feeling: An Interview with Anaïs Nin,' interviewer Jeffrey Bailey (1976), *Conversations with Anaïs Nin*, 244.
106 Nin, *Incest*, 3.
107 Nin, *Diary*, 1:149.
108 Anaïs Nin, 'Winter of Artifice' (1939), *Winter of Artifice* (1942; repr. Chicago: Swallow, 1948), 89.
109 Nin, *House of Incest*, 40, 47, 39.
110 Nin, *Diary*, 1:11.
111 Nin, *Diary*, 2:221.
112 Nin, *Diary*, 1:77.
113 Nin, *Henry and June: From the Unexpurgated Diary of Anaïs Nin* (San Diego: Harcourt Brace Jovanovich, 1986), 34.
114 Nin, *Nearer the Moon: From 'A Journal of Love,' The Unexpurgated Diary of Anaïs Nin, 1937–1939* (New York: Harcourt Brace & Company, 1996), 125.
115 Nin, 'Winter of Artifice,' 95.
116 Ibid., 96.
117 Anaïs Nin, *House of Incest*, 30.
118 There are several instances in the text where it is not clear whether it is Jeanne or the narrator who is talking
119 Nin, *House of Incest*, 46–7.
120 Ibid., 69.
121 Nin, *Incest*, 51.
122 Nin, *Diary*, 1:4.
123 Nin, *Henry and June: From the Unexpurgated Diary of Anaïs Nin* (San Diego: Harcourt Brace Jovanovich, 1986), 32.
124 Nin, *Diary*, 1:5.
125 Ibid., 7.
126 Ibid., 107.
127 Nin, *Fire*, 58.
128 Nin, *Diary*, 1:260.

129 Nin, *Nearer the Moon*, 24.
130 Ibid., 38.
131 Nin, *Diary*, 1:106.
132 Ibid., 220.
133 Nin, *Incest*, 27.
134 Nin, *Diary*, 1:57.
135 Ibid., 109.
136 Nin, 'Winter of Artifice,' 105.
137 Ibid., 65.
138 Ibid., 61.
139 Ibid., 66.
140 Ibid., 117.
141 Nin, *House of Incest*, 39.
142 Ibid., 38.
143 Ibid., 39.
144 Ibid., 46–7.
145 Nin, *Diary*, 1:45.
146 Ibid., 11.
147 Ibid., 45.
148 Gide, *Dostoevsky*, 138.
149 Nin, *Diary*, 1:160.
150 Doughty, 'True Confessions?' 26.
151 Nin, *Diary*, 1:147.
152 Ibid., 106.
153 Ibid., 233
154 Ibid., 233–4.
155 Estelle C. Jelinek, 'Anais Nin: A Critical Evaluation' (1978), in *The Critical Response to Anais Nin*, ed. Philip K. Jason (Westport, CT: Greenwood, 1996), 47.
156 Anaïs Nin, *D.H. Lawrence: An Unprofessional Study* 1932 (Denver, CO: Alan Swallow, 1964), 50.
157 Nin, *Incest*, 203.
158 The text that Durrell is citing here as *Notes*, however, is actually a quotation from Dostoevsky's *Raw Youth*, which may be Durrell's mistake, but is more likely a deliberate mystification of the reader on his part.
159 Richard Pine, *Lawrence Durrell: The Mindscape* (London: Macmillan, 1994), 424.
160 Kenneth Rexroth, 'Lawrence Durrell' (1960), *Critical Essays on Lawrence Durrell*, ed. Alan Warren Friedman (Boston: G.K. Hall, 1987), 25.
161 Ibid., 27–8.

162 Lawrence Durrell, introduction (1960), *The Black Book,* 13.
163 Ibid., 14.
164 Ian MacNiven, *Lawrence Durrell, A Biography* (London: Faber and Faber, 1998), 132.
165 LD to HM, end December? 1936, *The Durrell-Miller Letters 1935–80*, 35.
166 MacNiven, *Lawrence* Durrell, 150.
167 Durrell, *The Black Book*, 57.
168 Ibid., 58.
169 Ibid., 186.
170 Ibid., 34.
171 Ibid., 201.
172 Ibid., 199.
173 Ibid., 52.
174 Ibid., 85.
175 Ibid., 196.
176 Ibid., 196.
177 Ibid., 185.
178 Ibid., 38.
179 Ibid., 69–70.
180 Ibid., 80.
181 Ibid., 51.
182 Ibid., 34.
183 Ibid., 216.
184 Ibid., 197.
185 Ibid., 40.
186 Ibid., 56.
187 Ibid., 43.
188 Ibid., 81.
189 Ibid., 217.
190 Ibid., 40.
191 Ibid., 42.
192 Ibid., 203.
193 Ibid., 43.
194 Ibid., 88.
195 Ibid., 41.
196 Ibid., 217.
197 Ibid., 217.
198 Ibid., 126.
199 Ibid., 214.
200 Ibid., 234.

201 Ibid., 244.
202 Ibid., 45.
203 Ibid., 48.
204 Ibid., 192.
205 Ibid., 53.
206 Ibid., 193.
207 Ibid., 195, 194.
208 Ibid., 193, 194.
209 Ibid., 195.
210 Ibid., 196, 199.
211 Ibid., 192.
212 Ibid., 192.
213 Ibid., 212.
214 Ibid., 212.
215 Ibid., 211.
216 Ibid., 216.
217 Ibid., 213, 214.
218 Ibid., 244.
219 Ibid., 214.
220 Ibid., 215.
221 Ibid., 143.
222 Ibid., 229.
223 Ibid., 105.
224 Ibid., 71–2.
225 Ibid., 249.

Chapter 8: Pragmatics of Influence, the Dostoevsky Brand, and Dostoevsky Codes

1 S.L. Frank, 'Dostoevskii i krizis gumanizma,' ['Dostoevsky and the Crisis of Humanism'] *Put'* (Paris) 17 (12 February 1931); repr. in *Russkie emigranty o Dostoevskom* [*Russian Émigrés on Dostoevsky*] (St Petersburg: Andreev i synov'ia, 1994), 196–7, 203.
2 Harold Bloom, *The Western Canon: The Books and Schools of Ages* (New York: Harcourt Brace, 1994), 11.
3 See Maria Bloshteyn, 'Dostoevsky and the Beats,' *Canadian Review of Comparative Literature* 28 (June-September 2001): 218–42.
4 See Maria Bloshteyn, 'Dostoevsky and the South,' *Southern Literary Journal* 37 (Summer 2004). Also see Iu. Sokhriakov, 'Tvorchestvo F. M. Dostoevskogo i realisticheskaia literatura SShA 20–30-kh godov XX veka (T. Draizer,

Sh. Anderson, F. Skott Fitsdzheral'd)' ['Dostoevsky's Work and the American Realistic Literature of 1920s and 1930s (T. Dreiser, S. Anderson, F. Scott Fitzgerald)'], *DostoevskiiMaterialy i issledovaniia* [*Dostoevsky: Materials and Research*] 3 (1978): 243–55.

5 See Maria Bloshteyn, 'Rage and Revolt: Dostoevsky and Three African-American Writers,' *Comparative Literature Studies* 38.4 (2001): 277–309.

Appendix A

1 René Wellek, 'A Sketch of Dostoevsky Criticism,' *Dostoevsky: Collection of Critical Essays* (Englewood Cliffs, NJ: Prentice Hall, 1962), 13.

2 Georgii Fridlender, *Dostoevskii i mirovaia literatura* [*Dostoevsky and World Literature*] (Moscow: Khudozhestvennaia literatura, 1979), 7.

3 Victor Terras, 'Samoe glavnoe,' *Dostoevsky and the Twentieth Century: The Ljubljana Papers* (Cotgrave, Nottingham: Astra, 1993), 5.

4 Wellek, 'A Sketch of Dostoevsky Criticism,' 7.

5 Helen Muchnic, *Dostoevsky's English Reputation: 1881–1936* (Northampton, MA: Smith's College, 1939), vi.

6 Gilbert Phelps, *The Russian Novel in English Fiction* (London: Hutchinson's University Library, 1956), 9.

7 The usefulness of Phelps's study is seriously impaired by a puzzling lack of proper documentation. Little to no bibliographic information is provided for the sources he cites and, occasionally, the cited text's author and title are also left out.

8 A.N. Nikoliukin, 'Dostoevskii v perevode Konstans Garnet,' ['Dostoevsky in the Translation of Constance Garnett,'] *Russkaia literatura; istoriko-literaturnyi zhurnal* [*Russian Literature; A Historical-Literary Journal*] 2 (1985): 154–62.

Appendix B

1 See Reed Way Dasenbrock, 'Lawrence Durrell and the Modes of Modernism,' *Twentieth Century Literature: A Scholarly and Critical Journal* 33 (Winter 1987): 516.

Selected Bibliography

Dostoevsky

Writings and Correspondence

F.M. Dostoevsky. *F.M. Dostoevskii: Polnoe sobranie sochinenii v tridtsati tomàkh* [*collected Works of Dostoevsky in Thirty Volumes*] Academy of Sciences. Leningrad: Nauka, 1976–90.

Location of Main Archives

Rossiiskii gosudarstvennyi arkhiv literatury i iskusstva (RGALI) [Russian State Archive of Literature and Art] but also in various repositories concentrated mainly in Moscow and St. Petersburg. For more specific information see *Opisanie rukopisei F.M. Dostoevskogo* [*A Description of the Manuscripts of F.M. Dostoevsky*]. Ed. V.S. Nechaeva. Moscow: 1957.

Main translations into English up to and including the 1930s (Chronologically arranged within the categories).

MAJOR WORKS
a) *Brothers Karamazov* [*Brat'ia Karamazovy*] and *The Legend of the Grand Inquisitor* [*Legenda Velikogo Inkvizitora*] (1879–80)
The Legend of the Grand Inquisitor. Trans. Madame Blavatsky. The *Theosophist.* 3. 2/3 (November and December 1881).
The Brothers Karamazov. Trans. Constance Garnett. London: Heinemann; New York: Macmillan, 1912.

The Legend of the Grand Inquisitor. Trans. S.S. Koteliansky. *New Age.* October and
November 1925. Published as a separate book with an introduction by D.H.
Lawrence in 1930.
b) *Crime and Punishment* [*Prestuplenie i nakazanie*] (1866)
Crime and Punishment. Trans. Fredrick Whishaw. London: Vizetelly, 1886 (repr.,
Everyman).
Crime and Punishment. Trans. Constance Garnett. London: Everyman, 1914.
c) *Diary of a Writer* [*Dnevnik pisatelia*] (1873–80)
Pages from the Journal of an Author. Trans. S.S. Koteliansky and J. Middleton
Murry. Boston: John W. Luce, 1916.
d) *The Idiot* [*Idiot*] (1868)
The Idiot. Trans. Fredrick Whishaw. London: Vizetelly's Russian Novels, 1887
(repr., Everyman).
The Idiot. Trans. Constance Garnett. London: Heinemann, 1913.
e) *The Insulted and the Injured* [*Unizhennye i oskorblennye*] (1861)
Injury and Insult. Trans. Fredrick Whishaw. London: Vizetelly's One Volume
Novels, 1886.
The Insulted and the Injured. Trans. Constance Garnett. London: Heinemann, 1915.
f) *Notes from the Dead House* [*Zapiski iz mertvogo doma*] (1860–2)
Buried Alive, or Ten Years of Penal Servitude in Siberia. Trans. Marie von Thilo.
New York: George Munro; New York: Henry Holt; London: Longmans
Green, 1881.
Prison Life in Siberia. Trans. J. Sutherland Edwards. London: John & Robert
Maxwell, 1887.
The House of the Dead. Trans. Constance Garnett. London: Heinemann;
New York: Macmillan, 1915.
g) *The Devils* [*Besy*] (1871–2)
The Possessed. Trans. Constance Garnett. London: William Heinemann;
New York: Everyman, 1914.
Stavrogin's Confession; and The Plan of the Life of A Great Sinner. Trans. S.S.
Koteliansky and Virginia Woolf. Richmond: L. & V. Woolf at the Hogarth
Press, 1922.
h) *A Raw Youth* [*Podrostok*] (1875)
A Raw Youth. Trans. Constance Garnett. London: Heinemann, 1916.

SHORTER FICTION
A Christmas Tree and a Wedding, and an Honest Thief. Trans. Nevill Forbes.
Oxford: Clarendon, 1917.
The Eternal Husband and Other Stories. [Includes *The Double* and *A Gentle Spirit*].
Trans. Constance Garnett. London: Heinemann, 1917.

The Friend of the Family and the Gambler. Trans. Frederick Whishaw. London: Vizetelly, 1887.

The Friend of the Family; or, Stepanchikovo and its Inahbitants, and Another Story [Netochka Nezvanova]. Trans. Constance Garnett. London: Heinemann, 1920.

The Gambler and Other Stories. [Includes *Poor People* and *The Landlady.*] Trans. Constance Garnett. London: Heninemann, 1917.

The Honest Thief and Other Stories. Trans. Constance Garnett. London: Heinemann, 1919.

Poor Folk. Trans. Lena Milman. Preface by George Moore. London: Mathews and Lane, 1894.

The Uncle's Dream and the Permanent Husband. Trans. Frederick Whishaw. London: Vizetelly, 1888.

White Nights and Other Stories. Trans. Constance Garnett. London: Heinemann, 1918.

CORRESPONDENCE

Letters of Fyodor Dostoevsky to his Family and Friends. Trans. Ethel Colburn Mayne. New York: Macmillan; London: Chatto and Windus, 1914.

Letters and Reminiscences. Trans. S.S. Koteliansky and J. Middleton Murry. London: Chatto and Windus, 1923.

New Dostoevsky Letters. Trans. S.S. Koteliansky. London: Mandrake, 1929.

Dostoevsky's Letters to His Wife. Trans. Elizabeth Hill and Doris Mudie. Ed. Prince D.S. Mirsky. New York: Richard E. Smith, 1930.

Criticism

Abood, Edward F. *Underground Man.* San Francisco: Chandler and Sharp, 1973.

Adelman, Gary. *Retelling Dostoyevsky: Literary Responses and Other Observations.* Lewisburg: Bucknell University Press, 2001.

Bakhtin, Mikhail. *Problemy poetiki Dostoevskogo.* [*The Problems of Dostoevsky's Poetics.*] 1929/1963. Moscow: Izdatel'stvo 'Khudozhestvennaia Literatura,' 1972.

Bazanov, V.G. et al., eds. *F.M. Dostoevskii, novye materialy i issledovaniia* [*F.M. Dostoevsky, New Materials and Research*]. Moscow: Nauka, 1973.

Belinskii, Vissarion. 'Bednye liudi. Roman Fedora Dostoevskogo.' ['*Poor Folk.* A Novel of Fedor Dostoevsky.'] 1847. *Polnoe sobranie sochinenii* [*Collected Works*], 363–4. Moscow: Izdatel'stvo Akademii Nauk SSSR, 1956.

Belknap, Robert L. *The Genesis of The Brothers Karamazov: The Aesthetics, Ideology, and Psychology of Text Making.* Evanston, IL: Northwestern University Press, 1990.

– *The Structure of* The Brothers Karamazov. The Hague: Mouton, 1967.

Belov, S.V., ed. *Russkie emigranty o Dostoevskom* [*Russian Emigres About Dostoevsky*]. St Petersburg: Andreev i synov'ia, 1994.

– ed. *F.M. Dostoevskii v zabytykh i neizvestnykh vospominaniiakh sovremennikov* [*F.M. Dostoevsky in Forgotten and Unknown Reminiscences of His Contemporaries*]. St Petersburg: Andreev i synov'ia, 1993.

Berdiaev, Nikolai. *Mirosozertsanie Dostoevskogo.* [*Dostoevsky's World-view.*] Paris: YMCA Press, 1934.

Bloshteyn, Maria. '"Anguish for the Sake of Anguish" – Faulkner and His Dostoevskian Allusion.' *International Faulkner Journal* 9.2 (Spring 2004): 69–90.

'Dostoevsky and the Beats.' *Canadian Review of Comparative Literature* 28 (June-September 2001): 218–43.

– 'Dostoevsky and the Literature of the American South.' *Southern Literary Journal* 37 (Fall 2004): 1–24.

– 'Rage and Revolt: Dostoevsky and Three African-American Writers.' *Comparative Literature Studies* 38.4 (2001): 277–309.

Bourne, Randolph. 'The Immanence of Dostoevsky.' *The Dial* (28 June 1917): 24–5.

Crowder, Colin. 'The Appropriation of Dostoevsky in the Early Twentieth Century: Cult, Countercult and Incarnation.' In *European Literature and Theology in the Twentieth Century: Ends of Time*, ed. David Jasper and Colin Crowder, 15–33. Basingstoke: Macmillan, 1990.

Davie, Donald. *Russian Literature and Modern English Fiction*. Chicago: University of Chicago Press, 1965.

Dell, Floyd. 'The Novels of Dostoevsky.' *New Review* (15 May 1915): 38.

– 'Untitled.' *The Masses* (April 1916): 28.

Delbert, David Doughty. 'True Confessions? 'The Underground Hero In Modern World Literature.' PhD dissertation, Pennsylvania State University, 1995.

Dimitrieva, A., ed. *F.M. Dostoevskii v russkoi kritike, sbornik statei* [*Dostoevsky and Russian Criticism*]. Moscow: Gosudarstvennoe izdatel'stvo khudozhestvennoi literatury, 1956.

Fiene, Donald M. 'Elements of Dostoevsky in the Novels of Kurt Vonnegut.' *Dostoevsky Studies* 2 (1981): 171–86.

Flath, Carol Apollonio. 'Demons of Translation: The Strange Path of Dostoevsky's Novels into the English Translation.' *Dostoevsky Studies* n.s. 4 (2005): 45–52.

Flynn, Dennis. 'Farrell and Dostoevsky.' *MELUS* 18.1 (Spring 1993): 113–25.

Frank, Joseph. *Dostoevsky.* 5 vols. Princeton: Princeton University Press, 1976–2002.

Fridlender, Georgii. *Dostoevskii i mirovaia literatura* [*Dostoevsky and World Literature*]. Moscow: Khudozhestvennaia literatura, 1979.

– ed. *Dostoevskii: materialy i issledovaniia* [*Dostoevsky: Materials and Research*]. Leningrad: Nauka, 1976.

Garin, I. I. *Mnogolikii Dostoevskii* [*Manyfaced Dostoevskii*]. Moscow: Terra, 1997.

Gerigk, Horst-Jürgen. *Die Russen in Amerika: Dostojewsikij, Tolstoij, Turgenjew und Tschechow in ihrer Bedeutung für die Literatur der USA*. Hurtgenwald: Guido Pressler, 1995.

Gide, André. *Dostoevsky*. Trans. J.M. Dent. 1925, London: Secker and Warburg, 1949.

Grossman, Leonid. *Poetika Dostoevskogo* [*Dostoevsky's Poetics*]. Moscow: Gosudarstvennaia Akademiia Khudezhestvennykh Nauk, 1925.

Hearn, Lafcadio. 'A Terrible Novel.' 1885. In *Essays in European and Oriental Literature*, ed. Albert Mordell, 189–94. London: William Heinemann, 1923.

Ivanchikova, E.A. *Sintaksis khudozhestvennoi prozy Dostoevskogo* [*The Syntax of Dostoevsky's Literary Prose*]. Moscow: Nauka, 1979.

Jackson, Robert Louis. *The Art of Dostoevsky: Deliriums and Nocturnes*. Princeton: Princeton University Press, 1981.

– *Dialogues with Dostoevsky: The Overwhelming Questions*. Stanford: Stanford University Press, 1993.

– *Dostoevsky's Quest for Form*. New Haven: Yale University Press, 1966.

– *Dostoevsky's Underground Man in Russian Literature*. S-Gravehage: Mouton, 1958.

Kariakin, Yurii. *Dostoevskii i kanun XXI veka* [*Dostoevsky and the Beginning of the Twenty-First Century*]. Moscow: Sovetskii pisatel', 1989.

Kaye, Peter Paul. *Dostoevsky and English Modernism, 1900–1930*. Cambridge: Cambridge University Press, 1999.

Kjetsaa, Geir. *Fyodor Dostoyevsky: A Writer's Life*. Trans. Siri Hustvedt and David McDuff. New York: Fawcett Columbine, 1987.

Klessmann, Stefan. *Deutsche und amerikanische Erfahrungsmuster von Welt. Eine interdisziplinäre, kulturvergleichende Analyse im Spiegel der Dostojewskij-Rezeption zwischen 1900 und 1945*. Regensburg: Roderer Verlag, 1990.

Lary, N.M. *Dostoevsky and Dickens: A Study of Literary Influence*. London and Boston: Routledge and Kegan Paul, 1973.

– *Dostoevsky and Soviet Film: Visions of Demonic Realism*. Ithaca, NY: Cornell University Press, 1986.

Lavrin, Janko. *Dostoevsky and his Creation: A Psychocritical Study*. London: Collins, 1920.

– *Dostoevsky: A Study*. New York: Macmillan, 1947.

Leatherbarrow, W.J. *Fedor Dostoevsky, A Reference Guide*. Boston, MA: G.K. Hall, 1990.

– ed. *Dostoevskii and Britain*. Oxford: Berg, 1995.

Likhachev, D. S. '"Nebrezhenie slovom" u Dostoevskogo.' ["Indifference for the Word" in Dostoevsky's Works'] In *Dostoevskii: materialy i issledovaniia* [*Dostoevsky: Materials and Research*], ed. G.M. Fridlender, 30–41. Leningrad: Nauka, 1976.

Lobas, Vladimir. *Vsemirnaia istoriia v litsakh: Dostoevskii.* 2 vols. Moscow: ACT, 2000.

Lynch, Michael. *Creative Revolt: a Study of Wright, Ellison, and Dostoevsky.* New York: Peter Lang, 1990.

Manning, C.A. 'Dostoevsky and Modern Russian Literature.' *Sewanee Review Quarterly* 30 (1922): 286–97.

Moser, Charles A. 'The Achievement of Constance Garnett.' *American Scholar* 57.30 (1988): 431–8.

Motyleva, T. 'Dostoevskii i zarubezhnye pisateli XX veka' ['Dostoevsky and Foreign Writers of the Twentieth Century']. *Voprosy literatury* 5 (1971): 113–18.

Muchnic, Helen. *Dostoevsky's English Reputation: 1881–1936.* Northampton, MA: Smith's College, 1939.

Murry, Middleton, J. *Fyodor Dostoevsky, A Critical Study.* London: Martin Secker, 1916.

Nikoliukin, A.N. 'Dostoevskii v perevode Konstans Garnet' ['Dostoevsky in the Translation of Constance Garnett'] *Russkaia literatura; istoriko-literaturnyi zhurnal* [*Russian Literature; A Historical-Literary Journal*] 2 (1985): 154–62.

– *Vzaimosviazi literatur Rossii i SshA: Turgenev, Tolstoi, Dostoevskii i Amerika* [*The Interrelations of Russian and American Literatures: Turgenev, Tolstoi, Dostoevskii and America*]. Moscow: Nauka, 1987.

Pachmuss, Temira. 'Dostoevsky and America's Southern Women Writers: Parallels and Confluences.' In *Poetica Slavica: Studies in Honour of Zbigniew Folejewski*, ed. J. Douglas Clayton and Gunter Schaarschmidt, 115–26. Ottawa: University of Ottawa Press, 1981.

– 'Dostoevsky and T.S. Eliot: A Point of View.' *Forum of Modern Language Studies* 12 (1976): 82–9.

Peyre, Henry. *French Literary Imagination and Dostoevsky and Other Essays.* Tuscaloosa: University of Alabama Press, 1975.

Phelps, Gilbert. *The Russian Novel in English Fiction.* London: Hutchinson's University Library, 1956.

Peace, Richard. *Dostoevsky's Notes from Undergound.* London: Bristol Classical Press, 1993.

Powys, John Cowper. *Dostoievsky.* New York: Haskell House, 1946.

Relzor, B.G., ed. *Dostoevskii v zarubezhnykh literaturakh* [*Dostoevsky in Foreign Literatures*]. Leningrad: Nauka, 1978.

Rosenshield, G. 'Crime and Redemption, Russian and American Style: Dostoevsky, Buckley, Mailer, Styron and their Wards.' *Slavic and East European Journal* 42.4 (1998): 677–709.

Scanlan, James. *Dostoevsky the Thinker.* Ithaca, NY: Cornell University Press, 2002.

Sokhriakov, Iu. I. 'Traditsii Dostoevskogo v vospriiatii T. Vul'fa, U. Folknera i D. Steinbeka' ['Traditions of Dostoevsky in the Reception of T. Wolfe, W. Faulkner, and D. Steinbeck']. *Dostoevskii. Materialy i issledovaniia* [*Dostoevsky; Materials and Research*] 1980:4. 144–58.

– 'Tvorchestvo F. M. Dostoevskogo i realisticheskaia literatura SShA 20–30kh godov XX veka (T. Draizer, Sh. Anderson, F. Skott Fitsdzheral'd)' ['Dostoevsky's Work and the American Realistic Literature of 1920s and 1930s (T. Dreiser, S. Anderson, F. Scott Fitsgerald)'] in *Dostoevskii. Materialy i issledovaniia* [*Dostoevsky: Materials and Research*] 1978:3. 243–55.

Stepanian, K., ed. *Dostoevskii v kontse XX veka* [*Dostoevsky at the End of the Twentieth Century*]. Moscow: Izdatel'stvo 'Klassika plius,' 1996.

Suslova, Apollinaria. *Gody blizosti s Dostoevskim* [*The Years of Intimacy with Dostoevsky*]. 1928. Ed. A.S. Dolinin. New York: Serebriannyi vek, 1982.

Terras, Victor. *A Karamazov Companion: Commentary on the Genesis, Language, and Style of Dostoevsky's Novel.* Madison of University Wisconsin Press, 1981.

– 'Samoe glavnoe' ['The Most Important']. *Dostoevsky and the Twentieth Century: The Ljubljana Papers*, 3–7. Cotgrave, Nottingham: Astra, 1993.

Tunimanov, V.A. 'Posleslovie' ['Afterward']. *Besy* [*The Devils*]. Leningrad: Lenizdat, 1990.

Ulanovskiaia, Bella. 'Mozhet li solntse rasserditsa na infusoriiu … ' ['Can the Sun Become Angry at an Infusoria … ' 1974. In *Dostoevskii v kontse XX veka* [*Dostoevsky at the End of the Twentieth Century*], ed. K. Stepanian, 604–21. Moscow: Izdatel'stvo 'Klassika plius,' 1996.

Vogüé, E. M. *Le roman russe.* Paris: Librairie Plon, 1886.

Wasiolek, Edward. 'Dostoevsky and *Sanctuary.*' *Modern Language Notes* 74 (1959): 114–17.

Wellek, René. 'A Sketch of the History of Dostoevsky Criticism.' *Dostoevsky; A Collection of Critical Essays*, 1–15 Englewood Cliffs, NJ: Prentice-Hall, 1962.

Wilkinson, Myler. *The Dark Mirror: American Literary Response to Russia.* New York: Peter Lang, 1996.

Weisgerber, Jean. *Faulkner et Dostoievski: Confluences et influences.* Brussells: Presses universitaires de Bruxelles, 1968.

Zakharov, Vladimir. 'Paradoksy priznaniia: problema 'traditsii Dostoevskogo' v kul'ture XX veka' ['The Paradoxes of Recognition: The Problem of "The Dostoevsky Tradition" in the Culture of the XX Century']. In *Dostoevsky and the Twentieth Century: The Ljubljana Papers*, ed. Malcolm V. Jones, 19–35. Nottingham: Astra, 1993.

Lawrence Durrell

Major Writings

The Alexandria Quartet: Justine, Balthazar, Moutolive, Clea. 1957–1960. London: Faber and Faber, 1988.
Antrobus Complete. London: Faber and Faber, 1985.
The Avignon Quintet: Monsieur, Livia, Constance, Sebastian, Quinx. 1974–1985. London: Faber and Faber, 1992.
Bitter Lemons. London: Faber and Faber, 1957.
The Black Book. 1938. New York: Dutton, 1960.
Blue Thirst. Santa Barbara: Capra, 1975.
Caesar's Vast Ghost. London: Faber and Faber, 1990.
Cities, Plains and People. London: Faber and Faber, 1946.
Collected Poems. London: Faber and Faber, 1960.
Collected Poems 1931–1974. Ed. James A.Brigham. London: Faber and Faber; New York: Viking, 1980.
The Dark Labyrinth. 1947. London: Faber and Faber, 1961.
Esprit De Corps: Sketches From Diplomatic Life. London: Faber and Faber, 1957.
The Ikons. London: Faber and Faber, 1966.
An Irish Faustus: A Modern Morality in Nine Scenes. Birmingham: Delos, 1987.
A Key to Modern British Poetry. Norman: University of Oklahoma Press, 1952.
Nunquam: A Novel. London: Faber and Faber, 1970.
Panic Spring: A Romance. London: Faber and Faber, 1937. (Published under the pseudonym of 'Charles Norden.')
Pied Piper of Lovers. London: Cassell, 1935.
A Private Country. London: Faber and Faber, 1943.
Prospero's Cell: A Guide to the Landscape and Manners of the Island of Corcyra. London: Faber and Faber, 1945.
Reflections on a Marine Venus: A Companion to the Landscape of Rhodes. London: Faber and Faber, 1953.
Sappho: A Play in Verse. London: Faber and Faber, 1950.
Sicilian Carousel. New York: Viking, 1977.
Spirit of Place: Mediterranean Essays. 1969. Ed. Alan G. Thomas. London: Faber and Faber, 1988.
Stiff Upper Lip. London: Faber and Faber, 1958.
The Tree of Idleness. London: Faber and Faber, 1955.
Tunc. London: Faber and Faber, 1968.
Vega and Other Poems. London: Faber and Faber, 1973.
White Eagles Over Serbia. London: Faber and Faber, 1957.

Location of Main Archives

Lawrence Durrell Collection at the University of Southern Illinois–Carbondale; Lawrence Durrell Collection at The British Library; Bibliothèque Lawrence Durrell at University of Paris X (Nanterre).

Correspondence and Interviews

Art and Outrage: A Correspondence About Henry Miller Between Alfred Perlès and Lawrence Durrell (With an Intermission by Henry Miller). London: Putnam, 1959.
The Durrell-Miller Letters 1935–80. Ed. Ian S. MacNiven. London: Faber and Faber, 1988.
Lawrence Durrell and Henry Miller: A Private Correspondence. Ed. George Wickes. London: Faber and Faber, 1963.
Lawrence Durrell: Conversations. Ed. Earl G. Ingersoll. Madison, NJ: Fairleigh Dickinson University Press; London: Associated University Presses, 1998.
Letters to Jean Fanchette. Ed. Jean Fanchette. Paris: Editions Two Cities, 1988.
Literary Lifelines. The Richard Aldington – Lawrence Durrell Correspondence. Ed. I.S. MacNiven and Harry T. Moore. London: Faber and Faber, 1981.

Biographies and Criticism

Alexandre-Garner, Corinne. 'Black Snow in Winter: Anais in Paris – The Lawrence Durrell Connection.' *Anais Nin: Literary Perspectives*, ed. Suzanne Nalbantian, 236–53. New York: St Martin's, 1997.
– ed. *Lawrence Durrell: Actes Du Colloque Pour L'Inauguration De La Bibliothèque Durrell*. Nanterre: Université Paris-X, 1998.
– ed. *Lawrence Durrell Revisited: Lawrence Durrell Revisité*. Nanterre: Université Paris X, 2002.
Bair, Deidre. 'Writing As a Woman: Henry Miller, Lawrence Durrell, and Anaïs Nin in the Villa Seurat.' *Anaïs: An International Journal* 12 (1994): 31–8.
Bowker, Gordon. *Through the Dark Labyrinth: A Biography of Lawrence Durrell*. London: Sinclair Stevenson; New York: St Martin's, 1997.
Cartwright, Michael, ed. *On Miracle Ground: Proceediings of the First National Lawrence Durrell Conference*. Kelowna, BC: Department of English, Okanagan College, 1982.
Dasenbrock, Reed Way. 'Lawrence Durrell and the Modes of Modernism.' *Twentieth Century Literature: A Scholarly and Critical Journal* 33 (Winter 1987): 515–27.

Deus Loci: The Lawrence Durrell Newsletter. Ed. Ian MacNiven et al. Baltimore: Lawrence Durrell Society, 1976–.

Fraser, G. S. *Lawrence Durrell: A Study.* New York: Dutton, 1968.

Friedman, Alan Warren, ed. *Critical Essays on Lawrence Durrell.* Boston: G.K. Hall, 1987.

Hassan, Ihab. *The Literature of Silence: Henry Miller and Samuel Beckett.* New York: Alfred A. Knopf, 1967.

Herbrechter, Stefan. *Lawrence Durrell, Postmodernism and the Ethics of Alterity.* Amsterdam, Atlanta: Rodopi, 1998.

Kersnowski, Frank L., ed. *Essays on the Art of Lawrence Durrell.* Ann Arbor, MI: UMI Research Press, 1989.

– ed. *Into the Labyrinth: Essays on the Art of Lawrence Durrell.* Ann Arbor, MI: UMI Research Press, 1989.

Lillios, Anna, ed. *Lawrence Durrell and the Greek World.* London: Associated University Presses, 2004.

MacNiven, Ian. *Lawrence Durrell: A Biography.* London: Faber and Faber, 1998. 'A Room in the House of Art: The Friendship of Anais Nin and Lawrence Durrell.' *Mosaic: A Journal for the Interdisciplinary Study of Literature* 11.2 (1978): 37–57.

Markert, Lawrence W., and Carol Peirce, eds. *On Miracle Ground II: Second International Lawrence Durrell Conference Proceedings.* Kelowna, BC: Deus Loci; Baltimore, MD: University of Baltimore, 1986.

Nichols, Betsy, Frank Kersnowski, and James Nichols, eds. *Essays on the Humor of Lawrence Durrell.* Victoria, BC: University of Victoria Press, 1993.

Perles, Alfred. *My Friend Lawrence Durrell: An Intimate Memoir on the Author of* The Alexandria Quartet. Northwood, Middlesex: Scorpion, 1961.

Pinchin, Jane Lagoudis. *Alexandria Still: Forster, Durrell and Cavafy.* Princeton Essays in Literature. Princeton: Princeton University Press, 1977.

Pine, Richard. *Lawrence Durrell: The Mindscape.* London: Macmillan, 1994.

Raper, Julius Rowan, Melody L. Enscore, and Paige Matthey Bynam, eds. *Lawrence Durrell: Comprehending the Whole.* Columbia: University of Missouri Press, 1995.

Robinson, Jeremy. *Love, Culture & Poetry: A Study of Lawrence Durrell.* Kidderminster, Worcester: Crescent Moon, 1990.

Rook, Robin. *At the Foot of the Acropolis: A Study of Lawrence Durrell's Novels.* Birmingham: Delos, 1995.

Volkoff, Vladimir. *Lawrence le magnifique: essai sur Lawrence Durrell et le roman relativiste* Paris: Julliard: L'Age d'homme, 1984.

Weigel, John A. *Lawrence Durrell.* 1965. Rev. ed. Boston: G.K. Hall, 1989.

The World of Lawrence Durrell. Ed. Harry T. Moore. Carbondale: Southern Illinois University Press, 1962.

Henry Miller

Major Writings

The Best of Henry Miller. Ed. Lawrence Durrell. London: Heinemann, 1960.
Big Sur and the Oranges of Hieronymus Bosch. London: Heinemann, 1958. *Black Spring*. 1936. Paris: Obelisk; New York: Grove, 1963.
Books in My Life. 1952. London: P. Owen; Norfolk, CT: New Directions, 1969.
Colossus of Maroussi. 1941. Harmondsworth: Penguin, 1950.
The Cosmological Eye. New York: New Directions, 1939.
Crazy Cork. New York: Grove, Weidenfelt, 1991.
Henry Miller On Writing. Ed. Thomas H. Moore. New York: New Directions, 1964.
Joey: A Loving Portrait of Alfred Perlès Together with Some Bizarre Episodes Relating to the Other Sex. Volume III, Book of Friends. Santa Barbara, CA: Capra, 1979.
Just Wild About Harry: A Melo-Melo in Seven Scenes. New York: New Directions, 1963.
Moloch, or This Gentile World. 1928. New York: Grove, 1992.
My Bike & Other Friends; Volume II of Book of Friends. Santa Barbara, CA: Capra, 1978.
Notes on Aaron's Rod *And Other Notes on Lawrence From the Paris Notebooks*. Ed. Seamus Cooney. Santa Barbara, CA: Black Sparrow, 1980.
The Rosy Crucifixion: Nexus. 1960. New York: Grove, 1965.
The Rosy Crucifixion: Plexus. 1953. New York: Grove, 1965.
The Rosy Crucifixion: Sexus. 1949. New York: Grove, 1965.
Tropic of Cancer. 1934. New York: Grove, 1961.
Tropic of Capricorn. 1939. New York: Grove, 1961.
Sextet. Santa Barbara: Capra, 1977.
Smile at the Foot of the Ladder. 1948. Norfolk, CT: New Directions, 1959.
Stand Still Like the Hummingbird. New York: New Directions, 1962.
Wisdom of the Heart. New York: New Directions, 1941.
The World of Lawrence: A Passionate Appreciation. Ed. Evelyn J. Hinz and John J. Teunissen. Santa Barbara, CA: Capra, 1980.
The World of Sex. 1940. New York: Grove, 1959.

Location of Main Archives

Henry Miller Collection at the University Research Library, University of California–Los Angelos; The Miller Collection at the Harry Ransom Humanities Research Library at the University of Texas, Austin.

Correspondence and Interviews

Art and Outrage: A Correspondence About Henry Miller Between Alfred Perlès and Lawrence Durrell (With an Intermission by Henry Miller). London: Putnam, 1959.
Conversations with Henry Miller. Ed. Frank L. Kersnowski and Alice Hughes. Jackson: University Press of Mississippi, 1994.
Dear, Dear Brenda: The Love Letters of Henry Miller to Brenda Venus. Ed. Gerald Seth Sindell. New York: William Morrow, 1986.
The Durrell-Miller Letters 1935–80. Ed. Ian S. MacNiven. London: Faber and Faber, 1988.
Entretiens de Paris avec Georges Belmont. 1969. Paris: Éditions Stock-O.R.T.F., 1970.
Flash-Back: Entretiens de Pacific Palisades avec Christian de Bartillat. Paris: Éditions Stock, 1976.
Henry Miller's Letters to Anaïs Nin. Ed. Gunther Stuhlmann. New York: Putnam, 1965.
John Cowper Powys, Letters to Henry Miller. London: Village Press, 1975.
Lawrence Durrell and Henry Miller: A Private Correspondence. Ed. George Wickes. London: Faber and Faber, 1963.
Letters to Emil. Ed. George Wickes. New York: New Directions, 1989.
A Literate Passion: Letters of Anaïs Nin and Henry Miller, 1932–1953. Ed. Gunther Stuhlmann. San Diego: Harcourt Brace Jovanovich, 1987.
The Michael Fraenkel – Henry Miller Correspondence Called Hamlet. London: Carrefour, 1939.
Writer and Critic: A Correspondence with Henry Miller. Baton Rouge: Louisiana State University Press, 1968.

Biographies and Criticism

Armitage, Merle. 'The Man Behind the Smile: Doing Business with Henry Miller.' *Texas Quarterly* 4 (Winter 1961): 156–61. Repr. in *Conversations with Henry Miller*, Frank L. Kersnowski and Alice Hughes, 13–2. Jackson: University Press of Mississippi, 1994.
Bair, Deidre. 'Writing As a Woman: Henry Miller, Lawrence Durrell, and Anaïs Nin in the Villa Seurat.' *Anais: An International Journal* 12 (1994): 31–8.
Balliet, Gay Louise. *Henry Miller and Surrealist Metaphor: 'Riding the Ovarian Trolley.'* New York: Peter Lang, 1996.
Bartlett, Jeffrey. 'The Late Modernist.' In *Critical Essays on Henry Miller*, ed. Ronald Gottesman, 315–28. New York: G.K. Hall, 1992.

Baxter, Annette. *Henry Miller Expatriate*. Pittsburgh, PA: University of Pittsburgh Press, 1961.

Cleyet, George. 'The Villa Seurat Circle: Creative Nexus.' *Deus Loci: The Lawrence Durrell Quarterly* (June 1981): 1–6.

Dearborn, Mary V. *The Happiest Man Alive: Henry Miller, A Biography*. New York: Simon and Schuster, 1991.

Decker, M. James. *Henry Miller: and Narrative Form: Constructing the Self, Rejecting Modernity*. New York and London: Routledge, 2005.

Dick, Kenneth C. *Henry Miller: Colossus of One*. Sittard, The Netherlands: Alberts, 1967.

Ferguson, Robert. *Henry Miller: A Life*. London: Hutchinson, 1991.

Fraenkel, Michael. 'The Genesis of the *Tropic of Cancer*.' *Happy Rock: A Book About Henry Miller*, ed. Bern Porter, 38–56. Berkeley, CA: Bern Porter, 1945.

Gottesman, Ronald, ed. *Critical Essays on Henry Miller*. New York: G.K. Hall, 1992.

Hassan, Ihab. *The Literature of Silence: Henry Miller and Samuel Beckett*. New York: Alfred A. Knopf, 1967.

Jahshan, Paul. *Henry Miller and the Surrealist Discourse of Excess: A Post-Structuralist Reading*. New York: Peter Lang, 2001.

Jong, Erica. *The Devil at Large*. London: Chatto and Windus, 1993.

Lewis, Leon. *Henry Miller: The Major Writings*. New York: Schocken, 1986.

Mailer, Norman. *Genius and Lust: A Journey Through the Major Writings of Henry Miller By Norman Mailer*. New York: Grove, 1976.

Martin, Jay. *Always Merry and Bright: The Life of Henry Miller*. Santa Barbara, CA: Capra, 1979.

Mathieu, Bertrand. *Orpheus in Brooklyn: Orphism, Rimbaud, and Henry Miller*. The Hague: Mouton, 1976.

Moore, Harry T. 'Review of *Tropic of Cancer*.' *New York Times Book Review* (18 June 1961), 5.

Nexus: The International Henry Miller Journal. Ed. James Decker. Ann Arbor, MI: Roger Jackson, 2004–.

Orend, Karl. *The Brotherhood of Fools and Simpletons: Gods and Devils in Henry Miller's Utopia*. Paris: Alyscamps, 2005.

– *Cathedral of Light: Betty Ryan at the Villa Seurat*. Paris: Alyscamps, 2003.

– *Henry Miller's Red Phoenix: A Lawrentian Quest*. Paris: Alyscamps, 2006.

– 'Making a Place for Henry Miller in the American Classroom.' *The Chronicle of Higher Education* 50.18 (2004): 6–8; repr. in *Nexus; The International Henry Miller Journal* 2.1 (2005): 62, 65.

– *On the 70th Anniversary of 'Tropic of Cancer.'* Paris: Alyscamps, 2004.

Parkin, John. *Henry Miller, The Modern Rabelais*. Lewiston, NY: Mellen, 1990.
Perlès, Alfred. *My Friend Henry Miller: An Intimate Biography.* New York: John
    Day, 1956.
Poliak, G. 'Genri Miller i russkie na zapade. O russkoi versii romana.' ['Henry
    Miller and the Russians in the West; Concerning the Russian Version of the
    Novel.'] Introduction to *Tropic raka [Tropic of Cancer],* 313–15. Trans. Egorov.
    Moscow: Terra, 1994.
Porter, Bern, ed. *The Happy Rock: A Book About Henry Miller*. Berkeley: Bern
    Porter, 1945.
Powys, John Cowper. *Letters to Henry Miller*. London: Village Press, 1975.
Rembar, Charles. *The End of Obscenity: The Trials of* Lady Chatterley, Tropic of
    Cancer *and* Fanny Hill. New York: Random House, 1968.
Shifreen, Lawrence. 'Faction in the Villa Seurat.' *Deus Loci: The Lawrence
    Durrell Quarterly* 2 (1981): 1–19.
Wickes, George, ed. *Henry Miller and the Critics*. Carbondale: Southern Illinois
    University Press, 1963.

Anaïs Nin

Major Writings

Children of the Albatross. New York: Dutton, 1947; Denver: Swallow, 1966.
Cities of the Interior. (Includes *Ladders to Fire*, *Children of the Albatross*, *The Four-
    Chambered Heart*, and *Seduction of the Minotaur*.) 1959. Chicago: Swallow, 1974.
Collages. Denver: Swallow, 1964.
Delta of Venus: Erotica. New York: Harcourt Brace Jovanovich, 1977.
D.H. Lawrence: An Unprofessional Study. 1932. Paris: E.W. Titus; Chicago:
    Swallow, 1964.
The Diary of Anaïs Nin. Ed. Gunther Stuhlmann. New York: Harcourt, Brace
    and World.
    Vol. 1: *1931–1934* (1966, copublished with Swallow)
    Vol. 2: *1934–1939* (1967, copublished with Swallow)
    Vol. 3: *1939–1944* (1969)
    Vol. 4: *1944–1947* (1971) (Harcourt Brace Jovanovich)
    Vol. 5: *1947–1955* (1976)
    Vol. 7: *1966–1974* (1980)
The Early Diary of Anaïs Nin. New York: Harcourt Brace Jovanovich.
    Vol. 2: *1920–1923* (1982).
    Vol. 3: *1923–1927* (1983).
    Vol. 4: *1927–1931* (1985).

Fire: From A Journal of Love; The Unexpurgated Diary of Anaïs Nin. New York: Harcourt Brace, 1995.
The Four-Chambered Heart. New York: Duell, Sloan and Pearce, 1950; Denver: Swallow, 1966.
Henry and June: From the Unexpurgated Diary of Anaïs Nin. San Diego: Harcourt Brace Jovanovich, 1986.
House of Incest. 1936. Chicago: Swallow Press, 1958.
Incest: From 'A Journal of Love,' The Unexpurgated Diary of Anaïs Nin, 1934–1935. San Diego: Harcourt Brace Jovanovich, 1992.
In Favour of the Sensitive Man and Other Essays. New York: Harcourt Brace, Jovanovich, 1976.
Ladders to Fire. 1946. Chicago: Swallow, 1968.
Linotte: The Early Diary of Anaïs Nin, 1914–1920. Trans. from the French by Jean L. Sherman. New York: Harcourt Brace Jovanovich, 1978. (*Early Diary*, Vol. 1).
Little Birds: Erotica. New York: Harcourt Brace Jovanovich, 1979.
The Mystic of Sex and Other Writings. Ed. Gunther Stuhlmann. Santa Barbara: Capra, 1995.
Nearer The Moon: From 'A Journal of Love,' The Unexpurgated Diary of Anaïs Nin, 1937–1939. New York: Harcourt Brace & Company, 1996.
Novel of the Future. New York: Macmillan, 1968.
'Preface to the *Tropic of Cancer*.' 1934. New York: Grove Widenfeld, 1980. xxxi–xxxiii.
'Realism and Reality'. 1946. Repr. in *The Mystic of Sex and Other Writings*, ed. Gunther Stuhlmann, 23–31. Santa Barbara: Capra, 1995.
Seduction of the Minotaur. Denver: Swallow, 1961.
Under a Glass Bell. 1944. New York: Dutton, 1948.
Waste of Timelessness and Other Early Stories. Weston, CT: Magic Circle, 1977.
Winter of Artifice. 1939. Paris: Obelisk; *Winter of Artifice: Three Novelettes*. Denver: Swallow, 1961.
The White Blackbird and Other Writings. Santa Barbara, CA: Capra, 1985.

Location of Main Archives

Anaïs Nin Papers at University of California–Los Angelos.

Correspondence, Lectures, and Interviews

A Literate Passion; Letters of Anaïs Nin and Henry Miller 1932–1953. Ed. Gunther Stuhlmann. San Diego: Harcourt Brace Jovanovich, 1987.

Arrows of Longing: the Correspondence Between Anaïs Nin and Felix Pollak, 1952–1976.
   Ed. Gregory H. Mason. Athens: Swallow, Ohio University Press, 1998.
Conversations with Anaïs Nin. Ed. Wendy M. DuBow. Jackson: University Press
   of Mississippi, 1994.
A Woman Speaks: The Lectures, Seminars, and Interviews of Anaïs Nin. Ed. Evelyn
   Hinz. Chicago: Swallow, 1975.

Biographies and Criticism

Alexandre-Garner, Corinne. 'Black Snow in Winter: Anais in Paris – The
   Lawrence Durrell Connection.' In *Anais Nin: Literary Perspectives*, ed.
   Suzanne Nalbantian, 236–53. New York: St Martin's, 1997.
Anaïs: An International Journal. Ed. Gunther Stuhlmann. Becket, MA. 19 vol.
   1983–2001.
Bair, Deirdre. *Anaïs Nin: A Biography*. New York: Putnam, 1995.
– 'Writing as a Woman: Henry Miller, Lawrence Durrell, and Anaïs Nin in the
   Villa Seurat.' *Anais: An International Journal* 12 (1994): 31–8.
Barillé, Elisabeth. *Anaïs, Nin: Naked under the Mask*. Trans. Elfreda Powell.
   London: Lime Tree, 1992.
Evans, Oliver Wendell. *Anais Nin*. Carbondale: Southern Illinois University
   Press, 1968.
Fitch, Noel Riley. *Anaïs: The Erotic Life of Anaïs Nin*. Boston: Little, Brown, 1993.
Franklin, Benjamin, V., ed. *Recollections of Anaïs Nin*. Athens: Ohio University
   Press, 1996.
Hinz, Evelyn J. *The Mirror and the Garden: Realism and Reality in the Writings of
   Anaïs Nin*. New York: Harcourt Brace Jovanovich, 1973.
Jason, Philip. *Anaïs Nin and her Critics*. Columbia: Camden House, 1993.
– ed. *The Critical Response to Anais Nin*. Westport, CT: Greenwood Press, 1996.
MacNiven, Ian S. 'A Room in the House of Art: The Friendship of Anais Nin
   and Lawrence Durrell.' *Mosaic: A Journal for the Interdisciplinary Study of
   Literature* 11.2 (1978): 37-57.
Nalbantian, Suzanne. *Aesthetic Autobiography: From Life to Art in Marcel Proust,
   James Joyce, Virginia Woolf, and Anaïs Nin*. New York: St Martin's, 1994.
Anaïs Nin: Literary Perspectives. New York: St Martin's, 1993.
Richard-Allerdyce, Diane. *Anais Nin and the Remaking of Self: Gender, Modern-
   ism, and Narrative Identity*. DeKalb: Northern Illinois University Press, 1998.
Salber, Linde. *Tausendundeine Frau: die Geschichte der Anaïs Nin*. Reinbek bei
   Hamburg: Rowohlt, 1996.
Salvatore, Anne, ed. *Anaïs Nin's Narratives*. Gainesville: University Press of
   Florida, 2001.

Shapiro, Karl. 'The Charmed Circle of Anais Nin.' *The Criterion* 17 (October 1937). Repr. in *The Critical Response to Anais Nin*, ed. Philip K. Jason, 154–7. Westport, CT: Greenwood Press, 1996.

Schneider, Duane. 'Anais Nin in the *Diary*: The Creation and Development of a Persona.' *Mosaic* 11.2 (1978): 9–19.

Spencer, Sharon, ed. *Anais, Art and Artists: A Collection of Essays*. Greenwood, CT: Penkeville 1986.

Tookey, Helen. *Anaïs Nin, Fictionality and Femininity: Playing a Thousand Roles*. Oxford: Oxford University Press, 2003.

Bibliography of Other Works Cited

Anderson, Sherwood. 'To Eleanor Copenhaver Anderson' (29 April 1929). *Sherwood Anderson's Love Letters to Eleanor Copenhaver Anderson*. Ed. Charles E. Modlin, 9. Athens: University of Georgia Press, 1989.

– 'To Hart Crane' (4 March 1921). *Letters; Selected and Edited with an Introduction and Notes by Howard Mumford Jones, in Association with Walter B. Rideout*, 70–1. Boston: Little, Brown, 1953.

Atlas, James. 'The Age of the Literary Memoir is Now.' *New York Times Magazine* (12 May 1996), 25–7.

Belinskii, Vissarion. *Polnoe sobranie sochinenii [Full Edition of Collected Works]*. Moscow: Izdatel'stvo Akademii Nauk SSSR, 1956.

Berberova, Nina. *Kursiv moi; avtobiografiia [The Italics are Mine: Autobiography]*. 2nd rev. ed. New York: Russica, 1983.

Berdiaev, Nikolai. *Tsarstvo Dukha i tsarstvo Kesaria [The Kingdom of the Spirit and the Kingdom of Caesar]*. 1949. Moscow: Respublika, 1995.

Bloom, Harold. *The Anxiety of Influence*. New York: Oxford University Press, 1973.

– *The Western Canon: The Books and Schools of Ages*. New York: Harcourt Brace, 1994.

Breton, André. 'Limits not Frontiers of Surrealism.' In *Surrealism*, ed. Herbert Read, 93–116. London: Faber and Faber, 1936.

Brewster, Dorothy. *East-West Passage, A Study in Literary Relationships*. London: George Allen and Unwin, 1954.

Brewster, Dorothy, and Angus Burrell. *Dead Reckonings in Fiction*. New York: Longmans, 1925.

'Briefs on New Books; *Buried Alive; or Ten Years of Penal Servitude in Siberia*.' *The Dial* (May 1881): 15–16.

Brodsky, Joseph. 'Interv'iu *Vestnika*: Iosif Brodskii' ['*Vesnik* Interviews Joseph Brodsky']. *Vestnik* (Toronto) (11 February 1994): 6–7.

– *Less Than One: Selected Essays*. New York: Penguin, 1987.

Capote, Truman. *Conversations with Capote*. Interviewer and editor Lawrence Grobel. New York: New American Library, 1985.

Cleyet, George. 'The Villa Seurat Circle: Creative Nexus.' *Deus Loci: The Lawrence Durrell Quarterly* 4.4 (1981): 3–6.

Cowley, Malcolm. *Exile's Return: A Literary Odyssey of the 1920s*. New York: Norton, 1934.

Crane Hart. 'To Gorham Munson.' 23 December 1920. *The Letters of Hart Crane, 1916–1932*. Ed. Brom Weber. Berkeley and Los Angelos: University of California Press, 1965.

Dal', Vladimir. *Tolkovyi slovar' zhivogo velikorusskogo iazyka* [*Dictionary of the Living Russian Language*]. 2nd ed., 4 vols. Moscow: M.O. Vol'f, 1880–2.

Davie, Donald, ed. *Russian Literature and Modern English Fiction*. Chicago: University of Chicago Press, 1965.

Dell, Floyd. 'Review.' *The Masses* (April 1916): 28.

Dole, Nathan H. 'Contemporary Russian Literature.' *The Chautauquan* 8 (1888): 465.

Dos Passos, John. *The Fourteenth Chronicle: Letters and Diaries*. Ed. T. Ludington. Boston: Gambit, 1973.

Dreiser, Theodore. 'To James T. Farrell.' 20 January 1944. *Letters: A Selection*. Ed. Robert H. Elias. 3 vols. Philadelphia: University of Philadelphia Press, 1959. 3: 1002–3.

– 'To Simon and Schuster.' 26 March 1929. *Letters: A Selection*. Ed. Robert H. Elias. 3 vols. Philadelphia: University of Philadelphia Press, 1959. 2: 487–8.

– 'To Victor Smirnov.' 5 August 1932. *Letters: A Selection*. Ed. Robert H. Elias. 3 vols. Philadelphia: University of Philadelphia Press, 1959. 2: 595.

Ellison, Ralph. Interview. 'Ralph Ellison: Twenty Years After.' 1973. *Conversations with Ralph Ellison*. Ed. Maryemma Graham and Amrijit Singh. Jackson: University Press of Mississippi, 1995.

Eliot, T.S. *Selected Prose*. Ed. Frank Kermode. New York: Harcourt Brace Jovanovich, 1975.

– 'To Eleanor Hinkley' (23 July 1917). *Letters of T.S. Eliot*. Ed. Valerie Eliot. 2 vols. London: Faber and Faber, 1988. 1:189–90.

Emerson, Caryl. *The First Hundred Years of Mikhail Bakhtin*. Princeton, NJ: Princeton University Press, 1997.

Fraenkel, Michael. *Bastard Death: The Autobiography of an Idea*. Paris: Carrefour, 1936.

– *The Day Face and the Night Face*. New York: Irving Stettner, 1947.

France, Peter. 'The Rhetoric of Translation.' *Modern Language Review Supplement, One Hundred Years of MLR: General and Comparative Studies*. October 2005. http://mhra.org.uk/ojs/index.php/MLR/article/viewFile/3/34.

'French and German Books; *Littérature Contemporaine en Russie.' Scribners Monthly.* 10. 2 (June 1875): 256.

Ginsberg, Allen. *Collected Poems 1947–1980.* New York: Harper and Row, 1984.

Gold, Michael. 'Floyd Dell Resigns.' *New Masses* (July 1929): 10.

Goldman, Emma. *Anarchism and Other Essays.* New York: Mother Earth, 1917.

– *Living My Life.* 1931; New York: Alfred Knopf, 1971.

– *Social Significance of Modern Drama.* Boston: Richard and Badger, 1914.

Hassan, Ihab. *Radical Innocence: Studies in the Contemporary American Novel.* Princeton, NT: Princeton University Press, 1961.

Hemingway, Ernest. *The Green Hills of Africa.* 1935. New York: Scribner, 1963.

– *A Moveable Feast.* New York: Scribner, 1964.

Hemmings, F.W.J. *The Russian Novel In France, 1884–1914.* Oxford: Oxford University Press, 1950.

Howells, William Dean. *Criticism and Fiction.* New York: Harper and Brothers, 1892.

James, Henry. *French Poets and Novelists.* Leipzig: Tauchnitz, 1883.

– to Hugh Walpole.' 19 May 1912. In *The Letters of Henry James,* ed. Percy Lubbock, 2: 246. London: Macmillan, 1920.

Josephson, Matthew. *Life Among the Surrealists: A Memoir.* New York: Holt, Rinehart and Winston, 1962.

Kazin, Alfred. *On Native Grounds: An Interpretation of Modern American Prose Literature.* New York: Harcourt, Brace and World, 1942.

Kerouac, Jack. 'To Peter Orlovsky.' 24 August 1957. Columbia University, Butler Library, Spec Ms Collection Orlovsky, 1.

Lawrence, D. H. *Aaron's Rod.* 1922. New York: Viking Compass, 1961.

– *Selected Literary Criticism.* Ed. Anthony Beal. London: Mercury, 1961

– *Studies in Classic American Literature.* 1923. New York: Penguin, 1986.

Mackworth, Cecily. 'Montparnasse and 18 Villa Seurat.' *Twentieth Century Literature: A Scholarly and Critical Journal* 33.3 (1987): 274-9.

Manso, Peter. *Mailer: His Life and Times.* New York: Viking Penguin, 1985.

Mirsky, D. *Intelligentsia of Great Britain.* London: Victor Gollancz, 1935.

Morison, S.E., H.S. Commager, and W.E. Leuchtenburg, eds. *The Growth of the American Republic.* 7th ed., vol 2. New York: Oxford University Press, 1980.

Moser, Charles A. 'The Achievement of Constance Garnett.' *The American Scholar* 57.30 (1988): 431-8.

Nabokov, Vladimir. *Strong Opinions.* New York: McGraw-Hill, 1973.

Parrington, Vernon. *Main Currents in American Thought,* vol. 3: *The Beginnings of Critical Realism in America 1860–1920.* New York: Harcourt, Brace, 1934.

Pound, Ezra. 'To Robert McAlmon.' 2 February 1934. In *The Letters of Ezra Pound 1907–1941,* ed. D.D. Paige, 252. New York: Harcourt, Brace and Company, 1950.

Powys, John Cowper. *Autobiography*. 1934. London: Macdonald, 1967.
– *Visions and Revisions: A Book of Literary Devotions*. New York: G. Arnold Shaw, 1915.
'The Priest and the Devil.' [Story falsely attributed to Dostoevsky.] *Mother Earth Bulletin* (January 1910): 360–2.
Rank, Otto. *Don Juan. Une étude sur le double*. [Originally published as *Der Doppelgänger* in 1914.] Trans. S. Lautman. Paris: Denoël and Steele, 1932.
Robbins, Jack Alan, ed. *Granville Hicks in the New Masses*. Port Washington, NY: Kennikat, 1974.
Schumacher, Michael. *Dharma Lion: A Critical Biography of Allen Ginzberg*. New York: St Martin's, 1992.
Shifreen, Lawrence J. 'Faction in the Villa Seurat.' *Deus Loci: The Lawrence Durrell Quarterly* 5.2 (1981): 1–19.
Sinclair, Upton. *Mammonart: An Essay in Economic Interpretation*. Pasadena, CA: Published by the Author, 1925.
Spector, Herman. 'Liberalism and the Literary Esoterics.' *New Masses* (January 1929): 18.
Spengler, Oswald. *Decline of the West*. 1918–1922. Ed. Helmut Werner. Trans. Charles Francis Atkinson. New York: Alfred A. Knopf, 1962.
Vogüé, E.M. *Journal du vicomte E.-M. de Vogüé, Paris–Saint-Pétersbourg, 1877–1883*. Paris: Grasset, 1932.
Wechsler, Robert. *Performing Without a Stage: The Art of Literary Translation*. North Haven, CT: Catbird, 1988.
Wolfe, Thomas. 'To Scott Fitzgerald.' 26 July 1937. In *The Letters*, ed. E. Nowell, 643. New York: Scribner, 1956.
Wolkonky, Serge. *Pictures of Russian History and Russian Literature*. Boston, New York and London: Lamson, Wolfee, 1898.
Woolf, Virginia. *The Common Reader*. London: Hogarth, 1925.

Index

Dostoevsky by, 55, 63–5, 80, 100–1,
103, 104, 107, 131–6, 180–2; influence of, 20, 22, 23, 77, 176;
Lawrence, D.H., and, 59–60, 64, 80,
95, 101, 120, 130, 133–4, 178; literary underground and, vii, 17, 18;
Notes from Underground and, 146–57,
182; obscenity and, 18–9, 136–7;
philosophical discourse and,
117–18; proletariat leanings of, 50;
prose style and, 93, 100–2, 104–6,
113; psychoanalysis and, 119; reading of Dostoevsky by, 21, 43–4,
45–6, 56, 81, 100, 114, 177, 179;
reading of Dostoevsky commentators by, 46–7, 57–9, 63, 64, 100, 104,
111, 114, 119–20, 124; relationship
with June Miller, 48, 50, 51, 52,
69, 125, 126; relationship with
Lawrence Durrell, viii, 18, 20,
71–3, 76–7, 102, 168; relationship
with Anaïs Nin, viii, 18, 20, 52, 70,
73, 75–6, 77, 78–9, 80, 101, 120, 125;
reputation of, vii, 18–20; revolution in prose and consciousness,
and, 22, 65, 77, 79, 86, 113, 180;
Russian émigrés and, 53; serial
texts and, 111–12; suffering and,
122–4; surrealists and, 51, 53–4,
95–6, 98–9; understanding of
Dostoevsky's philosophy by,
116–18, 121–38; understanding of
Dostoevsky's style by, 100–2, 104,
105, 180; Villa Seurat Circle and,
viii, 18, 20, 22, 67–9, 74, 75, 77
– works: *Aller Retour New York,* 75;
Art and Outrage, 129, 205n8; Autobiographical Note, 93; 'Balzac and
His Double,' 58, 65; *Big Sur and the
Oranges of Hieronymus Bosch,* 147;

Black Spring, 43, 54, 68, 71, 75, 79,
81, 83, 86, 96, 98, 114; *The Books in
My Life,* 60, 63, 83, 100, 135, 208n87,
209nn92, 94, 99, 217n85, 220n5,
221nn35, 52, 222nn63, 73; *Colossus
of Maroussi,* 147, 221n51; *Crazy
Cock,* 69, 206n22; *Dear, Dear Brenda:
The Love Letters of Henry Miller to
Brenda Venus,* 211n58, 221n48; 'The
Enormous Womb,' 132; 'Un Être
Etoilique,' 75, 80, 87; 'First Impres-
sions of Greece,' 132; *The Hamlet
Letters (Hamlet Correspondence),* 75,
102, 132; *Joey: A Loving Portrait of
Alfred Perlès Together with Some
Bizarre Episodes Relating to the
Other Sex. Volume III, Book of
Friends,* 205n2, 209n107; *Just Wild
About Harry,* 206n35; *Max and the
White Phagocytes,* 68; 'Mlle
Claude,' 69; *Moloch,* 56, 69, 70, 81,
82; 'Mother, China and the World
Beyond,' 21, 205n7; 'Obscenity and
the Law of Reflection,' 137; 'Open
Letter to Surrealists Everywhere,'
54, 98–9, 108, 218nn116, 125;
'Reflections on the Death of Mish-
ima,' 222n71; 'Reflections on Writ-
ing,' 103, 107; *Rosy Crucifixion
Trilogy,* 50, 56, 81, 104, 105, 112, 117,
121, 123, 190, 210n11; *Nexus,* 57,
112, 207n68, 209n31; *Plexus,* 24, 47,
112, 122, 128, 135, 147, 209nn95, 96,
220nn6, 23, 221nn40, 41, 42; *Sexus,*
81, 112, 133; *Scenario (A Film with
Sound),* 71; *Smile at the Foot of the
Ladder,* 209n100; *Stand Still Like a
Hummingbird,* 218nn104, 108;
Sextet, 218n110, 221n47, 222n86;
Tropic of Cancer, 18, 19, 22, 57, 58,